THE BASIC BOOK OF
BUSINESS

The Basic Book of
BUSINESS

JOHN R. KLUG

CBI

CBI Publishing Company, Inc.
51 Sleeper Street
Boston, Massachusetts 02210

Library of Congress Cataloging in Publication Data

Klug, John R.   1945–
    The basic book of business.

    Includes index.
    1.   Business—Handbooks, manuals, etc.   I.   Title.
HF5356.K68   658.4   76-46588
ISBN 0-8436-0751-3

International Standard Book Number: 0-8436-0751-3

Library of Congress Card Catalogue Number: 76-46588

Printed in the United States of America

Designed by Bonnie Spiegel
Third Printing

CONTENTS

FOREWORD

Most small company owners and managers—even those who have been very successful—need help in further developing their management skills and knowledge. Help, however, is not easily obtained. Only a few small company owners and managers have the time or inclination to attend formal courses or programs. And few formal programs are directed toward the problems and concerns of small company managers. As a result, most small company managers seek their own development primarily through various efforts at self-education.

The most basic requirements for successful management of a small company is an understanding of key operating questions: what product features are important to customers, how costs vary with volume of production, what suppliers are reliable for quality and delivery, and so on. Traditionally, management acquires a practical, working knowledge of these areas through exposure and experience. For most small companies, this kind of expertise becomes a major competitive strength of the firm.

Unfortunately, understanding does not automatically follow from experience. When management is involved in many day-to-day decisions, emphasis must be given to finding solutions rather than studying the nature of the problems. As a result, the underlying causes of many problem situations are easily overlooked: inadequate production scheduling is seen as limited shop capacity, lack of cash planning appears as insufficient capital, and so on.

The power to conceptualize—to think about situations in general terms as well as specifics—enhances management's ability to anticipate and deal with problems and to utilize prior experience. Through exposure to business concepts which others have developed and improved over time, management finds new ways to approach old problems. Work with quantitative analyses permits the calculation of such things as economic order quantities and present values of investment alternatives. Formulation of decision trees assists in systematic analysis of complex decisions. Conceptualizing in more qualitative terms provides insight into situations where management has knowledge and understanding but has lost perspective. For example, thinking in terms of product life cycle and the marketing mix helps management recognize change and see a range of possible responses. Similarly, identifying strategic strengths and weaknesses assists in assessing corporate strategy.

In addition to the benefits gained from applying a number of concepts to small business situations, there are also specialized areas—corporate law, accounting, taxation (especially the 1976 Tax Act) and securities regulation—which, on occasion, are key to major management decisions. Each of these fields encompasses both basic concepts and substantive knowledge. Small firms, however, do not need, nor can they afford, full-time help in each of these areas. But neither can they always afford the penalties or opportunity costs of learning by experience. A reasonable compromise is for management to develop greater familiarity with these specialized fields in order to recognize situations where outside help should be sought.

In this book, John Klug presents a rich mixture of key business concepts and selected topics from specialized fields which should be of particular interest to managers of small companies. To make the material comprehensive yet readable, John has wisely elected to emphasize breadth and variety over fully detailed descriptions. At the same time, however, the elements of each area are described and discussed in enough detail for the reader to understand the nature of the area and to judge when additional readings or professional counsel would be helpful. For the owner and manager of the smaller firm, this book should give valuable exposure to important areas which few small company managers know enough about.

Patrick R. Liles
Associate Professor
Harvard University
Graduate School of
Business Administration

PREFACE

This book was written for owners or managers of small- and medium-sized businesses (less than 500 employees). This represents the great majority of American business people. It was not written for IBM or AT&T. They have enough money to afford management mistakes. You don't.

This book has only one purpose—to help you make or save money in your business. If you bought the book for some other reason, return it. It's not for you.

As you will discover when you begin reading this book, brevity and clarity are paramount. This book is not meant to be totally comprehensive or to make you an expert. Rather, it is intended to:

1. Be a reference of basic business information
2. Give you a sensitivity to issues so you know when to seek professional advice
3. Teach you a vocabulary so you can effectively and efficiently communicate with your advisors

Two caveats: first, tax and legal matters are always changing. Therefore, some of the material will get out of date. This should not concern you, however, because—again—the purpose of this book is to give you a basic knowledge of issues and techniques, not to be a reference of the latest tax rates.

Second, although you will know more about business and tax techniques than probably 95 percent of all business people after reading this book, do not substitute it for professional advice. Your accountant and lawyer should always be at your side as you make major business decisions.

For simplicity, a "life cycle" approach was used to organize this book. The first chapter deals with how to *organize* a new business, the second with how to *operate* the business, the third chapter with how to *sell out* and the fourth with hanging on to your well-earned money (*retirement and estate planning*).

Do not feel that you have to read the book from cover to cover. It's not a novel. Rather, go directly to whatever chapter serves your needs at the time.

The material for the book was gathered from two sources. The first is the Harvard Business School. As a graduate and later Research Associate of the school, I was able to avail myself of numerous case studies and professional management techniques. The second source was the real world and the school of hard knocks. As a small businessman myself and advisor to numerous others, I have too often seen inadequate business knowledge lead to unfortunate—sometimes disastrous—results. This book will help you avoid most of the pitfalls other business people have fallen into.

Finally, my challenges to you.

1. Use this book. It's not easy reading all the time, but it is reasonably clear and straightforward. Don't put it on a shelf to gather dust. Better to give it to a friend or send it back.
2. No need to read this book cover to cover. Do, however, familiarize yourself with all its contents so you know what type of information is available to you.
3. Always use the best accountants and lawyers available to you. If you can, use a partner in the largest major law firm near you and go with a good-sized accounting firm. Properly used, as a result of the knowledge you get from this book, they will be very cheap insurance.

Someone once said, the real basis of power was not to necessarily know everything—just where to find it out. This book will not teach you everything about business, but it will lead you to most of the sources of information you'll ever need.

John R. Klug

ACKNOWLEDGMENTS

Few endeavors of any merit are ever done alone, and this one is no exception.

First, I would like to thank Professor W. Earl Sasser of the Harvard Business School for his encouragement over the years and for his critique of much of the material.

Second, I would like to thank William C. Banks for his excellent editorial assistance and advice.

Also, I would like to thank Professor Thomas Brightwell from the University of Denver and Frederick Goldstein, Esq., of the Boston law firm of Csaplar & Bok for their excellent critique of the tax and legal aspects of the book.

Finally, and most importantly, I would like to acknowledge the support and assistance of my wife Carol, who endured many sacrifices as the book came together.

Part I
HOW TO ORGANIZE YOUR BUSINESS

CHAPTER 1

ORGANIZATIONAL OPTIONS

Huge, multinational corporations, such as General Motors and Exxon, have tens of thousands of shareholders and these companies must, for practical reasons, operate in corporate form. But smaller businesses have more options in selecting a business structure. The first and perhaps most vital step for any astute businessman is choosing the business form that best suits the needs of his individual circumstances.

You can always start right off modeling your company after Exxon by electing the standard corporate form. But if your firm is not quite that big yet, you might find that you can realize some handsome tax savings by electing the special Subchapter S corporation status. The Sub S enjoys most of the advantages of incorporation and yet avoids most of the drawbacks. Of course, you may want to stick with a proprietorship or partnership structure. In each case there are advantages and disadvantages in areas of management, owner's personal liability, the continuity of the firm, transferability of ownership, and costs to organize.

However, for most smaller businesses the choice of legal organizational form hinges on three major tax considerations:

1. Tax *rate* of profits.
2. Tax *treatment* of ordinary income/losses; capital gains/ losses; dividends.
3. *Fringe benefits* that are tax free or receive tax preferred treatment.

In addition to these *tax* considerations, there are other important considerations, such as:

- Does the owner wish to reinvest profits in the business or take them out of the business for personal use?
- Does the owner have profits or losses from other activities that he would like to offset against those of the business?
- Does the business initially expect to show losses?

The importance of these questions will be seen further on. But let's examine first the three dominant tax considerations listed above.

TAX RATES

Sole proprietorship and partnership income is combined with the owner/partner's personal income and is taxed as follows:

- The owner pays tax on the combined total of business and personal income at the individual progressive rate of from 14% to 70% with a special maximum tax of 50% on "earned"[1] income.
- Income from passive sources, such as dividends, is considered "unearned" and subject to tax up to the full 70% level.
- The proprietor may only treat 30% of business profit as earned income.
- The owner may deduct half of his net long-term capital gain and treat the other half as ordinary income, or he may pay 25% tax on the first $50,000 of gain and 35% on gain over $50,000 (the 35% represents the 50% deduction against the maximum 70% bracket).
- Estate tax is paid in full by the heirs if the business appreciates in value over the owner's lifetime. At the time of death the heirs pay estate tax on the full capital gain.

Corporations are entities in and of themselves and as such are separate and distinct from the owners of the corporation. They are taxed as follows:

- A corporation pays 20% tax on the first $25,000 of income, 22% on the next $25,000, and 48% on any remaining income.
- Long-term capital gain may be treated as ordinary income or the corporation may pay an alternative capital gain tax of 30%.
- If a corporation accumulates more than $150,000 and it cannot be shown that the excess amount is needed to run the company, a penalty tax of 27½% will be assessed against current earnings. In this way IRS urges corporations to pay the current income out as taxable dividends to the owners. (Note that a large company such as General Motors has, at any one time, many millions of dollars accumulated on hand, but these funds are needed in GM's day-to-day operations. Therefore, what constitutes an excess corporate accumulation depends on the particular circumstances.)
- The corporation's shareholders pay personal income tax on

---

[1] The Tax Reform Act of 1976 changes the term "earned" income to "personal service" income. The two terms will be used interchangeably throughout.

dividends received from the corporation. This constitutes, in effect, a "double tax" on the corporation's income.
- When ownership of a corporation is transferred upon the death of an owner, an estate tax is levied on the full fair market value of the ownership interest.

Subchapter S Corporations are taxed only once like a partnership and yet the owner may enjoy many of the tax free benefits and other advantages of a corporation. These benefits will be explained further on.

TAX TREATMENT OF INCOME/LOSSES; CAPITAL GAINS/LOSSES; DIVIDENDS

Different business structures merit different treatment of certain kinds of gains and losses. You must select and weigh the kind of treatment that best suits your needs.

Income, Capital Gains, and Dividends

Treatment of Special Income Items Such as Tax Exempt Interest and Dividends. Owners of a corporation, unlike partners or proprietors, must pay tax on some corporate income that would normally be tax free or tax favored if the individual or partner received the income rather than the corporation. If, for example, the corporation wishes to distribute income from tax exempt municipal bond interest or lower taxed net long-term capital gain, this income loses its tax favored status and is fully taxable as ordinary income to the shareholder. On the other hand, a corporation is entitled to exclude from its income 85% of any dividends received from another corporation, whereas an individual (proprietor-partner) must pay full tax on such dividend income, less a $100 exclusion. So the corporation has the advantage on dividend income and the proprietorship has the advantage when it comes to tax free or tax favored income.

Although in some cases a corporation may be at a disadvantage in distributing otherwise tax favored income, a corporation, if qualified, may elect Subchapter S status for a year in which there is anticipation of large capital gain. As a "Sub S," the corporation will pay no double tax on the income distributed for that year.

Getting Money Out. If your goal is to get money out of the company immediately, the Subchapter S or proprietorship forms often are best because you avoid the corporate double tax on income. Remember, a corporation pays tax on its income and then, when the income is distributed as dividends, the stockholder pays another tax at personal income tax rates. However, in the Sub S and noncorporate forms, company income is taxed only once—as personal income.

But don't shy away from the ordinary corporate form for a small business out of fear of the double tax. There are ways to reduce it or to get around it entirely. If profits don't get too high, the double tax can be greatly reduced by one or more of the following methods:

- The corporation can pay interest on loans from the owner.
- The corporation can employ family members.
- The owner may take as large a salary as is reasonable.
- The corporation can accumulate earnings up to a reasonable extent and later distribute the accumulation as capital gain.
- Accumulated earnings may be retained by the corporation by holding corporate stock until death. These techniques will be explained in detail in subsequent sections.

Reinvesting.   If your goal is to reinvest for expansion of your business, the standard corporate form will often be better because the income can be divided into two groups. Part of the income (up to $50,000 per year) can be accumulated for the expansion and taxed at the corporate rate of 20-22%, and the other part can be taken out as salary by the owner. This division of income is not possible in the noncorporate forms. In the proprietorship and partnership forms, all the business income is taxed to the owners at their personal tax rates before it may be reinvested for expansion. Quite often the result is that this business income ends up being taxed on considerably higher rates than the 20-22% corporate tax rate on the first $50,000 of corporate income.

Personal Holding Company (PHC).   Finally, be warned that there is such a thing as a *personal holding company* status if more than 60% of income is from passive income, such as interest, rent, or a personal service contract. There is a penalty tax of 70% if your corporation is declared a personal holding company. See page 25 for more details.

Losses

Capital Loss.   Treatment of losses can be just as important as treatment of gains. For the corporation, long term *capital loss* may not be used to offset current income. It may only be used to offset capital gains from three years back to five years forward. An individual, however, may deduct 50% of his long term capital loss (up to $2,000 in 1977 and $3,000 in 1978 and beyond) from his current ordinary income. If his capital loss results in more than the deductible amount, he may carry the extra loss over to the next year and so on until the loss is used up.

Operating Loss.   A proprietor may use a net *operating loss* to offset current income that he may have from other sources. A corporation may not do this. A corporation may only use a net operating loss to offset income in previous or future years. Therefore, if you are considering starting a new business and you anticipate start up losses, you would be better off with a noncorporate or Sub S status.

TAX-FREE OR TAX-FAVORED FRINGE BENEFITS

Fringe benefits in effect increase an employee's after-tax compensation by absorbing some important living costs. The special fringe benefits available to corporate owners-employees that are not generally available to proprietors and partners should be considered carefully when deciding whether or not to incorporate your business. The Subchapter S corporation offers most of the fringe benefits of a corporation without losing the tax advantages of a proprietorship. The following are some of the more important fringe benefits available to corporate employees:

- *Medical Reimbursement Plan.* This plan allows certain employees and their dependents to be reimbursed directly by the corporation for their medical expenses. This kind of plan may be set up to favor higher paid employees of the corporation, but may not be offered only to certain individual stockholders. It must be a plan for an entire class of employees.
- *Employee Death Benefits.* Upon the death of an employee, a corporation may pay the family or the estate of the decedent up to $5,000. This amount is not tax free if the deceased employee had the right to receive the payment while living. Proprietors and partners do not qualify for this benefit.
- *Group Health Insurance.* Under this plan the corporation buys insurance to cover the medical expenses of employees and their dependents. The corporation deducts the cost of the premium, but the employee does not include the value of the benefits or premium payments in his gross income. Such medical insurance is not a business expense for proprietors and partners. They may only deduct the premium as an itemized personal medical expense subject to certain limitations.
- *Profit Sharing and Pension Plans.* A corporation may contribute up to 15% of an employee's salary into a profit sharing plan. This contribution is deductible to the corporation and it is invested where it compounds and appreciates tax free. Upon retirement, the employee receives his share of the fund at a lower tax cost. In the case of a combined profit sharing and pension plan, the corporation may contribute up to 25% of the salary. The plan need not include *all* the company's employees, but it must include *most* of the employees. Under the "Keogh" or "HR-10" plan, proprietors and partners may only contribute up to 15% of earned in-

come or $7,500 (whichever is less) to a profit sharing or pension plan. (For more detail on retirement plans see Part 4.)

The pension and profit sharing plans for a Subchapter S corporation combine the features of a corporate plan and the Keogh plan. Generally, the rules are similar to those of a corporation.

However, there is an exception in the case of a stockholder-employee who owns more than 5% of stock. His contribution is taxable to the extent that it exceeds 15% of his salary or $7,500, whichever is less.

- *Group Term Life Insurance.* A corporation may purchase term life insurance for a representative group of employees and deduct the cost of the premium. The amount of insurance may be larger for corporate officers and the insured representative group may be limited to all salaried employees, to the exclusion of hourly wage employees. The insurance is tax free to the employees and stockholder-employees up to $50,000 of coverage. Insurance over $50,000 is taxable to the employee based on a small part of the premium payment.
- *Deferred Compensation Plans.* A corporate officer can arrange to defer part of his salary until after retirement. He then pays tax on the deferred part when he is in a lower tax bracket. Proprietors and partners may make no such arrangements.
- *Entertainment and Travel Expense.* Personal entertainment and travel expense is not deductible, but *business* entertainment and travel expense is deductible. Unfortunately, it is sometimes difficult to tell the one from the other. It becomes even more difficult to tell them apart when the personal owner of the business, the proprietor, claims the deduction. But a corporation is a separate entity, distinct from the owner. Therefore, it is often easier to justify travel and entertainment on a corporate expense account.

MAJOR NONTAX CONSIDERATIONS

In addition to the major tax considerations discussed above, there are several nontax factors to weigh before deciding how to organize your business. The major ones are:

1. Personal Liability
- The liability of a corporate stockholder is limited to his stock interest, unless, of course, he uses the corporation for a fraudulent activity or personally endorses a corporate obligation.

- General partners have unlimited liability, but a limited partner, who has no voice in management, is liable to the extent of his investment in the partnership.
- A proprietor has unlimited liability.

2. *Capital Resources*
- A corporation can sell different classes of stock and debentures to raise capital and thus can raise capital with comparative ease.
- A partnership can raise capital by bringing in additional partners. Also, each partner has a personal borrowing capacity.
- A proprietor's ability to raise capital is limited by his personal resources and his credit.

3. *Relative Difficulty of Formation*
- Generally, a corporation is the most expensive and difficult structure to form. Also, the corporation is subject to franchise taxes and state regulations.
- A partnership is easier to form than a corporation but generally requires some legal documentation.
- A proprietorship is the least expensive and easiest business structure to form.

4. *Transferring Ownership*
- Relatively speaking, corporate stock is more easily transferable and marketable than is an interest in a proprietorship or partnership.
- The number of people interested in buying into a partnership is generally limited, and a partner can often only sell his interest to a copartner. If he sells his interest to an outsider, he must usually get the other partner's approval.
- A proprietorship is usually the least marketable business form.

5. *Management*
- Authority within a corporation is usually carefully structured and easily recognizable to everyone.
- A partnership often has the least recognizable hierarchy and this can sometimes lead to confusion for employees and outsiders.
- A proprietorship has clear lines of authority and decision making power since the owner is the proprietor.

6. *How Long Will It Last?*
- Corporations usually have indefinite life. Their existence does not depend on the continued participation of certain individuals.
- Partnerships and proprietorships can be dissolved through transfer of ownership or upon the insolvency, death, or insanity of any owner.

BUSINESS ORGANIZATIONAL STRUCTURES

| | TAX CONSIDERATIONS | | | NON TAX CONSIDERATIONS | | | | | |
	Tax Rates	Treatment of Gains & Losses	Fringe Benefits	Personal Liability	Capital Resources	Difficulty of Formation	Transferring Ownership	Management	Continuity
Proprietorship	Same as owner's personal income tax rate	Business and its owner are single taxable entity.	Keogh Plan	Unlimited	Personal resources and credit	No filing fees and minimum formal regulation	Freely transferable	Proprietor has total authority with minimum formal regulation	Business dissolved at death of owner
Partnership	Same as partner's personal income tax rate	Profits flow directly to partners in proportion to ownership. Special rules cover the flow of losses to partners.	Keogh Plan	Unlimited for general partners. Confined to amount of investment for limited partners.	Sale of additional partnerships plus personal credit of partners	No filing fees and minimal formal registration. Written articles advisable	All general partners must usually consent to transfer	Usually ruled by majority vote of general partners.	May be dissolved at withdrawal or death of general partner
Standard Corporations	Profits taxed at corporate level at 20% for first $25,000, 22% on the next $25,000 and 48% thereafter.	Profits and losses do *not* flow directly to shareholders. Losses in one period may be offset against taxable cor-	1. Medical 2. Health 3. Life Insurance 4. Profit sharing and pension plan	Limited to amount of investment	Access to capital is through sale of bonds and stock.	Generally costs the most to set up. Statuatory requirements vary by state of	Any portion of ownership freely transferable by sale of stock.	In control of a board of directors elected by shareholders	Continuity unaffected by death or withdrawal of shareholder.

	Long term capital gain may be treated as ordinary income or else pay capital gain tax of 30%	porate income of other years	5. Deferred compensation			incorporation and place of business			
Sub S Corporations	Taxed the same as a proprietorship or partnership	Profits and losses flow directly to owners Losses may be deducted from other personal income only up to the amount of the owner's basis in the Sub S corporation plus any debt owed him.	Same as standard corporation EXCEPT pension contribution for stockholder employee with more than 5% of stocks is taxable at higher rate	Limited to amount of investment	Same as standard corporation	Same as standard corporation	Same as standard corporation	Same as standard corporation	Same as standard corporation

CHAPTER 2

THE SPECIAL CASE OF SUBCHAPTER S CORPORATIONS

The name "Subchapter S" comes from the part of the 1958 IRS Code that specifically authorizes a qualified corporation to *elect* to be *taxed* as a *partnership*. A Sub S corporation is permitted virtually all the benefits of incorporation, but it doesn't have the major disadvantage—double taxation. Subchapter S corporations are also referred to sometimes as pseudocorporations, tax option corporations, or small business corporations.

In an ordinary corporation, profits are first taxed at the *corporate* level and then any dividends paid out to shareholders are again taxed as income at the *personal* level. With a Sub S corporation you pay tax only once (and probably at a lower rate than the corporation would pay). For example, if you own 51% of a Sub S corporation that made $10,000 this year, you would pay tax only once—on $5,100 of income on your *personal* tax return. If you had personal losses from other sources to offset this income, you might wind up paying little or no tax at all.

Without having to worry about the corporate double tax a Sub S can enjoy special tax advantages of a partnership, including splitting income with family members who are in lower tax brackets and shifting income to a lower tax year. A Sub S is also allowed most of the advantages of incorporation referred to in the previous section. These are: protection from personal liability; permanence and continuity; ease of transferring business interest; business paid health and group life insurance; tax-free reimbursement of medical expenses; a more tax sheltered plan for profit sharing and pensions. There is one hitch though—you must qualify to make the Sub S election.

CHECKLIST TO QUALIFY FOR SUB S ELECTION

1. *Number of Shareholders.* Must be ten or less for the first five years of corporate existence. After that, up to fifteen shareholders.

2. *Shareholders' Status.* Must be individuals (or estates). No corporations, partnerships, or nonresident aliens. In limited circumstances, trusts may be shareholders.
3. *Class of stock.* Only one class of stock allowed.
4. *Passive income.* No more than 20% of income from *passive* sources (i.e., royalties, rents, dividends, interest, annuities.) However, this restriction may be waived during the first two years of operation if passive income is less than $3,000.
5. *Affiliation.* A Sub S corporation cannot be a member of an affiliated group of corporations.
6. *Location.* It must be a domestic corporation.

HOW TO MAKE A VALID SUB S ELECTION

If you qualify for Sub S (and most small- and medium-sized businesses do), all you do is file Form 2553 with the IRS notifying them that you wish to be taxed as a Sub S corporation. Note, however:

- All shareholders must consent to the election in writing. The election must be made within one month of beginning business for a new corporation. For an already established corporation, the election must be made thirty days prior to or after the beginning of the applicable tax year.
- Once you make the election, it is valid until you cease to be qualified or revoke the election with the IRS. You can revoke the election voluntarily at any time by having each shareholder revoke his consent in writing. You then file this with the IRS. A new shareholder may terminate a corporation's Sub S status if he acts within sixty days to revoke the election. If your Sub S status ends, your corporation may not elect again for five years without IRS approval.

All sound a bit complicated? Actually, it's not, and every businessman should give serious thought to becoming a Sub S corporation. Remember, you get all the benefits of incorporation—without the major disadvantage of double taxation. The profits from the business are taxed only *one* time and only at your *personal* tax rate.

DETAILS ON HOW A SUB S IS TAXED

As previously stated, for federal taxation a Sub S is treated as a partnership. Generally, all of the capital gain, taxable income, or net operating losses pass through to the shareholders without tax to the Sub S itself. Instead, the shareholders must report their pro rata share of the Sub S income on their personal tax return and pay tax on any income or capital gain. Similarly, if there is a corporate operating loss, the shareholders deduct their share of the loss from other personal income they may have. But there is one exception to this tax treatment in the area of capital gains.

If the corporation has not been a Sub S since its inception or for the preceding three years, and if the capital gains exceed the corporation's other income, then the tax-free pass-through of capital gain is limited to $25,000. Capital gain in excess of $25,000 is taxed first to the Sub S and then to the shareholders.

The following offer more specifics on Sub S taxation:

- *Income Splitting.* The income of a Sub S is distributed to anyone who is a shareholder on the *last day* of the company's tax year. The shareholder is not required to have held stock earlier in the year. This means that on the last day of a big profit year you may give stock to your children and shift the income from your higher tax bracket to their lower bracket.
- *Throw back rule.* Sub S shareholders usually pay tax on cash dividends the year they receive them, but there is a special "throw back" rule that states that if a cash dividend is paid within two and one-half months of the end of the *corporation's* tax year, the dividend is considered to have been paid during that year. For example, if both you and your corporation are on a calendar year tax basis and the corporation pays a cash dividend during the first two and one-half months of 1978, the dividend may be treated as if it had been paid in 1977. In other words, it may be thrown back as income to your 1977 tax return.
- *Switching income to a lower tax year.* If your personal tax year differs from that of your Sub S corporation, you may be able to shift your income to a lower tax year. You may pay tax on the corporation's profit either as it is paid out to you as a dividend or on the last day of the company's tax year. Therefore, if you are on a calendar tax year and the fiscal year of your Sub S ends February 28, you may take a taxable dividend in December or you may delay taking the income until the following year, whichever course offers less tax.
- *Sub S as long as you need it.* You may terminate your Sub S status at any time as described on page 17. This means you may take advantage of the tax benefits of the Sub S for as long as it suits your needs. You have an option with this structure, but once you terminate the election, you may not elect again for five years.
- *Tax on undistributed income.* Since a Sub S does not pay corporate tax, the shareholders must pay their pro rata share

of Sub S income, *even if* the income is retained in the corporation and not paid out to the shareholders at the end of the company's fiscal year. In later years this income may be distributed without further tax. For example, suppose you are the sole shareholder in a Sub S that makes $25,000 profit this year and you take out $10,000 as dividends, leaving $15,000 in the company. You must pay personal income tax on the full $25,000. However, at any time in the future you may take the $15,000 out without further tax, as long as the corporation is still a Sub S.

TAX SAVING OPPORTUNITIES

Mid-year Incorporation and Sub S Election.   Proprietors or partners may make a substantial one-time saving by incorporating in the middle of the year and immediately electing Sub S status. This is made possible by the progressive tax rate for individuals. The idea is to split up your proprietorship and Sub S incomes so you can file tax returns for two short periods, each of which falls into a lower tax bracket. However, you must be sure that the date you select for the end of your new Sub S fiscal year occurs in the year following Sub S election (i.e., if you elect Sub S in 1977, you must be sure that your new corporate fiscal year ends in calendar 1978).

Here's how it works: If your proprietorship normally earns $40,000 a year on which you might pay $11,300 in tax, you can save money by electing Sub S at mid-year. For example, on June 30, 1977 you've earned $20,000 and now you incorporate and elect Sub S status with a corporate fiscal year ending March 31, 1978. At the end of 1977 you file a personal tax return and pay the tax on the $20,000 your proprietorship earned in the six months of that year, about $3,300 tax. On March 31, 1978 you pay tax on nine months of operation as a Sub S in which you earned $30,000. You pay $6,600 tax on your nine months earnings as a Sub S and begin a normal twelve month corporate tax year on April 1, 1978. Instead of paying about $14,000 tax for the fifteen month period's earnings, you pay only $9,900 for the combined six month and nine month periods. Admittedly, this requires some fiscal finesse, but this technique resulted in a tidy one-time-only saving of $4,100 in our example. That's well worth a trip to your accountant or tax lawyer for further details.

Avoidance of Unreasonable Accumulation Tax Penalty.   An ordinary corporation is permitted to accumulate up to $150,000 of past earnings, but if it accumulates more than that and cannot show that the excess is needed for the operation of the business, the corporation must pay an "unreasonable accumulation" penalty tax of from 27½ to 38½% *in addition to* the regular corporate income tax. But a Sub S corporation is not subject to normal corporate taxation so it is not affected by the unreasonable accumulation penalty tax. Therefore, timely Sub S election and deft use of the dividend throw back rule can help an ordinary corporation to avoid this penalty tax. Here's how:

A corporation that meets Sub S election criteria discovers at year's end that its earnings are surprisingly high and that it may face a penalty tax for unreasonable accumulations. So, within thirty days before or after the first day of the new tax year, the shareholders elect Sub S status and declare a dividend in the first two and one-half months of the new year. This dividend is then thrown back to the previous year and the corporation is considered to have paid its previous year's excess earnings out as a dividend in that (the previous) year. As a result, there is no penalty tax. This rule applies even though the company was an ordinary corporation during the previous year.

Sub S Election Before Disposition of Major Corporate Asset. If the impending sale of a corporate asset promises to yield a substantial gain, it is likely that you do not want the gain to be taxed first to the corporation and then again to you as an individual. Instead, you can avoid the corporate double tax by electing Sub S status before the sale. Of course, take care that the $25,000 capital gain pass-through limitation does not affect the matter.

Return to Regular Incorporation. If you have already elected Sub S status, remember that you can switch back to the regular corporate form without any tax cost at any time. One reason to do this would be to have the first $50,000 of corporate income taxed at 20–22% rather than at your personal rate which could be higher. But after the return to regular incorporation, you may not elect Sub S for five years.

Sub S Election Before Corporate Liquidation. You may elect Sub S status before you liquidate your corporation to avoid the regular double tax on the sale of corporate assets. And naturally, if you incur losses during liquidation, Sub S election allows you to take a deduction as an individual.

Multiple Sub S's. If you own two corporations, Sub S election for both allows you to offset the gains of one against the losses of the other. This is not allowed in the case of regular corporation.

Combine Sub S Operating Losses with Personal Income to Save Taxes. If you elect Sub S for your corporation, you may deduct corporate loss from your other personal income. If you retain regular corporate status, you may only carry an operating loss back three years to offset prior corporate income and obtain a corporate tax refund. Any excess loss after carryback can then be carried forward to offset future corporate income.

As you can see, you may not deduct the losses from a regular corporation from your personal income. You may, however, elect Sub S for a year in which you anticipate losses and then return to regular incorporation the following year, if you wish. Note that personal loss deduction from your Sub S may not exceed the amount you paid for your stock (its *basis*) plus any corporation debt due you.

PROBLEMS TO AVOID WITH A SUB S

Loss Carryover. A corporation with a net operating loss carryover from years preceding its Sub S election may not use the loss carryover while it maintains a Sub S status. The carryover may be resurrected and put to use if the Sub S reverts to a regular corporation within the original five year carryover period. While the corporation remains Sub S, the carryover is put into a state of suspense.

Maintain Sub S Qualification. You must maintain your Sub S qualifications after election if you wish to retain your Sub S status. Remember that in the first five years you may have no more than ten shareholders who are individuals or estates (no corporation, or nonresident aliens) and your corporation must be domestic and not a member of an affiliated group. Only one class of stock is allowed and at least 80 percent of income must be bona fide, earned (not passive) income.

Salaries. A Sub S must pay reasonable salaries to its working shareholders before income is divided among all shareholders.

Deductibility of Operating Losses. Operating losses incurred by a Sub S are passed through directly to the shareholders who then deduct them from their personal incomes. Again, deduction of losses is limited to an amount *equal to the basis of the shareholder's stock and any corporate debt owed to him.* Excess loss above this amount is wasted.

Sub S Reversion. If your Sub S corporation reverts back to an ordinary corporation, be certain to distribute the retained income on which the shareholders have already paid tax. If you do not distribute it when you terminate your Sub S election, it will become taxable dividend when the ordinary corporation later distributes it to the shareholders. Of course, the throw back rule allows Sub S dividends to be distributed within two and one-half months of the end of the Sub S year.

Dividend Exclusion. An ordinary corporation may exclude from taxable income 85 percent of any dividends it receives from ownership of stock of other corporations. A Sub S corporation is entitled to no such deduction.

CHAPTER 3

SPECIAL ISSUES

HOW TO INCORPORATE TAX FREE

If you follow certain rules, you can incorporate your proprietorship or partnership tax free.

1. Transfer of assets from the proprietorship or partnership must be made only in exchange for stock or long term obligations of the corporation.
2. The person or persons who transferred property to the corporation must own at least 80% of the corporation's stock immediately after the exchange.

If the exchange satisfies the above two conditions and doesn't involve any of the following conditions, the incorporation is tax free. If, on the other hand, any one of the following three conditions are involved, there will be at least a partial tax.

1. *Liabilities in Excess of Assets*
   If you transfer $30,000 in assets and $35,000 in liabilities to a corporation, you have a taxable gain of $5,000. The rule is that transferred liability in excess of the adjusted basis of the transferred property is considered taxable gain. Here the term "liabilities" also includes property subject to liability.
2. *Personal Service*
   Personal service is not deemed property in this kind of tax free transfer. If personal service is exchanged for stock, a taxable income is created to the extent of the value of the personal service. In other words, if a person trades his skill and experience for 40% of the stock in a corporation, he must pay tax on the fair market value of the stock he receives.
3. *Bad Debt Reserve*
   If a proprietor transfers his accounts receivable as property exchange for corporate stock, he may have to treat any funds in a bad debt reserve account (for which he has taken annual deductions) as taxable income.

If you are caught in this kind of situation, there are a few things you can try to reduce the tax liability. You can elect Sub S for your corporation to avoid corporate tax so that the corporation's bad debt deduction for the new receivables passes directly to you. Or you can transfer your good receivables to the corporation and hold onto the dubious accounts. Finally, you may sell your receivables to a third party at a discount. In this last case you would want the amount of the discount to be less than the tax (that would be due) on the transfer of the reserve account to the new corporation. As long as the discount is less than the tax, you will be ahead.

SECTION 1244 STOCK

The term "1244 stock" comes from Section 1244 of the Internal Revenue Code, which deals with so-called small business stock.

Section 1244 was adopted by Congress as a means of encouraging investment in small incorporated businesses by giving a special tax break to investors. According to this part of the code, up to $25,000 ($50,000 if a joint return) per year of deductions against *ordinary* income can be taken for loss on the common stock of a small business corporation. This rule applies whether the loss is incurred by selling the stock or its becoming worthless while you hold it. However, several strict rules must be followed to qualify as 1244 stock.

- Only *common* stock (voting or nonvoting) of a *domestic* corporation may be designated.
- Such stock cannot be issued for more than $500,000, and the entire capital of the corporation cannot be more than $1 million.
- A *written* plan has to be adopted calling for the issuing of the stock within two years (and no other stock offering may be outstanding at the time of issue).
- The stock must be issued for money or property (not stock, securities, or services).
- The corporation must be an *operating* company and have derived over 50% of its revenue for the last five taxable years (or during its entire existence if less) from other than passive sources (royalties, rents, dividends, etc.).

Now, here are several points to consider:

1. Because of the special tax benefits, you may be better off purchasing 1244 stock rather than making a loan to a new company. If the business goes bad, you won't be caught in the troublesome area of trying to qualify the bad debt as a *business* loss (ordinary deduction) as opposed to a nonbusiness loss (short term capital deduction).

2. If you have a loss on 1244 stock but still have faith in the company, you can establish a loss (and the deduction) by selling the stock and then repurchasing shares later. However, to avoid classification as a "wash sale," don't buy the new shares for thirty days before or after the sale date.

3. Consider qualifying a new business as a Sub S corporation as well as under Section 1244. That way you will get personal deductions from *operating* losses (Sub S) as well as an ordinary deduction if the whole firm goes bad (1244).

As a final bit of information, the IRS says that the cost of preliminary research to investigate a new business is not deductible unless you subsequently go into the business. Therefore, whether you are an entrepreneur or an investor, consider incorporating and making a 1244 election *before* you spend any money. This way you will get an ordinary loss deduction if things don't work out.

PROBLEMS TO AVOID

Thin Incorporation

"Thin incorporation" refers to the capital structure of a new corporation. Quite often business people will transfer part of their assets to a new corporation as an equity investment in exchange for stock and part as a loan, a debt investment. The tactic employed here is that the corporation can deduct the interest it pays on the loan and, as the debt is repaid, capital is returned tax free. In addition to avoiding the double tax by paying *interest* instead of *dividends* to the shareholder, thin incorporation also allows profits to be accumulated to repay debts without risking penalty tax for unreasonable accumulation. But there are problems.

Incorporation is tax free only if the proprietor or partner receives stock and securities in exchange for his transferred assets. For this reason the corporation's debt instrument must qualify as a security. To avoid having the IRS regard the interest payments as disguised dividends, be sure that proper notes are drawn up to reflect evidences of debt.

The IRS and the tax courts get very suspicious if they don't see a true debtor-creditor relationship. The following will help to convince them of your good intentions:

*   Establish the debt in your accounts, show it on the financial statements, and record it in the minutes.
*   See that the ratio of debt to equity in the corporation does not exceed 3½ to 1.
*   Be sure there is a written unconditional promise to pay a reasonable, fixed rate of interest at proper intervals and that

the payment of interest does not depend on corporate earnings.

- Try to establish some evidence that outside creditors would have seriously considered making the same loan you did.
- The debt holder should have the right to sue and enforce payment and the debt should not be subordinate to other creditors.
- The amount of debt should be reasonable and it should be clear to the IRS that if interest and payments are made on schedule, the debt can be paid off in the normal operation of the business.

However, before you leap into thin incorporation consider the potential disadvantages. The debt may affect the corporation's credit rating and it commits the corporation to regular payments of interest and principal that could strangle cash flow at the wrong time.

Unreasonable Compensation

Basically there are three ways to take money out of an incorporated business: (1) salary, (2) dividends, and (3) tax-free benefits, such as a medical reimbursement plan. Clearly, the best route is tax-free benefits, but the law strictly limits the amount and type of benefits you can receive. Between salary and dividends, there is a decided advantage to salary. Even though both salary and dividends are treated as ordinary income to the individual, only salary payments are deductible to the corporation. As a result salary emerges as the most practical and taxwise way to get money out of most businesses. The trouble is the IRS knows this, too, and often attacks salaries as "unreasonable" and requires a portion to be treated as dividends.

The optimal salary from a tax standpoint isn't necessarily the best salary from all standpoints. First, you must consider the economic situation of your company. It simply may not be able to pay out all you would like as salary. The second consideration is your standard of living. You may not be able to live on a salary that works out best in terms of taxes. Finally, there is the IRS to contend with. A favorite Treasury strategy is to claim that the salary paid is excessive and that part must either be treated as a dividend (and the corporation will lose the deduction) or be repaid to the corporation. While there are no hard and fast rules, here are several factors the IRS considers when checking the reasonableness of officer-shareholder salaries:

1. *Qualifications.* What is the education and experience of the individual?
2. *Competitors.* What salaries are paid to comparable individuals in other companies in the industry?
3. *Scope of work.* What is the size and complexity of the business and nature of the individual's work? Is the individual full- or part-time?

4. *Dividend history*. Does the company have a history of paying dividends or do salaries vary from year to year to minimize dividends?

- *Other means of compensation*. If corporate earnings are rising and salaries are going up while dividends remain constant or are even omitted, you will probably face IRS scrutiny. In this case there are a couple of alternate strategies. The first is for officer-shareholders to perform certain services on a "for fee" basis. So long as the services are needed by the corporation and the fee is comparable to that paid to outsiders, the amount should be allowed. A second possible strategy is to enter into an arrangement with the corporation so that you are paid a base salary plus a percentage of sales. As long as the contract was consummated at arm's length and the percentage was reasonable at the time, high compensation results will not necessarily mean a disallowance of the deduction.

- *Don't shortchange yourself in the early years*. Many businessmen pay themselves low salaries in the early years because that is all their companies can afford. Later, as the dollars start to roll in, they raise their salaries to compensate—only to have the increase treated as excessive by the IRS. The solution is to pay yourself a reasonable salary from the beginning and have the corporation give you a note for any amount it can not afford to pay. Realize, of course, that the amount of the note must be taken into personal income. This way, the corporation gets the deduction in the current period and later, when you get your back pay, there should be no problem with the IRS. If you have been in business for some time and have underpaid yourself to build up corporate funds, be sure to have the corporate records show how much you were underpaid. This way, when you eventually raise your pay, you will be able to show the IRS that the increase is justified in light of your past undercompensation.

- *Repayment Agreement*. A good protective tactic in the area of unreasonable salary is to have a written salary agreement that stipulates that you will repay any salary that the IRS deems excessive. Put this written agreement into the corporate minutes. Then, if the IRS does declare part of your salary to be unreasonable, you may repay the excess salary (which you have already paid tax on) and treat this repayment as a personal deduction. Naturally, the corporation loses its deduction for the amount you repay, but it does, after all, get the money back. This way, even if the IRS makes you return part of your unreasonable salary, both you and your corporation are right back where you would have been had you not been paid the excessive amount. There is no penalty for trying. Later you can try again to get money out of the corporation either under different circumstances or through other means.

Fending Off the Accumulated Earnings Tax

Corporations are allowed to accumulate up to $150,000 of earnings, but if they exceed that amount, they must be able to justify the excess to the IRS or else pay a penalty tax on the excess. Although the excess that brought on the penalty tax may have been built up gradually over the years, the penalty tax is computed on the corporation's annual taxable income. If an earnings accumulation is deemed unreasonable by the IRS, the company must pay 27½% on the first $150,000 of its annual income and 38½% of income over $150,000 *in addition* to the regular corporate income tax.

There are three ways to avoid the penalty tax on accumulated earnings.

1. *Elect Sub S Status.* If the company elects Sub S status, the accumulation is directly taxed at the shareholder's personal rate whether the earnings are distributed or not.
2. *Pay the Excess Out in Dividends.* If the excess is paid out as dividends to the stockholders in an ordinary corporation, the usual double tax is paid on the earnings. But this might be preferable to paying the penalty tax. Also, the throw back rule allows dividends paid in the first two and one-half months of a new tax year to be deemed part of the previous year.
3. *Prove That the Excess is Needed for Operation of the Business.* Finally, how do you prove that the excess is needed for the continued operation of the company? The corporation should be able to show specific plans for the accumulated funds and evidence of intent and conduct toward accomplishing the plans. The following are some of the accepted planned uses for accumulated earnings:

- To acquire a new business. It need not be related to the corporation's business.
- Planned construction for replacement or improvement of facilities.
- Expansion for increased production, diversification, or acquisition of a source of supply.
- Working capital for an operating cycle. (The cycle goes from cash to inventory to sales to accounts receivable and back to cash.)
- Retirement of preferred stock.
- Retirement of the corporation's debt.
- A reserve fund for uninsurable events like lawsuits, proposed changes in legislation, a strike threat, etc.

- Loans or investments which ensure the continuation of a business relationship with suppliers and customers.

The above allay IRS suspicions. Below are a few conditions that arouse IRS suspicions.

- Large cash balances.
- Significant investments in certificates of deposit or marketable securities.
- Long term loans to stockholders.
- Rapid turnover in receivables.
- Corporate monies spent for the personal benefit of shareholders.
- Minimal inventory requirements.
- High premium life insurance policies on the lives of stockholder-employees.

Personal Holding Company Status

It might seem ideal to form an investment corporation and have the corporation buy stock, using the allowed 85% dividend exclusion deduction. Then, instead of paying tax on the dividends in accordance with your personal income tax rate, you could let the dividend accumulate in the corporation at a cost of only 3.3% (15% of dividend income times the 22% corporate tax rate). But it doesn't work this way. You don't want to have a personal holding company (PHC) which the IRS would frown upon and would tax at a rate of 70% plus the usual corporate tax rate.

A corporation is considered to be a PHC if it meets two criteria: (1) More than 50% of its outstanding stock is owned by five or fewer individuals at any time during the last half of the year. (2) 60% or more of its adjusted ordinary gross income is made up of passive income, such as interest, royalties, income from personal service contracts, dividends, annuities, (some) rent income and compensation paid to the corporation by its stockholders for use of company property. If your corporation meets *both* criteria, the PHC penalty tax will be assessed unless the PHC income is paid out as dividends.

In regard to ownership restrictions, a stockholder is considered the owner of shares held in his name by members of his family, relatives, other corporations and partnerships in which he has ownership interest. This attribution of ownership is common in close corporations. Therefore, the trick is to avoid meeting the income criterion.

Dividends and interest are obviously passive income that will be examined for the 60% passive income test. Income from leases to shareholders is also generally considered passive income. Your tax advisor should carefully look over your sources of income to see whether or not it will put you in a PHC status.

It is advisable to play it safe in the area of the PHC. Beware of falling with in the five person 50% ownership restriction and be certain that no more than 59% of the corporation's earnings is from passive sources.

HOW TO FORM A FAMILY PARTNERSHIP

A family partnership allows a proprietor to split his income with family members who are in a lower tax bracket. By paying less tax on the same income, the collective wealth of the family increases. And it should also be noted that a proprietor's estate tax will be reduced as well, because his children already own part of the business.

Since a family partnership can save a great deal on taxes, special rules have been established to prevent abuse of this structure. A family partnership may include husband, wife, children, grandparents, grandchildren, or a trust set up for these persons. Special family partnership rules do not apply to partnerships that include a brother, a sister, an in-law, an aunt, or an uncle.

In addition to adhering to the laws governing a general partnership, a family partnership must follow these special rules:

- If a child is to be a partner, his interest must be held under a trust or a guardianship. The guardianship of a minor must be reviewed annually by a court. A minor of any age may be a partner.
- A family member may be a partner only if capital (equipment, inventories, plant, etc.) is an income producing factor. In a service industry the family member must regularly perform a valuable service.
- The donor or seller of a partnership interest must take out a reasonable salary for his service before the remaining profit is divided among the family partners, if capital is a material income producing factor. A new partner may not receive a greater proportion of profit than the old partner.
- The donor or seller of the partnership interest can retain management control, but only so far as is consistent with transfer of interest in true ownership. In other words:
1. The old partner may not control the assets so that he owns them and leases them to the partnership.
2. All partners must agree on the distribution of profit.
3. The new partner must have an unlimited right to liquidate his interest.
4. The new partner must be treated publicly as a partner.

Some additional details on family partnerships:

- The gift of a partnership is subject to gift tax. But you can usually get around this tax by giving a small piece of the business to the new partner each year, the value of which does not exceed the annual $3,000 gift tax exclusion per donee.

- A spouse's share of the profits or the share belonging to a minor may be left in the partnership for the purpose of business expansion. However, a child must withdraw sufficient profit to pay his own income tax. If the parent pays it for him, the payment might be subject to gift tax.
- No matter how much income a child receives from the partnership, the parent may continue to claim him as a dependent (so long as he is a student or under nineteen). If your spouse is a partner, you will not reduce your annual income because you will still file a joint return. However it may reduce your future estate tax and your spouse may benefit from Social Security coverage.

Part II
HOW TO OPERATE
YOUR BUSINESS

CHAPTER 4

BASIC MANAGEMENT OVERVIEW

STRENGTHS AND WEAKNESSES OF A SMALLER BUSINESS*

Many small businessmen (those who employ less than five hundred people) worry that larger competitors will drive them out of business. However, small businesses actually do have many significant advantages over large companies. Knowledge of these strengths—and weaknesses—will help you avoid costly mistakes and protect your business from encroachments by competitors.

Small company weaknesses

Financial limitations. Balancing "cash in" and cash out" is a struggle, especially when a company is trying to expand. Instead of receiving the red carpet treatment by financiers when floating a loan, the small businessman is often made to feel like a second-class citizen. And small companies can't use credit as a selling tool as readily as companies with large financial reserves. Additionally, many small companies have trouble staying afloat while waiting for their products to win acceptance in the marketplace.

Manpower problems. Small companies cannot pay top salaries and provide the opportunities and status normally associated with a big company job. Small company management must also concentrate on the day-to-day problems of running the business and generally have little time left to think about the company objectively.

Higher direct costs. A small company cannot buy raw materials, machinery, or supplies as cheaply as a large company or obtain a large producer's economies of scale. So per unit production costs are usually higher for a small company, but overhead costs are generally somewhat lower.

Too many eggs. A large diversified company can take a licking in one sector of its business and still remain strong. This is not so for the small busi-

---

*Portions of this article are condensed from: Alfred Gross, "Meeting the Competition of Giants," *Harvard Business Review*, May–June 1967.

ness with only a few product lines. A small company is vulnerable if a new product doesn't catch on, if one of its markets is hit by a sharp recession, or if an old product suddenly becomes obsolete.

Lack of acceptance. The public accepts a large company's products because its name is well known and usually respected. A small company must struggle to prove itself each time it offers a new product or enters a new market. Its reputation and past successes in the marketplace seldom carry weight.

Small company strengths

Personal touch. Customers will often pay a premium for personalized attention. In fact, in many industries where product and price differences are minimal, the human factor emerges as a prime competitive advantage.

Greater motivation. Top management of a small company normally consists of the owners or major stockholders. Consequently, they work harder, longer, and with more personal involvement. Profits and losses have more meaning for them than salaries and bonuses have to employees of a larger company.

Greater flexibility. The small company has the prime competitive advantage of agility. A big business cannot close a plant without opposition from organized labor or even raise prices without possible intervention from Washington, but a small company can react quickly to competitive changes. A small company also has shorter lines of communication. Its product lines are narrow, its markets limited, and its factories and warehouses close. It can quickly spot trouble or opportunity and take appropriate action.

Less bureaucracy. Grasping the big picture is difficult for executives of large companies. This "management myopia" leads to redundant actions and bureaucratic inefficiencies. In a small business the whole problem can be understood readily, decisions can be made quickly, and the results can be checked easily.

Unobtrusive. Because it is not readily noticeable, the small company can try new sales tactics or introduce new products without attracting undue attention and opposition. Large companies also are constantly faced with proxy battles, antitrust actions, and government regulations.

Opportunities in the giant's shadow

Too many businessmen panic in the face of competition from a large company and overcompensate by drastic price cuts, expanded services, or the introduction of unproven products. The most important rule is never compete head on with a giant—you'll invariably lose. Here is a plan of action for circumventing the competition:

> *Aim at specialized market segments.* To maximize sales volume and production efficiency, large companies concentrate on the needs of average customers—often bypassing large market segments that desire specialized products or services. By carefully studying the unique needs of this market, the small business-

man can usually find numerous opportunities that are both secure and profitable.

Localize your business. Certain local preferences exist for almost every product and service. For example, food, beverages, clothing, and household items have regional and local variances. Large companies cannot efficiently cater to individual markets. In national promotions, the giant must appeal to as many and irritate as few people as possible. Its copy becomes bland and generalized. Stress the uniqueness of your localization by using local people, backgrounds, and motifs in your advertising.

Personal touch. No large company can compete with the personal touch of a smaller local businessman. Don't become so absorbed in your operational problems that you fail to get out to see customers. In those cases where you are not competitive in price, extra personal service can often swing the sale your way.

Conclusion

In an expanding economy large companies generally concentrate on expanding markets and new product areas, bypassing lower yield market segments. Sometimes, however, the opposite is true. To maintain sales, the large company begins to enter more specialized market segments, threatening smaller businesses. Be alert to this potential threat and take action to protect yourself.

HOW TO FORMULATE A BUSINESS STRATEGY

Formulating a corporate strategy is an imposing-sounding undertaking. On one hand you might say, "That's just for huge conglomerates—not for my relatively simple business." But, you might be surprised if you knew how many large firms are floundering because they don't have a coherent or consistent strategy—or just how many little firms are rapidly getting larger because they do!

What is a Corporate Strategy?

Strategy—no panacea or mystery—consists of three simple but profound questions that you should regularly ask yourself:

- What business am I really in?
- What is happening in the business environment that could affect my company?
- How do I organize all the resources I have (human, financial, material, etc.) to meet the business challenge ahead?
  In other words, strategy means to constantly ask, "Where am I going—and how do I plan to get there?"

Why Is a Business Strategy Important?

Because if you don't know where you are going, how can you ever get there? Strategy formulation forces you to:

- Focus on the *future* as well as on your present problems.
- Consider *risks* and obstacles ahead and plan adequately to meet them.
- Define your corporate *purpose.*
- Set *objectives* to meet your goals.

Business Definition

What business are you *really* in? This is the first mistake many businessmen make. Let's take a classic example:

Earlier this century, there was hardly an industry more powerful than the railroads. Today many are practically bankrupt. What happened? Well, the railroads were insular and isolated in their thinking. They scoffed at the idea that trucks could ever carry volumes of freight as efficiently from place to place as the railroads. And, of course, to think of carrying major cargo by air—well, that was ridiculous. Or so it seemed at the time. They defined their business as railroading and it was king! What they failed to realize until too late was that they were really in the *transportation* business. Rather than integrate naturally into other transportation businesses, including trucking and the airlines, which they could have done, they stuck to the rails and fought a bitter battle to try and kill other forms of freight and passenger haulage. Today, the results of the myopic and literal, rather than *functional,* definition of their business is all too evident.

And so it is that first you must define your business in functional, not product, terms. What do you *do* for your customers—not what do you sell them. McDonald's doesn't sell just hamburgers and french fries—they also sell quality, service, and convenience. That's what the customer wants. Hamburgers he can get anywhere.

Environmental Trends

Once you have properly defined your corporate purpose, you must then assess how *social, political, economic,* and *technological* trends affect your business. For example:

Social. If you are in high fashion, what does the back-to-nature movement mean to you?
Political. What effect will such governmental actions as price controls, taxes, zoning restrictions, or import quotas have on your business?
Economic. How is your business affected by changes in interest rates, the general economic climate, or inflation? (And what about raw materials and the energy shortage? If you are in trucking, lack of energy is obviously an ominous threat. If you

are in the insulation business, it could be a splendid opportunity.)

Technological. Is there danger of technological obsolescence in your business? What must you do to keep up? Can you *afford* to keep up?

What Resources Do You Have?

In other words, once you've considered the risks and opportunities ahead for your business, what capabilities do you have to cope with them? What are your *strengths* and *weaknesses* in each of the following areas?

> *Human.* Do you have enough people, and can they be properly trained to shift to a slightly (or perhaps radically) different type of business?
>
> *Financial.* What money will be required and how can it be made available?
>
> *Physical.* Will new or different facilities, machinery, or raw materials be needed?

Strategic Choices and Internal Consistency

After you have defined your business and assessed relevant environmental trends and your capabilities to cope with them, you must choose among several strategic options, such as:

- Maximize short-term or long-term profits.
- Invest in present markets or expand into new markets.
- Invest profits back in the company (growth) or commit to shareholders (dividends).

You must insure, however, that your strategy is *internally consistent.* For example, rapid short-term growth is not consistent with paying out most profits as dividends. In addition, analyze if the proposed strategy is acceptable in terms of:

- *Risk.* A subjective judgment based on (1) resources available for commitment, (2) duration of commitment, (3) proportion of total resources committed to a single venture.
- *Time Horizon.* How long until results are evident? How long do you have?

Conclusion

A major problem of managers in many companies is that they are completely preoccupied with day-to-day problems. They never have the time to appraise current performance and assess the long-term needs and prospects of their business. It is a form of ad hoc decision-making—not management. In brief, take time to *manage* your company.

HOW TO MAKE YOUR BUSINESS SUCCEED
BEYOND ONE GENERATION—THE SEARS EXAMPLE

Many managers are so engrossed in the day-to-day operational details of running their businesses (and surviving) that they sometimes lose sight of where their companies are going. Often studying the experiences of other successful companies can yield a rewarding sense of perspective. Here's a brief case study of one of the most consistently successful companies in the country. It is no accident, as you will see.

In the Beginning . . .

Sears, Roebuck and Company was founded around the turn of the century with the objective of tapping a totally separate and distinct market—the farmer. Separate because his isolation made other distribution channels virtually inaccessible to him; distinct because his needs were different in many respects from urban counterparts'.

To reach this market, new distribution channels had to be created. Merchandise had to be produced for the farmer's specific needs and made available at low prices. Finally, the merchandise and company had to have a reputation for reliability and honesty, since the farmer's geographic isolation made it impractical for him to inspect the merchandise beforehand or seek redress if swindled. To accomplish these needs, innovations were necessary in five distinct areas:

> *Supply.* Arrangements had to be made with vendors to furnish to Sears the quantity and quality of goods needed.
> *Distribution.* The mail order catalog had to be developed as a substitute for big city shopping.
> *Quality.* The famous (and revolutionary at the time) guarantee of "your money back and no questions asked" was initiated.
> *Processing.* A mail order plant had to be built to inventory huge quantities of merchandise and process large numbers of customer orders.
> *Organization.* When Sears began, there were no buyers, accountants, artists, clerks, etc., with the necessary skills. Everything had to be developed.

While Richard Sears gave the company its name, it was Julius Rosenwald who oversaw the necessary innovations and built the initial enterprise. Rosenwald is not only the father of Sears but of the twentieth century distribution revolution. By targeting a specific market and building an organization to serve it, by the end of World War I Sears grew into a national institution with its "wish book," the only literature, outside of the Bible, found in many farm homes.

A Major Strategic Shift

The second phase of Sears's growth began in the 1920s and was dominated by General Robert E. Wood. When Wood joined Sears, the original market was rapidly changing. The farmer was no longer isolated; he now had an automobile to take him to town where he could shop. Hence, many of the systems and innovations instituted by Rosenwald were no longer appropriate.

At the same time a vast urban market was developing that consisted of lower-income groups who were rapidly acquiring both the money and the desire to buy the same goods as upper class consumers. It was Wood who perceived that the country was becoming one large homogeneous and mobile market. As a result of this analysis, Sears made the decision to make a major strategic shift and switch its emphasis to retail stores equipped to serve both the more mobile farmer and the city dweller.

Still More Innovation

A whole series of innovations were necessary to implement the new thrust of the company:

> *Merchandise.* Many items had to be redesigned—goods appropriate for the farmer had to be changed to appeal to the mass market. New suppliers had to be created and often trained by Sears.
> *Management.* Running a retail store is different from a mail order business. For almost fifteen years Sears's greatest bottleneck was a shortage of retail store managers. Internal management development programs were begun and became the models for many other companies.
> *Organization.* Mail order was a highly centralized operation for Sears. Running retail stores throughout the country required a complete shift to a decentralized organizational structure. Everything possible was done to encourage local autonomy.
> *Site Selection.* Major innovations were necessary to determine the optimum location for new stores. The suburban shopping center, which is thought to be a relatively recent phenomenon, is really a copy of many of the concepts developed by Sears before World War II.

Modern Day

The automobile changed Sears's market once and seems to be affecting it again. Pollution, gas shortage, and lack of parking all affect the urban shopper today. Also, more women are entering the work force and so have less time to shop. Many customers are shifting back to catalog-ordering—although more often by phone than by mail. In short, Sears must run as fast today as they did seventy-five years ago.

The major conclusion we can draw from the Sears's story is that *people* determine the destiny of any business. It took Rosenwald twenty-five years to build the basic enterprise—and Wood another twenty-five to insure its continued growth. In contrast, it took Sewell Lee Avery only a few years to wreck Sears's only major competitor, Montgomery Ward, by his premonition of a depression following World War II.

As you struggle to stay on top of your business, keep one eye on the future. *Few businesses are successful beyond one generation simply because they cannot adapt to the ever-changing competitive environment.*

BUSINESS OPPORTUNITIES YOU MAY NOT HAVE CONSIDERED —SHOULD YOU OFFER A SERVICE?

It may surprise you to learn that over two thirds of our gross national product is created by services, and nine out of every ten new jobs are created in the service sector of the economy. Businessmen come in contact with services every day. Perhaps you should take a few moments to learn a little more about this fastest-growing part of the US economy.

Just What is a Service?

Keep a list of every purchase where you end up empty-handed. For example, you may pay rent, an insurance premium, or a highway toll. Or you may see a doctor, go to a movie, take a trip, or have a plumber unstop a drain. In each case, you have purchased a service—you received something for your money, but it was not tangible.

Actually, there are many definitions of a service, but they all revolve around two main characteristics. One is intangibility; the other is that *production and consumption of a service occur almost simultaneously.* A dinner in a fine restaurant or at a hamburger stand certainly involves a tangible product, but in both cases, the meal is produced and consumed over a relatively short period of time, so restaurants and fast-food chains are also generally referred to as service establishments.

What is Different About a Service?

There are several differences between services and goods. Here are a few:

> *No ownership.* It is easy to transfer possession of physical property, whether a house or a bottle of aspirin. Services, on the other hand, cannot be owned or patented. This results in a very fast product life cycle for new service innovations. When Hertz offered the Number One Club that cut red tape, note how quickly the Wizard of Avis followed.
> *Interaction of buyer and seller.* Since production and consumption occur almost simultaneously, the buyer and seller must come together, so the physical location of operating units can be very important.
> *No inventory.* Unlike a goods-producing business where one can create a backlog of inventory to meet seasonal needs or peak demand, services cannot be stored. Only the *capability* to produce can be stockpiled. A consulting firm can take on extra professionals in anticipation of an increasing workload, but until additional work actually comes in, the individual cannot produce.
> *Cannot be transported.* Unlike manufactured goods, services cannot be transported to the consumer. As a result, a service business tends to have many units—each run as a separate busi-

ness. Much of the impetus behind the franchise boom was to obtain competent, committed managers to own and run local units.

Difficult to define quality. The quality of most services (except perhaps food) is difficult for the consumer to evaluate. How can one accurately measure the quality of medical care, management consulting, or education? And what can be done if the quality is not up to expectations? You generally cannot send a service back any more than you can give back a plane trip. As a result, the reputation of the service producer for providing quality is of major importance. And because the provider of the service generally comes in direct contact with the consumers, education and training of employees, agents, franchisees, and other people involved in the business are very important. In effect, training is often a service firm's only lever on quality control. Such emphasis on training has led to the establishment of McDonald's Hamburger University and Holiday Inn's Holiday University.

Why Have We Become a Service Economy?

Sixty-seven percent of the gross national product, 70% of the jobs, and 45% of personal consumption dollars go for services—and the figures are steadily rising. The reasons are simple:

First, the development of many services is a result of today's increased emphasis on experiences rather than possession of physical goods. We are encouraged to *do* our own thing, not own our own thing.

The second reason is the need for specialization due to exploding technological changes and new informational requirements. Consultants, computer time-sharing companies, personnel agencies, leasing companies, and many other services are used by businesses because of their need to specialize where they have a definite competitive advantage and leave supporting services to be performed by others.

Implications for the Businessman

The continued trend toward a service-dominated economy is inescapable. Coca-Cola is marketing a multi-media learning system to the education market. Upjohn has started a company called Homemakers that performs paramedical and housekeeping chores for newly discharged hospital patients. Gerber is moving from baby foods into nursery schools, daycare centers, and insurance. Maytag is offering to lease washers to make it easier for would-be purchasers.

In short, more and more companies realize that future growth will be in services. No matter how bad the times, over half of service expenditures are relatively fixed commitments. Take a look at what you sell. Is there a related service you could offer? Services could improve your sales and profits in our increasingly service-oriented economy.

HOW TO GET COMMITMENT FROM YOUR EMPLOYEES—MANAGEMENT BY OBJECTIVES*

According to Webster, an objective is "that toward which effort is directed; an aim or end of action; goal."

A laborer was asked to dig a three-foot hole beside a building. After completing the job his foreman asked him to dig another a few feet away. The foreman then requested a third hole and a fourth. Finally, the man threw down his pick and shovel and shouted, "I quit!" Although well-paid, he refused to aimlessly dig holes in the ground. As soon as the foreman told him that the purpose was to locate a broken drainage pipe, the man went back to work and willingly dug until the pipe was located.

A New Era

Most employees today are just like the laborer above. They seek fulfillment, self-expression, and meaning in their work. As a result the era of the hard-nosed manager and management by pressure is giving way to "management by objectives." MBO is one of the dominant management philosophies of the 1970s and has been used successfully by an impressive number of companies throughout the world.

What is MBO?

MBO is based on two simple, but powerful, concepts:

- The clearer the idea employees have of where a business is going, the better the chance it has of getting there.
- Real progress can only be measured in relation to what one is striving toward.

When these concepts are put into action, MBO consists of three concrete steps:

- Superiors and subordinates *jointly* agree on the overall goals of the organization.
- Each manager's major area of responsibility is delineated, and his specific performance objectives are jointly agreed upon.
- These objectives serve as guides for operating the unit and assessing the performance of its members.

Efficiency vs. Effectiveness

Traditional management philosophies focus on efficiency; MBO is based on effectiveness. Most managers encourage "workmanship" and "doing a good

---

*For further information on management by objectives, see John N. Humble, *How to Manage by Objectives*, The American Management Association.

job." But the danger is that the manager will confuse efficiency in digging holes (doing things right) with effectiveness in solving drainage problems (doing the right things). Successful management, therefore, goes beyond setting production quotas or standards of workmanship. It is the art of obtaining *organizational commitment to the overall goals of the company.* Without this focus on the big picture, effort throughout the company can become misdirected; and friction, frustration, and conflict will inevitably result.

Job Descriptions

Does your business have job descriptions? If they contain such behavioral words as administers, maintains, organizes, plans, and schedules, you can be sure they are not very useful as an operating guide. Other companies have job descriptions that identify the manager's position in the organization: reports to, authorizes, coordinates, delegates, approves. These, too, are ineffectual. Only when a job description emphasizes *outputs* does it become effective. It might deal with sales and costs and the authority to increase or decrease staff, use overtime, change products or services, rearrange work flow, or modify production patterns. It does little good to tell a man what he will administer and to whom he will report if he does not have objectives. Objectives tell him what he is working toward and how his progress will be evaluated.

Setting Objectives

The first step in setting objectives is to clarify the company's overall goals. Typically, these are stated in terms of sales and profitability, although sometimes such factors as market standing, productivity, and social responsibility are also mentioned.

The second step is to determine all the key factors that contribute toward meeting these overall goals. They could include:

- Optimum business areas
- Profitability by line of business
- Productivity
- Financial and physical resources
- Management resources
- Employee performance and attitude

Once determined, specific objectives are usually arranged in hierarchical fashion. (See chart on page 42.)

Where Goals Go Astray

Many executives make these mistakes when setting objectives for their subordinates:

- Goals set too low to challenge the individuals (underload).
- Goals set too high (overload).

SIMPLIFIED MBO CHART
TYPICAL HIERARCHY OF OBJECTIVES.

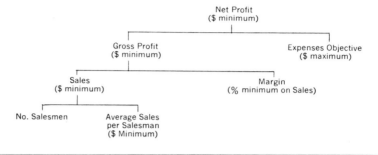

- Goals not measurable.
- Too many goals.
- Too long or short a time period.
- Imbalanced emphasis.
- Real obstacles to achieving specific goals ignored.
- Intermediate target dates by which to measure the subordinates' progress not set.
- Rigidity. Subordinates not allowed to seize new opportunities or targets in lieu of stated goals.

To Insure Success

The strength—and weakness—of MBO is that it appears to be simple to introduce. To insure success, several factors must be present: (1) top management must be intimately involved and dedicated to making the program work; (2) subordinates must be confident that they will be evaluated on how well they meet their objectives; (3) objectives must be jointly set by superior and subordinates; and (4) the MBO program cannot become clogged with paperwork.

MBO is not a panacea to pin things down. If anything, it introduces flexibility up and down the line. Hence, a climate conducive to creativity and expression by subordinates must be encouraged.

HOW TO ORGANIZE TO GET THE JOB DONE

What is an organizational structure and why is it so important? Consider the analogy of a football team coming to the line of scrimmage. The way resources are deployed and what sort of formation is used obviously depends on the competitive situation and what the team is trying to accomplish. It's the same way in business. Like a football team, a business organization is people who must be properly organized to be effective. *No business, whether it is large or small, can prosper and grow without an appropriate organizational structure.*

Types of organizational structure

Size is a major factor that influences what organizational structure is best for a particular business. As a business grows, managerial style as well as organizational shape must also change, or the company may be effectively stymied.

Entrepreneurial stage. Most small companies (those employing up to about twenty-five people) are characterized by *lack* of organizational structure. Here, the owner-manager gets involved in almost everything—selling, accounting, manufacturing, hiring/firing, and buying. Typically, the company has few product lines at this stage.

Functional structure. In order for a business to grow beyond about twenty-five employees, the owner-manager must devote more time to higher-level problems and less to daily operations. As a result, a second echelon of middle management must be developed to take over the specialized functions, such as sales, production, and administration. The shift from the entrepreneurial stage to a functional structure is usually gradual, and the dividing line is somewhat arbitrary. However, the key to a successful transition is the owner's ability to *delegate responsibility* to subordinates and to work *through* people rather than supervising the work directly. Many business owners cannot make this shift from entrepreneur to manager and their companies often stagnate or fail completely. The functional structure is highly adaptive and used by most medium-sized companies as well as many large ones. It works best when there are *relatively few products using similar production processes and distribution channels.* For example, the Thomas J. Lipton Tea Company is organized functionally as is Goodyear Tire, Standard

ENTREPRENEURIAL STAGE

Oil of Ohio, and the Aluminum Company of America (ALCOA). However, a functional structure has several serious weaknesses:

- *Profit responsibility.* Each functional area (sales, production, etc.) tends to think only in terms of costs. Only top management has direct responsibility for profits.
- *Parochialism.* Each functional specialty tends to think only of its own problems. For example, it can be difficult to coordinate the insular perspectives of production and sales. Production may be concerned with even work flow and minimal disruptions while sales may promise a customer early delivery. Conflict naturally arises.
- *Market responsiveness.* A functional structure can be unresponsive to shifting demand since no one has overall responsibility for each product. For example, the production department can be busily cranking out Product A without learning from the sales department that Product A just isn't selling. For a functional structure to work successfully, therefore, the burden is on top management to carefully monitor and coordinate each functional area.

Product structure.   To overcome the weaknesses of a functional structure, many companies use a product-oriented structure in which the company is structured according to its primary products instead of its functional areas.

The chief advantage of this structure is that each product manager can be given overall profit and loss responsibility for his particular product. As a result, decisions are decentralized and the company can be more responsive to the marketplace. The great disadvantage of this structure, however, is that it can result in expensive duplication of functional specialties. For example,

FUNCTIONAL STRUCTURE

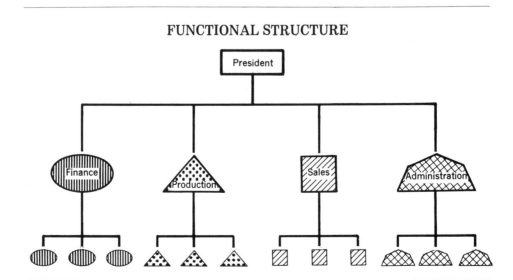

PRODUCT STRUCTURE

instead of one production manager for the whole company, a different one may be needed for each product.

Project management or matrix structure. To overcome the expense of a product structure and still retain control of certain important products, some companies use what is known as a matrix structure. With this type of organization, a manager is assigned the responsibility of coordinating a particular product with each functional area. He reports directly to top management. By cutting across functional areas, however, the structure has an inherent instability, and it is best applied to products needing intensive but rather short-term attention.

*How to design an organizational structure
for your company*

No matter how big your company is, consider its organizational structure. You don't need to draw up formal charts and distribute them to employees—many managers don't. Nevertheless, *you* should have a clear idea of how your company is organized. Here is a summary of the factors to consider once you are beyond the entrepreneurial stage.

- *Competitive situation.* If the market in which you operate is stable and predictable, a functional structure is probably best. A product structure is more appropriate when the

PROJECT MANAGEMENT STRUCTURE

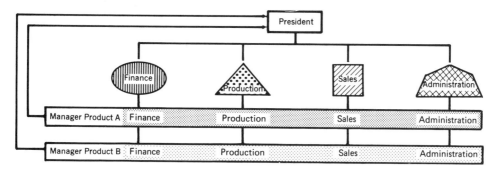

competitive situation is volatile and decisions must be made quickly at a decentralized level.

- *Cost.* A functional structure is more efficient in terms of manpower. However, if many products are being produced, the time to coordinate all products with each functional area may obviate any real savings. In such a case, a product structure may be more appropriate.
- *Type of product.* Products that are heavily research and development-oriented or likely to require continual updates or modifications usually fit best in a matrix or a functional structure. However, if the product is well established and primary emphasis is on sales rather than development, the more market-oriented product structure is generally best.

SPECIAL PROBLEMS—CONFLICTS THAT PLAGUE FAMILY BUSINESSES*

The entrepreneur/founder

Most successful small- and medium-sized companies are started and run by business executives who are essentially entrepreneurs. However, their own business success often results in intense personal and family problems that are rarely encountered by professional managers of larger companies. Psychological research reveals three general causes for these problems:

- An entrepreneur characteristically has unresolved conflicts with his father. Because of his discomfort when under supervision, he starts his own business both to outdo his father and to escape authority.
- An entrepreneur's business is simultaneously his baby and his mistress. When anyone else tries to obtain any power, including family members, trouble results. This dominance and centralization of power is why so many organizations cannot grow beyond the entrepreneurial stage and often decline or fail when the founder ages or dies.
- For the entrepreneur, the business is essentially an extension of himself and a medium for personal gratification and achievement. While he may be concerned with what happens to the business after he dies, generally that concern takes the form of thinking about what kind of monument he can leave behind rather than making sure that the business can continue to thrive and grow without him.

*Portions of this article were condensed from: Harry Levinson, "Conflicts that Plague Family Businesses," *Harvard Business Review*, March–April 1971.

Father/offspring rivalry

The entrepreneur-founder often has difficulty dealing with his children. While consciously he would like to pass the business on to his children, unconsciously he is afraid to give up his "baby," his source of social power, and whatever else the business may mean to him. Most of all, the father unconsciously needs to assert himself and demonstrate competence. "After all, I'm the one who built this business and no one else can make it run the way I can." As a result, the father really doesn't want his children to take over the business because he's afraid that he may be displaced as the central figure. The result is predictable. The children feel increasingly frustrated by a lack of true autonomy and authority commensurate with their maturity. The father looks on the children as ungrateful, implies that they will never be able to run the business, and refuses to retire, despite repeated promises to do so. And, of course, even if the children do gain control, the scion cannot win. No matter how much they improve the business, their contribution will always be minimized. "After all their father really built that business."

Sibling rivalry

The rivalry between children for parental approval begins early in life. In a succession situation, the problem can become especially acute if the parent shows that he favors one child over the other. The natural result is continuous family conflict.

- *Perceptions of the eldest child.* Traditionally, the oldest child succeeds his father. This custom reaffirms the perception of the younger sibling (or siblings) that the oldest is indeed the favorite. Also, because the oldest is generally largest, physically strongest, and most knowledgeable merely because of age, the younger children rarely have the opportunity to match the skills, competence, and experience of the eldest. By that time, the nature of the relationship is so well established that the oldest sibling has difficulty regarding the younger ones as adequate and competent. Moreover, because the eldest is in earlier and longer contact with his parents, their control efforts fall heaviest on him. The result is that older children tend to expect more of themselves and control themselves more rigidly than younger children. Being already a harsh judge of himself, the eldest is likely to be an even harder judge of his younger siblings.
- *Perceptions of the younger child.* The younger sibling attempts to compensate for the effects of the childhood relationships by carving out a niche of the business that he can nurture in order to prove his capabilities. He guards it jealously and resents any incursion into his domain. Even if the siblings own equal shares of the business and are all on the board, the younger feels subservient, and friction and

distrust are likely to occur. Furthermore, if for some reason the younger replaces the oldest, and particularly if the latter becomes subordinate to him, the younger often feels guilty for having usurped the supposedly rightful role of the senior.

Other relatives

In some families, it is expected that any relative who wants to join the business can do so. The results can be devastating, especially if the jobs are sinecures. The chief executive of a family business naturally feels a heavy responsibility to preserve and enlarge the family fortunes. If he is weighed down by unproductive relatives, internecine warfare results, bringing casualties but no peace. Rational planning and decision making are frustrated, and often the only solution is to sell the business. This solution is costly because it results in loss of the business as a means of employment, betrayal of a family tradition, and dissolution of close ties that have been maintained through the business.

What can be done

- *Father-offspring rivalry.* Most entrepreneur-fathers are unable to resolve this problem themselves because they find it difficult to accept outside advice. In these cases, it is generally advantageous for the children to form their own ventures. This can often be done under the corporate umbrella or outside it without deserting the father. For example, one father in retailing set up a store in different communities for each of his children. While collaborating on overall policy and buying, each child could run his own store, and the father also could continue to run his.
- *Sibling rivalry.* It is important for siblings to realize that their relationship recapitulates ancient rivalries. And since there is love and hate in all relationships, theirs cannot, by definition, be pure. Nevertheless, they should confront and discuss the worries, anger, fears, and disappointments they cause each other. If this does not help, they should consider separate organizations.
- *Relatives.* Few family businesses can sustain regeneration over a length of time solely through family members. Every family business must give thought to eventually bringing in outside professional management. In some cases, family members have gotten entirely out of day-to-day business operations while forming a trust to oversee their interests. This enables the family to act in concert and fosters cohesion while also preserving the family's role in the business.

CHAPTER 5

AIDS IN MAKING PROPER DECISIONS

GROWING A DECISION TREE

Every businessman has to make decisions. Whether they are routine or agonizingly complicated, decisions are what the business runs on, and anything specifically designed to help with that process is worth knowing about.

What is a decision tree?

A decision tree is a simple mathematical tool enabling the planner or decision maker to:

- Consider various courses of action.
- Assign financial results to them.
- Modify these results by their probability of achievement.
- Make comparisons to determine the best alternative.

Actually drawn out on a piece of paper with a branch for each course of action and for each event that could stem from such actions, the structure does look like a tree laid on its side.

How does it work?

A decision tree is used to structure business problems and present in a formalized way the decision process that every executive is probably doing intuitively. The clearest way to explain this is through an example. In this instance, a commonplace business decision is reduced to a decision tree.

The president of Acme Tool Company has the opportunity to invest $50,000 in an exciting project. After carefully considering all the data and information, he is convinced that Acme will make a $250,000 profit if the project succeeds. However, the company is bound to lose the whole $50,000 investment if the idea fails. Furthermore, the project is more likely to fail than succeed. Being ruthlessly objective about it, he and the company's treasurer agree that the chances of succeeding are only 40 percent, implying that the probability of failure is 60 percent. Both acknowledge, however, that the loss of $50,000 is far from disastrous. They are faced with a "go/no-go" decision and quickly draw up a decision tree (Decision Tree 1). The two men then multiply out the financial consequences of the alternatives by the agreed probability that either will occur.

The value of success is put at $100,000 ($250,000 × 0.4), while the loss from failure is assigned –$30,000 (–$50,000 × 0.6). Adding the two financial results together, a positive cash flow of $70,000 is deduced from the *go* choice against nothing from the *no-go* decision. The treasurer looks concerned, but the president explains he is doing no more than playing the odds on the upside potential against the downside risk. He rationalizes by saying that if he could make the same decision ten times, he would succeed four times for a positive cash flow of $1,000,000 (4 × $250,000) and fail six times for a loss of $300,000 (6 × $50,000)—altogether a net cash flow of $700,000 or an average of $70,000 each time.

The treasurer accepts the theory but correctly points out that, in reality, the project can only be done once, not ten times, and that a $70,000 gain will not be made. It will either be a larger profit of $250,000 or a complete loss, not a theoretical figure in between. Wouldn't it be better to pursue an alternate project, he says, where, for the same investment, they could possibly make a $100,000 profit and, in the worst possible case, at least get their $50,000 back and break even.

The president looks at the proposal. He agrees with the treasurer's figures, and they both agree that the chance of success is about 60 percent for the second project versus 40 percent for the first project. It is obviously better to go with the second. Acme cannot lose, and it stands a better chance of making $100,000.

Just to put the issue beyond doubt, they draw up another decision tree to compare the alternatives (Decision Tree 2). Both are amazed to discover that the first project is still the better decision. The assigned value of the first is $70,000 (as before), while the value of the second is only $60,000 ($100,000 × 0.6) + ($0 × 0.4).

The conclusion goes against intuition—it is clear that *the best business decision is not necessarily to prepare for the most likely event* or to take the most cautious approach. Needless to say, the above example is rather simplistic, and, in practice, the problems committed to decision trees are generally diverse and complex. Nevertheless, the technique can be a useful

DECISION TREE 1

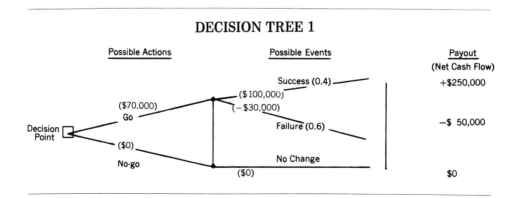

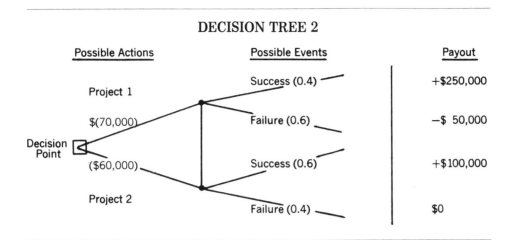

DECISION TREE 2

Possible Actions	Possible Events	Payout

After image: Project 1, $(70,000), Decision Point, ($60,000), Project 2; Success (0.4) +$250,000; Failure (0.6) −$ 50,000; Success (0.6) +$100,000; Failure (0.4) $0

discipline whenever the problem has more separable elements than the decision-maker can comfortably take account of in his own head.

Not a mechanical substitute

It is important to recognize that a decision tree is far from being a mechanical replacement for executive judgment and experience. Both these qualities, together with all hard facts and data available, are essential inputs to the three basic steps to drawing up the decision tree:

1. Stipulate what *decision alternatives* are to be considered in the analysis of a problem.
2. Make an *assessment of the probabilities* of the occurrence of each uncertain event.
3. Quantify possible *financial consequences* of the various alternatives.

After this has been done, the arithmetic will do the rest. Large corporations have computer programs to handle the mathematics when the problem is complex, and "the tree gets so bushy, it is positively hairy," but the input to the problem must depend on nonmechanical items.

Benefits of growing a decision tree

1. The discipline involved in tabulating alternatives, determining the financial consequences, and assessing the probabilities of various outcomes forces a careful and complete consideration of the factors to be taken into account.
2. The gamble of decision-making is reduced. The prudent businessman acts when the odds of highest payoff are in his favor. It is the gambler who deviates from the odds.
3. Better decision analysis can be logically performed and if properly communicated, can remove the burden of being

cautious in the interest of job security rather than in the best interest of the company.

LINEAR PROGRAMMING*

One problem facing business people today is how to get maximum efficiency and profits from existing facilities. For example, a manufacturer must decide how to use his machinery to get the most output at minimum costs; a retailer is concerned with how much floor space to allocate to different products to get maximum sales and profits. Each situation involves the question of how to allocate *limited resources* (machines and shelf space) among *competing demands* (Product X or Product Y) to *maximize profits.*

What is linear programming?

Linear programming is a rather imposing title for a commonly used management technique that helps solve resource allocation problems. The word programming simply means problem solving. The term *linear* comes from the expectation that relationships within the problem will be linear. For example, if it takes five hours to produce one item, then to produce two is presumed to require ten hours, and so on. A simple example should illustrate the technique.

How many sofas?

A small furniture manufacturer is attempting to set his production schedule for the coming month. The market is not the limiting factor, and he can sell any quantity of his two main products—tables and sofas—that the plant can produce. His objective is to produce tables and sofas in whatever combination maximizes total contribution to profit and overhead. For a table, the contribution (sales price less direct expenses) is $40 per unit, versus $60 per unit for a sofa.

At first glance, it would seem logical to produce only sofas, since they yield the highest contribution per unit. However, the tables and sofas require different production times.

PRODUCTION TIME FOR TABLES VS. SOFAS

Machine center	Capacity of center during month (hours)	Time required to produce (hours) Table	Sofa
A	1,200	2	1
B	2,000	2	3
C	1,000	1	2

*For further information on the many applications of linear programming, two excellent sources are: (1) *Introduction to Linear Programming* by R. Stansbury Stockton (Boston: Allyn and Bacon, Inc.), and (2) *A Primer of Linear Programming* by Kurt Meisels (New York: New York University Press).

The optimum production mixture

We know that our objective is to maximize total profit contribution and that each table yields $40 contribution versus $60 for a sofa. If we let "T" represent tables and "S" sofas, then the total profit contribution ("P") from any mixture of tables and sofas produced could be represented as: P = 40T + 60S.

Similarly, the time constraints at each of the machine centers can also be represented. We know that tables require two hours and sofas require three hours at machine center B. Each month the maximum number of tables and sofas would be processed when the number of tables processed times two hours per table plus the number of sofas times three hours each totals less than or equal to 2,000 hours. If you are confused, study the Optimum Production Mixture chart, which summarizes these relationships.

OPTIMUM PRODUCTION MIXTURE

This is the objective	*These are the constraints*	
Maximize total profit contribution (P) where: P = 40T + 60S	Machine center A	2T + 1S ≤ 1,200 hours
	Machine center B	2T + 3S ≤ 2,000 hours
	Machine center C	1T + 2S ≤ 1,000 hours

By using an algebraic method known as the *simplex* method, the above equations can be solved. As it works out, the optimum solution is to produce 462 tables and 269 sofas. No other production mixture will yield a greater total profit.

How can linear programming help you?

Linear programming can be used to maximize profits or minimize expenses whenever there are competing demands for limited resources. We've already described how it can be applied to manufacturing and retailing. Another common use is in transportation. For example, suppose you ship your products from three different warehouses. By using linear programming, you could minimize transportation costs while, at the same time, maintain a desired inventory level at each warehouse. This is accomplished by using linear programming to determine how much of each product to ship from each warehouse.

CRITICAL PATH ANALYSIS

The Critical Path Method (CPM) has been used in aerospace, construction, and research and development for some time, and now more and more businessmen are adopting it as an aid to their planning, scheduling, and cost control problems. The basic requirements are surprisingly simple—common sense and arithmetic—yet CPM can produce results that, as one project manager says, "are so good I wish we could keep it a secret."

The evolution of graphical control techniques

Whether building a new addition to a plant or planning a marketing campaign, businessmen have always faced problems whenever multiple, and often interrelated, tasks have to be completed in order to finish a particular job on time and within a budget. During the early 1900s, Henry T. Gantt developed the familiar bar chart or "Gantt" chart, as it is often called, that depicts a plan of action for completing tasks within a project according to a time schedule.

Gantt charts are useful for planning and scheduling, but they have one major limitation: they can't show the *interrelationship* of the various tasks within the project. (See Gantt chart below.) In other words, it is not clear which activities must be finished before others can begin. (See Critical Path Method.)

Development of the critical path method

In 1957 the Du Pont Company developed the critical path technique to help shorten the long time lag between completion of research and development on a new product and the construction of facilities for manufacturing the product. Basically, the technique consists of reducing a project to a graphic model called a "network plan" or "arrow diagram". Referring to the building example, let's condense it for simplicity and assume that there are only five tasks to be performed. First the house has to be framed, then plumbing and brickwork can be done simultaneously, and finally plastering and roofing can be completed. The project could be represented graphically with the flow of work represented by arrows. Each node (circle) represents the end of one activity and the beginning of another.

GANTT CHART FOR BUILDING A HOUSE

TIME (DAYS)

	5	10	15	20	25	30	35	40
Excavate	■							
Pour Foundation		■						
Frame			■					
Heating				■				
Rough Plumbing				■				
Wiring				■				
Brickwork				■				
Roof					■			
Plaster					■			
Finish Carpentry						■		
Finish Plumbing					■			
Paint							■	
Landscape								■

CRITICAL PATH METHOD

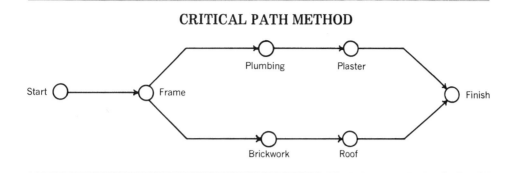

Preparing a critical path chart

Planning. Determine all the major activities of a project. Using the example above, framing, plumbing, etc., are each definite and separate tasks. Once this is accomplished, the interrelationship of the task must be established. For example, framing must be completed before plumbing and brickwork can begin; plumbing must be finished before plastering can start, etc.
Scheduling. Determine from experience the normal time necessary to complete each activity and note it within the nodes.
Control. Determine the longest path (in terms of time) through the arrow diagram. This is the *critical path* because *each activity along this route represents a bottleneck holding up completion of the overall project.*

Building a house on the critical path

On the next page is the completed CPM chart which corresponds in CPM format to the exact same activities shown in the previous Gantt chart format. Note that in the completed CPM chart the time to complete each activity is listed, and the interrelationship of all activities is clear. The critical path is the heavy line and is forty days long. Leeway or "float" on noncritical jobs (the amount of time they can be delayed without changing the critical path) can also be determined. With this stage completed, the businessman can see which jobs are critical to his finish date. For the other jobs he knows how much leeway or float time he has.

CPM as a cost-cutting tool

Once a manager knows which activities are critical to timely completion of a project, he can determine how to allocate his resources. For example, the builder above may decide that it is worth the cost to put extra men on plastering in order to finish the overall house in less time since plastering is on the critical path. Similarly, he can see that roofing and wiring are not on the critical path and may decide to reduce manpower in those areas. The ability to see the interrelationships between activities of a complex project and to make cost-saving changes is the great advantage of the critical path method.

COMPLETED CPM CHART

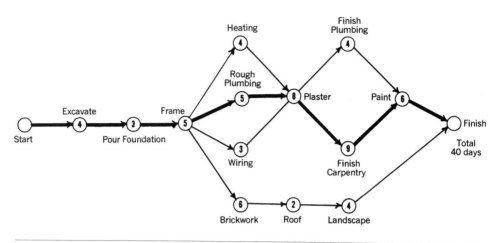

Conclusion

The critical path diagram can be as simple or complex as the project it represents. In some cases computer programs are built to handle the immense amount of data that can be involved in large-scale undertakings.

Even so, the logic and method of the critical path are basically straight forward. Their main purpose is improving the planning and scheduling of interrelated tasks by drawing out information that may be too complex to be left to intuition or experience—however expert. The economic benefits follow naturally from these processes. Try using CPM on the next complicated project you tackle. The discipline of breaking the project into stages and making time estimates to complete each phase should be well worth the effort.

THE LEARNING CURVE

The theory

Practice makes perfect. A task can always be done better each time it is repeated. In industry, the theory is just as simple. A worker learns as he works, and the more he repeats a task, the more efficient he becomes with the result that direct labor per unit produced declines. This decline in cost with cumulative experience is known as the "learning curve". And far from being esoteric and "nice to know but useless," the learning curve is an underlying characteristic of organizational activity that is crucially important to the business manager.

The practice

Even before World War II, when the learning curve theory was put to use in the aircraft industry, definite studies had shown that each time the number of units produced doubled, direct man hours per unit declined about 20%. Below is a classic example that shows how the learning curve resulted in progressively lower prices for the Model T Ford.

When the same curve is plotted on ratio paper (i.e., logarithmic coordinates), it actually becomes a straight line. In more recent years, it has been found that the learning curve describes not only the increasing skill of an individual or group of production workers, but the whole complex organism of a company—some in line function, others in staff. In other words, as the *cumulative output* of a company's product doubles, *all costs* attributable to the product (direct and indirect) decrease at a fairly predictable rate.

Practical application

Pricing. Whenever long production runs are being quoted, costs (in constant dollars) should decline by a definite percentage each time cumulative volume doubles. Knowledge of this fact could give you a competitive edge when pricing a job. (Only after the British government decided to let Rolls Royce go bankrupt because the RB211 engine could not be produced at a profit was it discovered that the government's cost estimates had not con-

FORD MODEL T PRICE EXPERIENCE CURVE
(1909—1915)

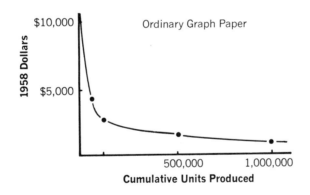

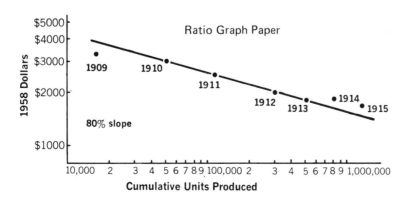

sidered the learning curve. According to many reports, the company would probably have at least broken even once the engine was in production.)

Strategic decisions. If you can grow faster than your competitors in a market, your costs will be lower (according to the learning curve) because of your greater cumulative experience. By undercutting the competitors, your market share will grow further, leading to lower production costs, and so on. However, to get the initial jump on competitors, you have to price at a loss until volume catches up and your costs begin to fall. This has been the Texas Instrument strategy in the calculator market. Cut prices, build market share, cut prices again until, eventually, most of the competition is driven out.

Cost control. If you *know* costs should decrease by a certain amount, you can take remedial action when the reduction does not occur.

Learning is a characteristic of all living organisms. But progress and growth —and reduced costs—do not always occur without stimulation and encouragement from management. Be aware that learning curves exist for competitors as well. If you don't find ways to cut costs as your productive experience grows, you may begin to lose your position in the marketplace.

CHAPTER 6

FINANCIAL ANALYSIS
AND CONTROL

WHY FINANCIAL ANALYSIS IS IMPORTANT
TO HELP YOU PROTECT YOUR COMPANY

From time to time you should take stock of your company and plan defensively to insure that your business remains viable and strong no matter what misadventures might lie ahead. How do you begin this process of defensive planning? First, you should define your company's "key success variables". Think about your business. What factors are crucial to its viability and success? Where do you have the most flexibility to respond to a changing business environment?

Income Statement

Certain factors are keys to success in every industry. A good way to learn some of the leverage points in your particular business is by looking at your business's score sheet—its income statement. Glance down each line and ask yourself, "How critically does this item affect my business: sales, labor, materials, interest expense, overhead? Which ones most vitally affect success?" No doubt they all seem important, so let's take a closer look.

Contribution vs. Fixed Costs

Proper management response to any change in sales or expenses depends heavily on two factors affecting your firm's cost structure:

- *Gross Margin, or So-Called "Contribution" From Your Products.* Defined as the net sales price less those expenses that vary directly with sales volume, i.e., "variable expenses".
- *Level of Fixed Costs.* Includes such expenses as rent, heat, administrative salaries, and depreciation, which do not vary appreciably with sales volume.

Cost Structure Matrix

The matrix of Fixed Costs vs. Contribution shows representative examples of each type of business. Take a look at your income statement and try to

COST STRUCTURE MATRIX

		High CONTRIBUTION (greater than 40% of sales)	Low (less than 40% of sales)
FIXED COSTS	High	Radio or T.V. Station Airline or Railroad Specialty Clothing Store	Truck Line Supermarket Machine Shop
	Low	Executive Placement Agency Real Estate Broker Insurance Agent	Janitorial Service Guard Service Temporary Hire (Kelly Girls)

identify which description best fits your firm. For example, if the majority of your expenses are fixed at your present volume level and your per unit contribution is less than 40 percent of the sales price, your firm would probably be best characterized as a high fixed cost, low contribution business.

Volume vs. Cost Dependent

What does all this mean for defensive planning? High fixed cost businesses, such as railroads or supermarkets, are critically *volume dependent*. They must keep sales up to be able to cover their fixed costs. That is why specialty clothing stores are so quick to go out of business if they ever falter on a fashion trend.

On the other hand, low contribution businesses, such as trucklines and most service companies, are critically *cost dependent*. In other words, since most of their revenue goes to paying variable expenses, any rise in these expenses (which cannot be passed on to the consumer) has a disastrous effect on profitability. It should be readily apparent that if you are in a high fixed cost and low contribution business, any adverse changes in sales volume and expenses have a doubly debilitating effect. For example, consider the truckers' plight when the speed limit was cut to 55 mph. They could not travel at normal speed (hence, sales capacity was effectively cut) and, at the same time, had to pay more for fuel (costs up)—all while not being able to pass the effect on to the consumer because of fixed ICC freight rates.

Capital vs. Labor Intensive

High fixed cost ("capital intensive") firms generally have substantial *money* tied up in plant and equipment while low fixed cost ("labor intensive") businesses usually have *people* as the critical resource. If yours is a capital intensive business, one of your main concerns should be financial management—adequate bank lines to allow for contingencies. On the other hand, a labor intensive firm's flexibility to reduce the work force during a downturn is a distinct advantage—take care not to lose it during union negotiations.

Pricing Structure

Inflation is the one constant we can count on. How flexible are your prices? To avoid getting trapped with older products with established and less flexible prices, perhaps you should consider an aggressive policy of introducing new products as soon as possible where you could establish prices at an attractive level.

Cash Management

Most businessmen have a fairly good feel for the lifeblood of their business— cash. They know what money is expected in, and what must be paid out. But one thing they practically never do is slip the receivables by one month. That's right: extend the date when your accounts receivable come in by just thirty days. Unless you have considerable cash reserves, you will probably be frightened when you see the result. Now, obviously, this won't happen overnight, but in every economic downturn, customers take longer to pay. Here are some defensive steps you can take to counteract this problem:

- *Accounts Receivable Management.* Watch all major accounts closely and take an aggressive stance with any late payers.
- *Bank Lines.* "Money is always available when you don't need it and rarely when you do," goes the cliche. It might be prudent to line up a standby loan now at the bank for possible use later.
- *Inventory Control.* Closely monitor your inventory. If sales are down, don't get caught with a large inventory. On the other hand, however, if raw materials are in short supply be certain to maintain an adequate inventory to cover any supplier delays.

Many businesses take the attitude that, if receivables slip, they will extend their payables accordingly. While this may be a formula for survival, it certainly is no way to build a business. Suppliers will remember who pays on time, *and as we enter a supply dominated economy, ready access to raw materials will progressively become a key ingredient to competitive success.*

CASH FLOW

What is cash flow?

Like any profession, business has many specialized and sometimes confusing terms. It's important to use them properly, however, because often bankers, lawyers, and other professionals will judge your commercial expertise simply by how well you handle your business vocabulary and a few simple business techniques.

Cash flow is a term that many people use, but not too many understand what it means. More often it is used in reference to a "cash flow statement" which is the *single most* important document to every businessman.

"Profits", "income", and "revenue" are all accounting terms. They may be important to Wall Street analysts and accountants, but they mean practically nothing to the average businessman. Cash is the lifeblood of any business and in most circumstances, cash does not equal *income*. For example, you have to meet your payroll with cash in the bank this week, although the item you have manufactured may not be sold for several weeks. And even after you sell the item (and recognize income on your books), you may not actually receive the cash payment for several more weeks. All the while you have to pay out cash. Keep this in mind—you can't spend income. You can only pay bills with cash.

Now let's see how to prepare a cash flow forecast. Let us assume that there is a new doctor in town who wishes to open a medical practice. He has approached the local banker with a cash flow projection. (See below.)

Let's go through this forecast point by point. First, note that the doctor plans to rent an office for $200 per month and pay $1,000 for his equipment in January. By February he will open his doors, hire a nurse for $500 per month, and begin to see patients. He expects business to be slow at first and patients won't start to pay until the next month (March). Also, some patients will probably have insurance, but because of the paperwork involved, no money will be received from insurance until May.

As you can see, the doctor estimates $1,200 Cash Out in January and nothing for Cash In for a Net Cash Flow of minus $1,200. In February it will be minus $700, which, added to the deficit from January, gives a Cumulative Balance of minus $1,900. Note that Net Cash Flow won't turn positive until July and the Cumulative Balance is negative until November.

What does this statement tell us? Well, it means that if you were the doctor, you would have to ask the banker for a line of credit of at least $3,400 which is your peak point of negative balance in June.

Now, how can we criticize this statement? If you were the banker, you would probably query several of the doctor's assumptions. For example:

- How confident is he of getting patients?
- What controls does he plan to use to make sure patients and insurance companies pay according to schedule?
- Will he need more equipment, nursing staff, or bookkeeper later?

CASH FLOW

		J	F	M	A	M
Cash In						
1 Patients				100	200	300
2 Insurance						100
	Total in	0	0	100	200	400
Cash Out:						
1 Equipment		1000				
2 Nurse			500	500	500	500
3 Rent		200	200	200	200	200
	Total out	1200	700	700	700	700
Net Cash Flow		(1200)	(700)	(600)	(500)	(300)
Cumulative Balance		(1200)	(1900)	(2500)	(3000)	(3300)

- Most importantly, how does the doctor plan to support himself? He has shown no figure for his own salary.

Hopefully you can now appreciate the importance of the cash flow statement. It is generally the first document that any lender wishes to see and can be the basis for you to control every aspect of your business. It can be prepared on a daily, weekly, or monthly basis. You can use it to project out as far as you feel comfortable in forecasting. Most importantly, it lets you see at any point in time where you are (or should be) in terms of business lifeblood—cash.

CONTRIBUTION ANALYSIS

One of the most important concepts for every businessman to understand is "contribution analysis". Its proper use is fundamental to practically all competent and knowledgeable decision making.

Definition of Contribution

Contribution is defined as the selling price of a product less the variable costs associated with its production and marketing.

Variable Costs

Business expenses can be broken down into variable and fixed categories (sometimes called direct and indirect expenses). By variable costs, we mean only those costs that *vary directly with the number of items produced*. These would include the direct costs of material, labor, shipping costs, and selling commission. For example, if you are making widgets and each one contains $1.00 of steel and costs $2.00 in direct labor to produce, it will have a variable cost per unit to manufacture of $3.00. Now let's say you pay $2.00 per

PROJECTION

J	J	A	S	O	N	D
400	500	750	1000	2000	2500	2500
200	300	300	350	350	350	350
600	800	1050	1350	2350	2850	2850
500	500	500	500	500	500	500
200	200	200	200	200	200	200
700	700	700	700	700	700	700
(100)	100	350	650	1650	2150	2150
(3400)	(3300)	(2950)	(2300)	(650)	1500	3650

WIDGET CONTRIBUTION

Selling Price		$10.00
Less Variable Costs		
Steel	1.00	
Labor	2.00	
Shipping	2.00	
Marketing (10% × $10)	1.00	
Contribution		$ 4.00

unit to ship the widget and you pay 10 percent commission to a salesman for selling it (based on a selling price of $10.00). The net contribution would be $4.00 per unit as shown above.

Fixed Costs

As we said before, variable expenses are those that vary according to the volume produced. Fixed expenses are those that *stay practically the same over a wide range of number of units produced.* These include such overhead items as heat, lights, water, rent, office staff, and manager's salary. Now, taking our simplified example, for every widget we produce and sell, we have $4.00 left over after paying all the variable expenses to "contribute" towards paying the fixed expenses (i.e., overhead) of the business and hopefully having something left over to provide a profit. That's why the term contribution is really an abbreviation of its full title "contribution to fixed overhead and profit." (See diagram on facing page.)

Why Is It So Important to Think in Terms of Contribution?

Every business has a certain capacity to produce within a given level of fixed overhead. Let's look at two examples. A machine shop has several different kinds of products it can produce and yet its overhead won't vary appreciably. Similarly, a consultant may be able to do several different kinds of studies and still his heat, water, lights, clerical costs, etc., will stay about the same. In both these cases the manager should always try to concentrate on that type of work that produces the highest *contribution* to the fixed overhead and profit.

Common Sense

That is just good common sense, of course, but most businessmen think in a different way. They either attempt to maximize sales or they try to maximize profit—not contribution. Let's take a couple more examples.

Sales

Given two nearly identical items on the shelf, one at $4.00 and one at $5.00, a merchandise manager should push the $5.00 item—right? Not necessarily. It depends on their relative contribution. The $5.00 item may have cost $3.00 (contribution = $2.00) while the $4.00 item cost $1.50 (contribution

SCHEMATIC DIAGRAM OF CONTRIBUTION
TO OVERHEAD AND PROFIT

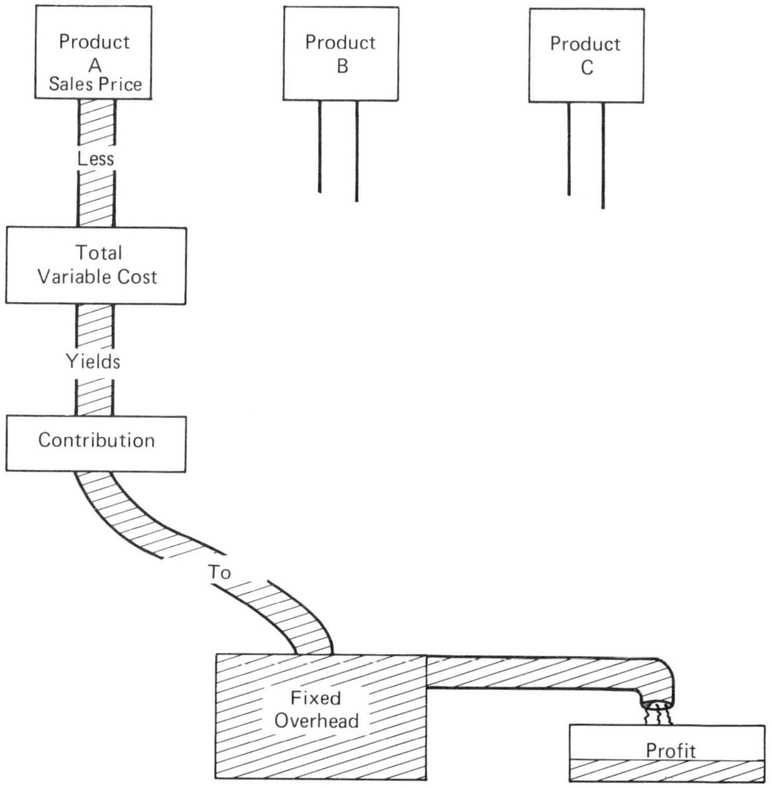

= $2.50). On this basis it would be better to focus attention on the $4.00 item and thereby not attempt to maximize sales dollars, but contribution.

Now before we begin to shift product lines or remove things from the shelf, let's refine our thinking one more step. It is not always possible to sell *just* high contribution items. What our merchandise manager should really consider is the optimum *mix* of merchandise to have a full product line and maximize *total* contribution per year. To do this, he may have to carry a few loss leaders. Also, turnover is important. Although the per unit contribution of the $5.00 item may be less, if you can sell it twice as fast, it would contribute more per year than the $4.00 item.

Profit

Other managers often try to maximize profit. But profit is an accounting term and depends on proper *allocation* of all the fixed costs such as depreciation, rent, water, heat, and lights. It is far easier and more accurate to maximize the *contribution* a given product *makes* to fixed overhead and profit. Consider the following minicase study. You manage a company that sells products A, B, and C.

Product A costs the most to make and sell, but you are forced to price it

PRODUCTS A, B, AND C

Product	Sales Price Per Unit	Sales Per Year	$ Sales	Direct Costs to Manufacture & Sell
A	$100	500 units	$50,000/yr	$90/unit
B	$100	500 units	$50,000/yr	$60/unit
C	$100	500 units	$50,000/yr	$30/unit

at only $100 because of competition. Product B provides a nice profit margin, but Product C is your real moneymaker because it is a new product and you have little competition thanks to patent protection. It will be difficult, however, to sell more than five hundred units per year of Product B or C because they have very specialized and limited markets. (See chart above.)

The total overhead for this company is $45,000 per year. No matter how you allocate the overhead (by product line, dollar sales, or units produced), it works out that Product A is a big money loser. (See chart below.) For every unit of Product A you sell, you lose $20. You should definitely drop it before you go broke—right?

Wrong! This is a classic trap that brings large and small companies alike to their financial knees and often to bankruptcy as it did a large and famous English aircraft manufacturer. Don't make the same mistake!

Let's restate the figures, but in terms of contribution. As you can see, Product A does contribute towards fixed overhead and profit. Obviously Products B and C contribute more per unit than Product A, but we assumed for purposes of this example that the market for Products B and C was fixed at five hundred units each. On this basis you should definitely not drop Product A so long as two factors are present:

- It has a positive contribution.
- It does not utilize productive capacity that could be used to produce higher contribution products than A.

Summary

Every well-run business must attempt to maximize contribution in a slightly different way. Supermarkets and retailers try to maximize contribution per year per square foot of floor space. Salesmen and doctors maximize contri-

PRODUCTS A, B, AND C: PROFIT AND LOSS

Product	Direct Costs to Manufacture & Sell	Overhead	Total Cost to Produce	Selling Price	Profit (Loss)	
A	$90/unit	$30/unit	$120	$100	($20)	Loss/unit
B	$60/unit	$30/unit	$90	$100	$10	Profit/unit
C	$30/unit	$30/unit	$60	$100	$40	Profit/unit

PRODUCTS A, B, AND C: CONTRIBUTION

Product	Selling Price	Direct Costs to Manufacture & Sell	Contribution
A	$100/unit	$90/unit	$10/unit
B	$100/unit	$60/unit	$40/unit
C	$100/unit	$30/unit	$70/unit

bution per working hour; airlines maximize contribution per flight hour and so on. You will find this concept vital in your decision making.

CALCULATING YOUR COMPANY'S BREAKEVEN

On of the most important planning and control tools available to the businessman is called "breakeven analysis".

Breakeven refers to the sales volume (either in dollars or units) at which a business neither makes a profit nor incurs a loss. In other words, it is the point where sales revenue just equals expenses. Using a simple graphic technique known as breakeven analysis, it is possible to calculate your company's breakeven level as well as analyze a number of important management problems, such as setting prices, projecting profit and loss at different sales volume levels, and estimating the impact of major capital expenditures on profitability.

Three main factors affect the profitability of every business:

- Sales volume
- Expenses
- Sales price

The problem is that each of these factors is dynamic, i.e., constantly changing. For example, what would be the profit level of your particular business if sales were off 10%, costs went up 5%, and your sales price per unit stayed the same?

Chances are you find it rather hard to give a quick answer. But businessmen face this situation every day—costs up, volume changing, should we raise our price, what will that do to profits? It's essential that you have an analytical method to help you make quick decisions concerning the key economic components of your business.

Fixed vs. Variable Expenses

Before we go much further, there are a couple of terms we should review. Almost all business expenses can be divided into two main categories that are explained and also shown graphically on the next page.

- Variable expenses vary in direct proportion to changes in sales volume or production, i.e., direct materials, direct labor, sales commission, and direct shipping expenses.
- Fixed expenses do not vary as sales or production volume change. These expenses remain constant within the existing plant and equipment capacity, i.e., property taxes, insurance, depreciation, administrative salaries, and rent.

There is another category of expenses known as semivariable that change with increases or decreases in sales or production, but not in *direct* proportion to such changes. Examples would be telephone service and advertising. For the most part, however, practically all expenses can be categorized as either fixed or variable; therefore, we will not concern ourselves with semivariable expenses at this time.

FIXED VS. VARIABLE EXPENSES

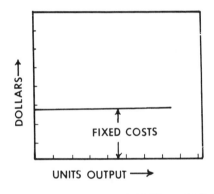

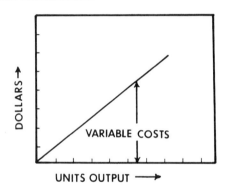

Total Costs

Now that we're again clear on the differences in fixed and variable costs, let's take a specific example and determine the *total* costs at any given volume level. Suppose that you are in the manufacturing business and your product sells for $1.30 each. Your direct costs per item are $.37 for materials, $.23 for direct labor, $.13 for salesman's commission, and $.07 for shipping expenses. Total variable costs, therefore, come to $.80 per item. Now, to run your plant costs $15,000 a month, come rain or shine, for depreciation, administration, taxes, and so on. Therefore, you have $15,000 of fixed costs per month. Taking the fixed and variable costs from the two graphs above and graphically adding them together, we can construct a graph that gives the total costs at any output level. (See Total Costs chart.)

To verify the figures, pick a point, such as 30,000 units of output. The fixed costs will be $15,000, and the variable costs will equal 30,000 units times $.80 per unit which equals $24,000. Therefore, total costs at a volume level of 30,000 units equal $15,000 fixed costs plus $24,000 variable costs or $39,000. This can be seen as point A on the chart.

TOTAL COSTS

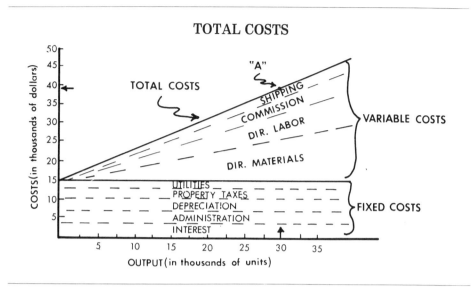

Determining the Breakeven Point

Now we need to determine the breakeven level for this particular business. As noted before, the sales price is $1.30 per unit. We can now superimpose a Sales Revenue line on the chart. Where the Sales Revenue line crosses the Total Costs line is the "breakeven point." At any sales volume less than this point, the company loses money—at greater volume the company makes money. The exact amount of the Profit or Loss (the area shown by hatch marks) is the difference in the Sales Revenue and Total Costs at the given volume level.

BREAKEVEN POINT

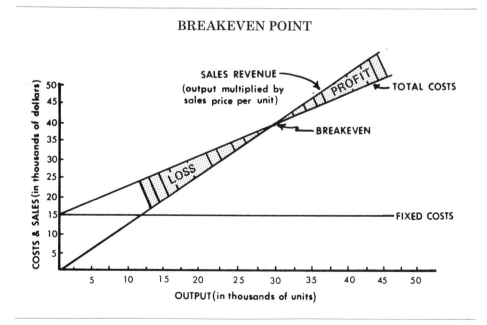

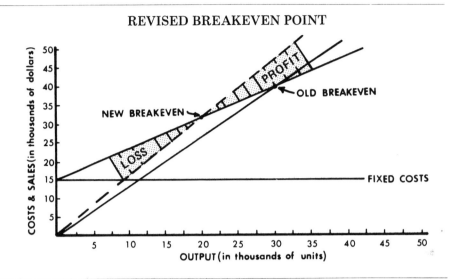

REVISED BREAKEVEN POINT

Solutions to Other Management Problems

As we mentioned earlier, breakeven analysis provides a flexible management tool to solve a number of problems involving the complex interrelationship of costs, volume, and profitability. Let's take one such problem and see how easily you might solve part of it using the techniques we have discussed.

Suppose that your manufacturing firm discussed above is considering raising prices from $1.30 to $1.50 per unit. You are concerned, however, that you analyze all relevant factors before making such a decision. How would you approach the problem?

Well, part of the solution is quite easy. You should analyze the result of the price increase on your firm's cost and profit structure. Above is the same chart as before, but this time we have plotted a new Sales Revenue line (dotted line) that projects the effect of the price increase.

As you can see, the price increase caused the breakeven point to shift rather dramatically from the previous 30,000 units to only about 21,000 units (21,428 to be exact). And, of course, the profit and loss areas shift as well. This information is essential because the question now becomes, what is the "price sensitivity" of the product? Although the company will make more profit *per unit* at the higher price, will the market absorb as many units as before? Breakeven analysis can't answer this final question, but it does aid management by providing a picture of profits at various prices and levels of sales.

Impact of Changing Costs on Profit

We looked only at varying *prices* in the above example, and projected the impact on profitability. Similarly you could study the effect of changing fixed or variable *costs* on your profit structure.

Summary

Breakeven analysis provides a flexible management tool to:

- Study information concerning volume, price, and expenses in an analytical manner.
- Determine expense and revenue projections under alternative management and economic assumptions.
- Control costs through the integration of breakeven analysis with budgeting techniques.
- Consider in a systematic manner the impact of price changes on profit.
- Project the impact of breakeven volume of major capital expenditures such as plant expansion.

What's your company's breakeven level? Don't ignore this valuable tool—it may give you insights into your business you've never had before.

TIME VALUE OF MONEY

The time value of money is a straightforward concept with widespread application to business decision making. Inflation makes an understanding of the time value of money more important than ever because money used inefficiently will quickly decline in value.

The mathematics of the time value of money is simple. Any businessman prefers $100 today as opposed to $100 next year because the $100 can be invested to earn as much as 10% to 12% at high interest rates. Or it can be invested in the business as working capital or in equipment purchases. Thus, $100 today is really worth $110 next year (at a 10% interest rate). This compounding process can be carried out for future years. (See below.)

Fortunately, there are tables that speed this process by supplying an appropriate multiplier—called the "accumulation factor." The original figure is multiplied by the accumulation factor to yield the final amount accumulated. In the example below, the accumulation factor for compounding at 10% interest for three years is 1.331 since $100.00 × 1.331 = $133.10. These factors can be found by specifying the annual interest rate and the number of years involved and entering tables in any standard accounting or finance textbook.

If you need to know how much to set aside today at 10% interest to

COMPOUNDING INTEREST

Year	Amount at beginning of year	Plus	One year's interest on that amount	Equals	Amount at end of year
1	$100.00	+	$100.00 × 10%	=	$110.00
2	$110.00	+	$110.00 × 10%	=	$121.00
3	$121.00	+	$121.00 × 10%	=	$133.10

PRESENT VALUE

χ	×	1.331	=	$100.00
Amount to be set aside		Accumulation factor		Amount to be accumulated

Therefore: $\chi = \$100.00 \times \dfrac{1}{1.331} = \$75.13$

accumulate $100 in three years, simply reverse this compounding process. At a 10% interest rate, the $75.13 is called the "present value" of $100.00 received three years from now. It is called present value because that amount, at the present, will grow to $100.00 in three years at a 10% interest rate. As shown, the present value can be easily figured by multiplying the desired amount by the inverse of the accumulation factor. This new multiplier, the *discount factor*, can be found in the same tables that contain accumulation factors. Abbreviated discount and accumulation factor tables are on pages 75 and 76.

A graphic display of the time value of money is shown. The center of the horizontal axis represents time zero, the increase in value from compounding is shown to the right, and the decrease in value from discounting is shown to the left. Note that both the amount of time involved and the interest rate affect the time value of money.

DISCOUNT AND ACCUMULATION FACTORS

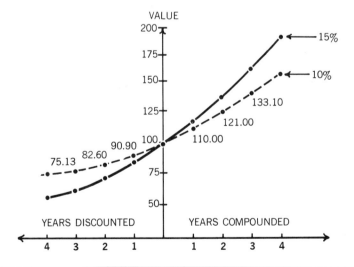

When to pay

Let's take a couple of common business problems and illustrate the importance of the time value of money concept. Suppose you are enlarging your plant and the contractor gives you the following payment options:

PRESENT VALUE OF PAYMENT OPTIONS

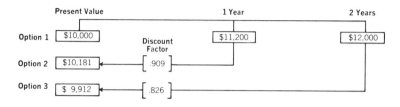

1. $10,000 when work begins,
2. $11,200 when work is completed (expected to be one year), or
3. $12,000 deferred payment plan (due in two years).

The time value of money can be used to compare these alternatives by discounting the payments in options (2) and (3) back to the time when work begins. At this point, the payments are on an equivalent basis, and we can compare their present values. Using a 10% interest rate, you eventually pay out more dollars under option (3), it has the lowest effective cost in terms of time value of money. So you should choose the third option. (See chart above.)

Lease or buy?

Another common decision faced by businessmen is the lease versus buy decision for facilities, office equipment, company vehicles, and so on. This decision involves differential cash flows over time, and the time factor must be analyzed.

Suppose you have the option of either purchasing office equipment with a five-year expected life or leasing the same equipment for five years. If the equipment costs $5,000 new with an anticipated trade-in value of $500 in five years and rents for $1,200 per year, the cash flows might be graphed as shown below.

LEASE VERSUS BUY OPTION

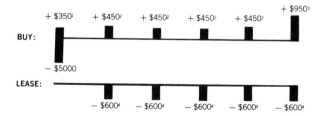

(Notes) 1. (Investment tax credit at 10%.)
2. (Depreciation tax shield at 50% tax rate.)
3. ($500 trade-in plus depreciation tax shield.)
4. ($1,200 lease payment net of 50% tax shield.)

NET PRESENT VALUE OF LEASE VERSUS BUY OPTION

BUY: Net Present Value = -\$5,000 + 500 + 450(.909) + 450(.826)

$$+ 450(.751) + 450(.683) + 950(.621) = -\$2,484$$

LEASE: Net Present Value = -\$600(.909) - 600(.826) - 600(.751)

$$- 600(.683) - 600(.621) \qquad = -\$2,275$$

The discounting aspect of this problem is straightforward. Because both cash outflows (purchase cost and lease fees) as well as cash inflows (investment credit, depreciation, and salvage value) are involved, the discounted figures must be algebraically added to determine the *net* present value of each alternative. (See chart above.)

As you can see, the correct decision is to lease since that alternative has the lowest net cost in terms of the time value of money. Actually, this decision probably goes against the intuitive judgment of many businessmen who would argue that buying costs less money (\$5,000 to purchase versus \$6,000 to lease) and that the cost to purchase is reduced even further by the effects of the investment credit (\$350) and salvage value (\$500). With this total difference of \$1,850 between lease and purchase, how could it possibly be cheaper to lease? What makes the difference is the *timing* of the cash flows. To buy required complete payment in year one, while the lease fees are paid out over the five-year period. When the time value of these dollars is considered, it definitely works out (as you can see from the figures above) that it is cheaper to lease.

Present value problems can sometimes get complicated in detail, but the effort will definitely be worth it in times of high cost money. Remember these steps when making time-value decisions, and you should avoid any trouble:

1. List the incoming and outgoing cash flows of each alternative.
2. Apply the appropriate tax rate to determine the *after* tax effect of these cash flows. Remember that lease fees and depreciation expenses are tax deductible. The investment credit yields an effective cash inflow because it directly reduces income taxes.
3. Select an interest rate representative of your investment opportunities. Do not set the rate too low. It should certainly be above current interest rates, and many companies consider the "opportunity cost" of their capital to be as high as 30%.
4. Discount the cash flows to arrive at the net present value.
5. Choose the alternative with lowest net cash outflow or highest net cash inflow.

ACCUMULATION FACTORS
[Value in the future of $1.00 received today]

Interest Rate

	5%	6%	7%	8%	9%	10%	12%	14%	15%	16%	18%	20%
1	1.050	1.060	1.070	1.080	1.090	1.100	1.120	1.140	1.150	1.160	1.180	1.200
2	1.102	1.124	1.145	1.166	1.188	1.210	1.254	1.300	1.322	1.346	1.392	1.440
3	1.158	1.191	1.225	1.260	1.295	1.331	1.405	1.482	1.521	1.561	1.643	1.728
4	1.216	1.262	1.311	1.360	1.412	1.464	1.574	1.689	1.749	1.811	1.939	2.074
5	1.276	1.338	1.403	1.469	1.539	1.611	1.762	1.925	2.011	2.100	2.288	2.488
6	1.340	1.419	1.501	1.587	1.677	1.772	1.974	2.195	2.313	2.436	2.700	2.986
7	1.407	1.504	1.606	1.714	1.828	1.949	2.211	2.502	2.660	2.826	3.185	3.583
8	1.477	1.594	1.718	1.851	1.993	2.144	2.476	2.853	3.059	3.278	3.759	4.300
9	1.551	1.689	1.838	1.999	2.172	2.358	2.773	3.252	3.518	3.803	4.435	5.160
10	1.629	1.791	1.967	2.159	2.367	2.594	3.106	3.707	4.046	4.411	5.324	6.192
11	1.710	1.896	2.105	2.332	2.580	2.853	3.479	4.226	4.652	5.117	6.176	7.430
12	1.796	2.012	2.252	2.518	2.813	3.138	3.896	4.818	5.350	5.936	7.288	8.916
13	1.886	2.133	2.410	2.720	3.066	3.452	4.363	5.492	6.153	6.886	8.599	10.699
14	1.980	2.261	2.579	2.937	3.342	3.797	4.887	6.261	7.076	7.988	10.147	12.839
15	2.079	2.397	2.759	3.172	3.642	4.177	5.474	7.138	8.137	9.266	11.974	15.407
16	2.183	2.540	2.952	3.426	3.970	4.595	6.130	8.137	9.358	10.748	14.129	18.488
17	2.292	2.693	3.159	3.700	4.328	5.054	6.866	9.276	10.761	12.468	16.672	22.186
18	2.407	2.854	3.380	3.996	4.717	5.560	7.690	10.575	12.375	14.463	19.673	26.623
19	2.527	3.026	3.617	4.316	5.142	6.116	8.613	12.056	14.232	16.777	23.214	31.948
20	2.653	3.207	3.870	4.661	5.604	6.728	9.646	13.743	16.367	19.461	27.393	38.338

Note: As you may note, the accumulation and discount factors at a given interest rate and year are the inverse of each other.

DISCOUNT FACTORS
[Value today of $1.00 received in the future]

Interest Rate

	5%	6%	7%	8%	9%	10%	12%	14%	15%	16%	18%	20%
1	.952	.943	.935	.926	.917	.909	.893	.877	.870	.862	.847	.833
2	.907	.890	.873	.857	.842	.826	.797	.769	.756	.743	.718	.694
3	.864	.840	.816	.794	.772	.751	.712	.675	.658	.641	.609	.579
4	.823	.792	.763	.735	.708	.683	.636	.592	.572	.552	.516	.482
5	.784	.747	.713	.681	.650	.621	.567	.519	.497	.476	.437	.402
6	.746	.705	.666	.630	.596	.564	.507	.456	.432	.410	.370	.335
7	.711	.665	.623	.583	.547	.513	.452	.400	.376	.354	.314	.279
8	.677	.627	.582	.540	.502	.467	.404	.351	.327	.305	.266	.233
9	.645	.592	.544	.500	.460	.424	.361	.308	.284	.263	.226	.194
10	.614	.558	.508	.463	.422	.386	.322	.270	.247	.227	.191	.162
11	.585	.527	.475	.429	.388	.350	.287	.237	.215	.195	.162	.135
12	.557	.497	.444	.397	.356	.319	.257	.208	.187	.168	.137	.112
13	.530	.469	.415	.368	.326	.290	.229	.182	.163	.145	.116	.093
14	.505	.442	.388	.340	.299	.263	.205	.160	.141	.125	.099	.078
15	.481	.417	.362	.315	.275	.239	.183	.140	.123	.108	.084	.065
16	.458	.394	.339	.292	.252	.218	.163	.123	.107	.093	.071	.054
17	.436	.371	.317	.270	.231	.198	.146	.108	.093	.080	.060	.045
18	.416	.350	.296	.250	.212	.180	.130	.095	.081	.069	.051	0.38
19	.396	.331	.276	.232	.194	.164	.116	.083	.070	.060	.043	.031
20	.377	.312	.258	.215	.178	.149	.104	.073	.061	.051	.037	.026

Note: As you may note, the accumulation and discount factors at a given interest rate and year are the inverse of each other.

CAPITAL INVESTMENT ANALYSIS

Any time a business invests money (capital) *today* in the hopes of earning a return on this money in the *future*, it has made a capital investment decision. It is vital that problems of this type be analyzed correctly because: (1) they often involve large amounts of money and (2) they generally lock the business into a course of action for several years. The most common types of capital investment decisions are:

- Expand plant vs. stay "as is"
- Lease equipment vs. buy
- Buy new equipment vs. keep the old
- Introduce new product vs. stick with the old

Steps in analysis

In each of these cases, the following steps must be considered:

1. *Alternatives.* All capital investment decisions involve alternatives. The starting point, therefore, is to be sure that the proper alternatives are being considered. For example, perhaps the decision should not be buy new equipment versus keep the old, but rather refurbish the old versus let it wear out. Or maybe the alternatives should not be introduce new product versus scrap old product, but rather introduce the new product on a regional basis versus go national. It is difficult to reach the right decision unless you analyze the right alternatives. Before proceeding, make a careful study of all the options and reduce the list to those that are relevant and most viable.

2. *Isolate relevant costs.* It is important to recognize which decisions are capital investment decisions.

- *Differential costs.* Since capital investment decisions involve alternatives, we are not concerned with the absolute cost of an alternative but only with the *difference* in cash flows between the alternatives.

- *Future cash flows vs. sunk costs.* Most accountants and business people worry about *past* costs saying, "What was our raw materials cost on that part?" or "What was our utility bill last quarter?" When analyzing a capital investment decision, however, *only future cash flows are relevant.* Any expenditures made in the past are considered "sunk", i.e., they can't be recouped and are therefore irrelevant to any decisions involving the future. This is a crucial (and sometimes difficult) concept to grasp. A couple of examples may clarify these concepts.

Buy new equipment vs. keep the old. This is a common problem that faces most business managers. First, consider *all* alternatives. For example,

if the old machine is broken beyond repair, there really is no analytical problem—it must be replaced. If, however, the old machine is working satisfac-
torily but a new one would be faster and more efficient, then we have a
genuine capital investment decision. Consider the following case: Company X
has an old machine with an estimated salvage value of $2,500. To replace
the old machine, which originally cost $7,000, with a new one will cost
$10,000 plus $2,000 to install it. This new machine will save $1,500 a year
in operating costs, has an estimated useful life of five years, and can be sal-
vaged for $2,000 at the end of that period. The company desires a 15% mini-
mum return on its investments. Should it buy the new machine?

First, it is vital to know how much money will have to be invested in the new
machine. Here we are concerned only with future costs. The book value of
the old machine (its cost less accumulated depreciation) is irrelevant as is its
original cost since both are past history. What is relevant is how much the
old machine can be sold for and anything else such as the investment tax
credit which will reduce the net cost of the new machine. Taking all these
factors into account, the net investment comes to $8,834.

The second step is to calculate the effect of savings from the new machine. In other words, what will be the return on the proposed investment?
Note that when we speak of savings, it means the *differential* in all costs to
operate the new machine versus the old. This includes labor, depreciation,
utilities, and maintenance. At first glance you might say, "We'll save $1,500
a year times five years plus the $2,000 we'll get when we scrap it—that
equals $9,500. That's well above our net investment of $8,834. Let's buy
it!" But you aren't going to realize those savings until sometime in the

SHOULD COMPANY X BUY NEW MACHINE.

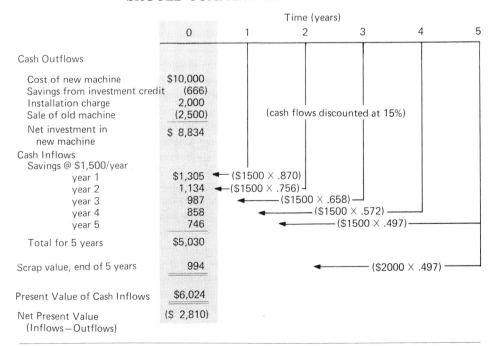

future, and the investment of $8,834 has to be made today. It's like comparing apples and oranges. We have to take the time value of money into account (see page 71) and discount those savings by the 15% you would like to earn on your money. Otherwise it could be a bad investment.

As you can see, when the savings are discounted at your desired 15% rate, the present value of the inflows is only $6,024 versus the $8,834 you would have to pay out today. You would technically lose $2,810 in net present value on your investment—certainly not a 15% return! There may, of course, be nonmonetary factors that influence the decision such as a requirement to buy new machinery to meet industrial safety standards. But simply on the basis of the above economic analysis, the proposal to buy the new machine should be rejected.

Introduce new product.   Suppose that Company Y has spent $25,000 to develop and test market a new product. The decision of whether or not to commit an additional $25,000 to go into full production and introduce the product nationwide is now before the board of directors. The vice president of marketing tells the directors, "We've spent $25,000 to develop and test market our new product. While I'll concede that the test market results weren't as good as we had hoped, we'll never know for sure if this product is a winner until we go national. We've got $25,000 in this thing already, and we stand a good chance of making $100,000 over the next five years before the competition catches up. We must protect our investment, and I for one think it's a good place to put our money." The treasurer, however, countered: "I agree we've spent a lot of money, but that's no reason to throw good money after bad. What we've spent is gone. We have to look at this product strictly on its future merits." With that, the treasurer distributed his analysis. (See New Product Proposal below.)

The treasurer continued, "I think several things should be apparent from this analysis. First, we are really considering making a capital investment of an additional $40,000, not $25,000 as was suggested, because increased working capital of $15,000 will be needed to finance accounts receivable

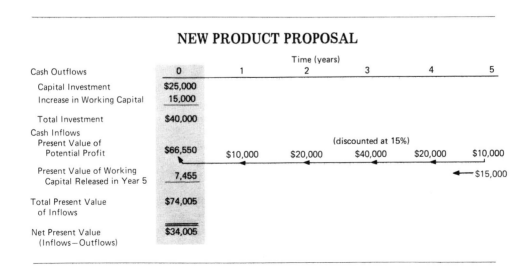

NEW PRODUCT PROPOSAL

Cash Outflows	Time (years)					
	0	1	2	3	4	5
Capital Investment	$25,000					
Increase in Working Capital	15,000					
Total Investment	$40,000					
Cash Inflows				(discounted at 15%)		
Present Value of Potential Profit	$66,550	$10,000	$20,000	$40,000	$20,000	$10,000
Present Value of Working Capital Released in Year 5	7,455					←$15,000
Total Present Value of Inflows	$74,005					
Net Present Value (Inflows—Outflows)	$34,005					

during the five years. We'll get it back, however, at the end, and I've shown its present value of $7,455 after discounting at our standard required return of 15%. The $25,000 we've already spent is not, as I've stated, relevant to this decision of whether to go ahead or not. The $100,000 we stand to make over five years is worth $77,500 today if discounted at our desired 15 percent rate of return. The net present value of this investment decision (inflows minus outflows) is $34,005. What we have to decide is whether comparable investment alternatives available to us yield more or less than this one. We should also determine the probability of our realizing the $100,000 figure we have been using. While this alternative yields a high rate of return if all goes well, I think the inconclusive test marketing results cast considerable doubt on the projected figures." After considerable discussion, the board agreed with the treasurer's assessment of the risks and voted down the proposal.

Conclusion

Many decisions that were made based on gut feel in the past can be subjected to critical, unemotional analysis with surprising results. Take a few minutes to review these techniques again. Don't worry unduly about whether you should stipulate a 10% or 20% return on your investments. It's the methodology and approach to these problems that are important.

RETURN ON INVESTMENT ANALYSIS

Return on Investment (ROI) analysis is an invaluable guide for profit planning. You can use ROI analysis for intercompany or interindustry comparisons and for various pricing, cost, inventory, and investment decisions. In your analysis, however, you must take care that consistent definitions of sales, profit, and total investment are applied to validate your comparisons.

Sources of Profit

As your products wind their way through your business and on to the customer, two factors determine how much dollar-return they will provide on your investment: margin and turnover.

$$\text{Margin} = \frac{\text{Profit}}{\text{Sales}} \quad \text{(i.e., what percentage profit do you make on sales)}$$

$$\text{Turnover} = \frac{\text{Sales}}{\text{Total Investment}} \quad \text{(i.e., the amount of sales to your total investment level)}$$

To insure the consistency we mentioned above, let's define our terms:

- *Sales.* Net (after returns and allowances) rather than gross sales.

- *Profit.* Net operating income before tax. Any items of non-operating income, such as income from leased property or interest, are excluded.
- *Total Investment.* All fixed and current assets normally used in the business to produce the net operating profit.

Note that the formula for Return on Investment could also be calculated as Profit divided by Total Sales. This short form is derived by a simple mathematical function in which the sales figures in the basic formula cancel each other. (See Basic Formula below.) While the answer obtained is the same, the short form ignores the fact that Return on Investment is influenced by *two* relationships: (1) profit to sales; and (2) total investment to sales. Both of these relationships must be recognized to localize the sources of change in Return on Investment. Each company should attempt to increase sales while simultaneously employing its resources in such a manner that it consistently increases its profit on total investment. The basic formula emphasizes this dual movement. Before we go any further, maybe you would like to go back and reread what we have covered. If you understand the basics, it is all downhill from here.

BASIC FORMULA FOR ROI

$$ROI = Margin \times Turnover$$

or substituting:

$$ROI = \frac{Profit}{Sales} \times \frac{Sales}{Total\ Investment}$$

Relationship of Operating Ratios

Simple as the basic ROI formula appears to be, it takes into consideration all the various items that go into a balance sheet and income statement. The chart on the top of page 82 presents a structural outline of the relationship of these items to Return on Investment and to each other.

Application of Basic Formula

Let's take a specific example to illustrate the use of the formula. The operations data on the chart that follows have been summarized from the income statements and balance sheets of two divisions of the PDQ Specialties Co. From the figures in the chart we can calculate the ROIs for each division.

PDQ SPECIALTIES COMPANY

Income Statement Data			Balance Sheet Data		
	Division A	*Division B*		*Division A*	*Division B*
Sales	$1,000,000	$1,000,000	Fixed Assets	$400,000	$400,000
Less Cost of Sales	900,000	900,000	Current Assets	200,000	400,000
Profit	$ 100,000	$ 100,000	Total Investment	$600,000	$800,000

Implications for Decision Making

Note that Divisions A and B made the same profits ($100,000). Also, they had the same amount of money invested in fixed assets ($400,000). Yet, the Return on Investment for Division A is significantly higher than Division B.

RELATIONSHIP OF OPERATING RATIOS

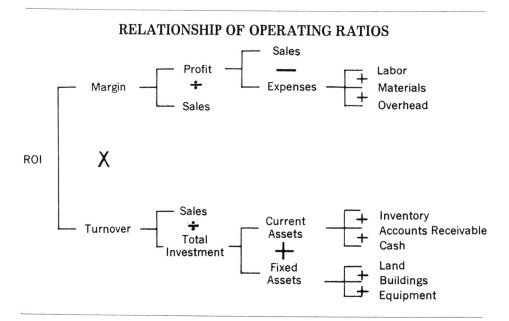

How could this be? We see from Division B's balance sheet that it has considerably more money tied up in current assets; in other words, inventory, accounts receivable, and cash. Now, there are two possible explanations. Either Division B is poorly run and has not properly managed its current assets, *or* Division B is in a considerably different business that requires significantly more inventory and involves slower paying customers than Division A. Whatever the case, it should be clear that to compare the two divisions in terms of profit level alone would be misleading. Only when we examine how *efficiently* they use their resources (i.e., by using ROI analysis) can we properly compare the two businesses and make competent management decisions.

ROIs FOR DIVISIONS A AND B

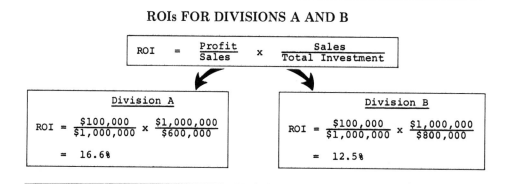

Methods of Improving ROI

Given this background, we can now consider how we might go about improving the efficiency and earning power of a business. Again, we must examine the two main components of ROI—margin and turnover. There are two ways to improve each item:

Margin

- *Increase sales revenue more than expenses* (i.e., charge considerably more for only slightly more of a product. A good example is a 10¢ pack of chewing gum—only a little more product for twice the previous price).
- *Cut expenses more than sales* (i.e., the shrinking candy bar at the same price is a classic example).

Turnover

- *Increase sales relatively more than total investment* (i.e., improve utilization and efficiency of present assets or replace old assets with considerably more efficient new assets).
- *Reduce total investment relatively faster than sales* (i.e., try to cut inventory levels and sell off or reduce other unproductive assets).

Summary

Return on Investment analysis provides the manager with an excellent tool to compare various operating entities both within and outside his own industry and firm. Take a few moments to compute your own company or division's ROI. Then walk around your business and ask yourself the question, "Does this asset help or hurt my overall return?" You will probably find it quite a revealing exercise.

CONTROLLING ACCOUNTS RECEIVABLE

Credit control is one of the most fundamental aspects of managing a business. Too often, however, managers relegate this function to others. This inattention can be especially dangerous if there are economic changes that impact directly on the cost, control, and management of credit sales.

How much are accounts receivable costing you?

When one business advances goods or services to another on credit, it is effectively loaning short-term working capital. Naturally, there is a cost associated with such capital that increases as (1) interest rates rise and/or (2) customers take longer to pay. The combination of these two factors can reduce profits, adversely affect cash flow, and in extreme cases, endanger the business. Here is a simple example:

The John Doe Tool Company borrows to finance its receivables and allows thirty days credit terms to customers. Last year it had sales of $5 million and has average accounts receivable outstanding of $410,000. The cost of money last year was 10 percent, making the cost to maintain this level of credit $41,000. This year, while sales remained constant, the borrowing cost rose to 13 percent, and average accounts receivable expanded to $640,000. The result was that the cost of extending credit to customers more than doubled to $83,200 per year ($640,000 × 13%)—an increase of over $42,000 that would have a direct impact on profits.

How to use the days credit formula

An easy way to track the health of credit sales is to monitor the average number of days customers take to pay ("days credit").

DAYS CREDIT FORMULA

$$\left(\frac{\text{Average accounts receivable outstanding}}{\text{Annual sales level}}\right) \times 365 = \text{Average days taken by customers to settle accounts}$$

Applying this formula, the Doe Company controller determined how long customers were stretching their payments.

DOE COMPANY DAYS CREDIT

Last year	*This year*
$\dfrac{\$410,000}{\$5,000,000} \times 365 = 30 \text{ days}$	$\dfrac{\$640,000}{\$5,000,000} \times 365 = 47 \text{ days}$

The Doe Company calculation showed that while last year customers were sticking to the thirty days credit allowed them, this year they were taking an average of seventeen extra days. While nothing could be done about the higher interest rates, this laxness in collecting the receivables incurred nearly $30,000 of the $42,000 overall increase in financing costs ($640,000 – $410,000 × 13% = $29,900). And, of course, this says nothing about the attendant cash flow problems.

Tightening up

On a routine basis, every manager should track (1) the number of days credit he has outstanding using the formula above, and; (2) the absolute cost of maintaining the current level of receivables. In addition, new accounts should be closely scrutinized. A standard operating procedure for evaluating a new credit candidate should include:

- Ask for and check all supplier and bank references.
- Independently check suppliers in your same type of business regarding the credit worthiness of the new account.
- Ask for the customer's recent audited financial statements.
- Set credit limits and terms and monitor the account in the first few months.
- Refer to Dun and Bradstreet where possible or applicable.

CHAPTER 7

BASIC ACCOUNTING TECHNIQUES

WHAT IS ACCOUNTING?

Accounting has often been called the "language of business". Every businessman uses accounting terms and concepts to describe the events that make up the existence of his business. The underlying purpose of accounting is to provide financial information about the business. This information is needed by the businessman himself, to help him plan and control the activities of his organization. It is also needed by others, such as banks, lessors, investors, creditors, or the public, who have supplied money to the business or who have some other interest that will be served by information about its financial position and operating results. The material contained in this section will help you to become conversant and comfortable in this extremely important language.

THE BALANCE SHEET AND INCOME STATEMENTS

Financial statements are the end products of the accounting process. They reveal a clear picture of the profitability and financial status of a business.

The two most important financial statements are the balance sheet and the income statement. These statements are summaries of all pertinent accounting information.

A *balance sheet* shows the financial position of a business *at a given point in time*, for example on the last day of the fiscal year. Some businesses prepare a balance sheet every month, some on a quarterly basis, but all businesses must prepare a balance at the end of the business year. This balance sheet contains a list of the assets and liabilities of a business as well as a description of the owner's equity.

An *income statement* describes profits and losses *over a period of time*. All businesses must prepare income statements at least once a year to satisfy the IRS. Of course, as with the balance sheet, some firms prepare income statements more than once during the year because they can provide managers with reliable indication of the company's progress.

How to Read a Balance Sheet

Everytime you sell products or services on credit, you are acting as a banker. Even though you may conduct periodic credit checks on your customers through Dun & Bradstreet and your bank, if one company becomes a major customer purchasing, say, 5% or more of your total sales, you should make your own analysis of that customer's financial condition. Many companies will not release their income statements, but you can invariably obtain a balance sheet, and this is where your analysis should center. Remember, too, that the condition of suppliers may also be important, particularly if you are buying long lead-time items.

No customer or supplier is immune from financial difficulty, nor are bankers infallible judges of corporate solvency. Here's a list of often overlooked points you should check to decide if a company is in a solid financial position.

Date. The balance sheet is a static snapshot of the financial condition of a company on one particular day of the year. Therefore, always try to obtain the most recent statement available—of the past month or quarter if possible.

Auditor's opinion. Most companies have their year-end financial statements audited by a Certified Public Accountant. The auditor prepares a statement describing the manner in which he conducted the audit and expresses his opinion as to the manner of preparation, consistency with prior periods, and fairness of valuation. Often an auditor will state that his opinion is "subject to" occurrence of some event or a particular accounting principle. In this case he is bringing some special item to your attention, and you should determine whether the qualification is serious. When no auditor's opinion is attached, remember that the figures have been prepared by company management and may be inaccurate or even deliberately misleading.

Footnotes. You can generally detect a company in trouble by carefully reading the footnotes to its balance sheet. This most often overlooked area should be the starting point of your analysis—not an afterthought. Important items to check are:

- *Contingent liabilities.* Debts that a company *may* owe do not show up on its balance sheet but could have an adverse impact on the condition of the firm.
- *Lease obligations.* Obligations for payments under leases are fixed obligations of the company and hence, a form of debt. Such fixed commitments do not show up on the balance sheet, however, and leasing is often referred to as "off the balance sheet financing". Check this area carefully.
- *Reserve for contingencies.* Many companies will set up a reserve account if they anticipate major losses from a setback, such as a product that failed, bad debts, or a fire. Check the reason for any reserve and assess whether it appears adequate to cover the potential loss.
- *Financial arrangements.* The balance sheet will tell you how much debt a company has. It will not give you such details as when sinking fund payments must be made, how much

remains on a line of credit, or the interest rate the company is paying. For these details, you should consult the footnotes.

- *Capitalized items.* Companies have the option of showing certain items as assets when, in fact, they may represent only intangibles. Examples that you should check include organizational expenses, goodwill, research and development expenses, and preopening expenses. To test the company's financial condition, eliminate intangibles from the balance sheet by deduction from net stockholders equity (otherwise known as "net worth"). If this results in a definite net worth or reduces total assets by more than 25 percent, further investigation is merited.

Other problem areas.

- *Cash.* Be aware of a large cash balance. If bank debt under current liabilities is equal to or greater than cash, the company may be engaged in window dressing to give the appearance of greater liquidity than it actually has.
- *Receivables.* A large portion of the receivables may be uncollectable. Prudent management will establish a reserve for bad debts. Make sure it appears reasonable.
- *Inventories.* Another significant asset, inventories may be worthless at liquidation. Valuation of finished-goods inventory at cost rather than net selling price is more conservative. Also, check the footnotes to see if the company uses FIFO or LIFO. FIFO is less conservative than LIFO but either is acceptable.
- *Net worth.* This is the most widely used indicator of a company's financial condition. It represents the difference between the value of assets and liabilities. However, you should look into the computation of net worth. It is made up of two primary items: *capital and surplus*, being the money paid in by the company's stockholders, and *retained earnings* (or deficit), being the accumulated result of the company's operations. A deficit indicates that losses have exceeded profits. If comparison with the previous year reveals an increased deficit, then the company may still be losing money.

Reading the balance sheet as a means of evaluating a company's financial condition may have its limitations owing to problems with valuating certain assets. However, your own analysis along with professional advice where necessary should help prevent losses.

How to Read an Income Statement

The interaction of an income statement and a balance sheet can be confusing. Basically, a balance sheet shows what assets a business has at a certain point in time and who has claim to them, giving the basic accounting equation: Assets equals Liabilities plus Owners Equity. This means that all the assets of any business are claimed by either: (1) the creditors, such as tradesmen, bond holders, or banks (*liabilities*) or (2) the owners, who have a right to whatever is left over (*owners equity*).

Whereas a balance sheet is a static snapshot of assets and liabilities, the income statement is a dynamic summary of the profits and losses of the business over a period of time. The illustration below shows this important difference.

As you can see from the illustration, an income statement bridges the time period between the two balance sheets. Any changes in the overall condition of a business from one period to another must be explained by the intervening income statement. Suppose that the XYZ Corporation has a balance sheet at the end of 1975 as shown on the top of the next page. Its $10,000 in assets are represented by $2,000 owed the bank, $3,000 in capital that the owners contributed, and $5,000 from past earnings that were retained in the business. As shown on its income statement, 1976 was a profitable year, and the company netted $7,800 after taxes. The question, therefore, is how to update the old balance sheet.

We can see from XYZ's income statement that all profits for 1976 were retained in the business. Total assets must, therefore, have gone up in 1976. To keep this new balance sheet in balance, an adjustment must now be made to its right side. This is done by taking the retained earnings as of the previous year ($5,000), adding the profits retained from the current year's operations ($7,800), yielding an updated retained earnings figure as of December 31, 1976 of $12,800. The basic accounting formula is now satisfied, and total assets equal liabilities plus owners equity.

The major elements of an income statement   Accountants have many formats for presenting income statements, but the one on the bottom of the next page is representative. The important thing is to obtain audited statements *with all footnotes*. Here is an explanation of the three major components of an income statement:

1.   *Revenues*

   • *Gross sales.* This component is the total invoice price of goods shipped, excluding sales taxes or excise duties, charged

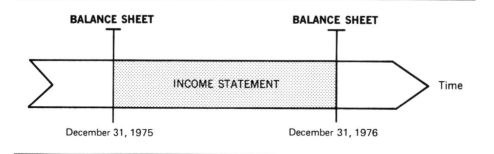

BALANCE SHEET		INCOME STATEMENT	BALANCE SHEET	
XYZ Corporation as of December 31, 1975		XYZ Corporation Calendar Year 1976	XYZ Corporation as of December 31, 1976	
ASSETS	LIABILITIES	Sales $100,000	ASSETS	LIABILITIES
Cash $2,500	Bank loan $2,000	Cost of goods sold 80,000	Cash $9,000	Bank loan $2,000
Inventory 7,500		Gross profit 20,000	Inventory 8,800	
		Overhead 10,000		
	OWNERS EQUITY Paid in capital $3,000	Profit before tax 10,000		OWNERS EQUITY Paid in capital $3,000
		Taxes @ 22% 2,200		
	Retained earnings 5,000	Profit after tax. 7,800		Retained earnings 12,800
		Dividends 0		
Total $10,000	Total $10,000		Total $17,800	Total $17,800
		Retained earnings . . . . $7,800 ⟶ =		

to the customer. Always check the footnotes to see how sales are "recognized". Significant differences can result depending on whether the company is on a cash or accrual basis, if installment reporting is used, or if goods are shipped on consignment.

- *Returns, allowances, and discounts.* Returns and allowances are sometimes deducted directly from gross sales. Discounts refer to reductions taken by customers for prompt payments, such as 2/10 net 30 days.

2. *Expenses*

- *Cost of goods sold.* The final amount of COGS is dependent on the inventory convention used. Companies on the "full

ABC CORPORATION INCOME STATEMENT

ABC Corporation Income Statement—Year ended December 31, 1976			Expense ratios (% of net sales)	Profit ratios (% of net sales)
Gross sales		$300,000		
less: Returns & allowances	2,000			
Discounts	4,000			
Net sales		294,000	100.0%	100.0%
less: Cost of goods sold		175,000	59.5%	
Gross profit		119,000		40.5%
less: Selling, general, & administrative	65,000		22.1%	
Depreciation	20,000		6.8%	
Operating profit		34,000		11.6%
less: Interest expense		9,000	3.1%	
Profit before tax		25,000		8.5%
less: taxes		5,500	1.9%	
Profit after tax		$19,500	6.6%	6.6%

cost" system sometimes engage in a practice at year's end known as "selling to inventory". This can materially distort profits. A switch to the LIFO system, depreciation policies, and capitalization procedures can significantly affect COGS and profits. Details on all these points should be checked in the footnotes, and any questions should be referred to your accountant.

- *Selling and G & A.* These expenses should be itemized, but sometimes they are combined. If not itemized, check the footnotes for any significant pension expenses, deferred compensation arrangements, bed debts, or unusually high officers salaries.

- *Interest expense.* This item can be a clue to how much debt the company owes if a balance sheet is not available.

3. *Profits*

- *Gross, operating, and PBT.* Gross profit is the difference when cost of goods sold is subtracted from net sales. Operating profit is the amount the business earns before any financing expense. Profit before tax, the amount of profit on which taxes are computed, is the final amount left after all expenses have been met.

- *Profit after tax.* Many business managers are confused to find that profits before and after tax are sometimes similar; in other words, little tax was paid even though there were healthy profits. Often the explanation is that there were significant investment credits or a healthy loss carry forward. Check the footnotes for details.

What the income statement shows. The significance of a company's income accounts can only be determined by comparing the current figures with: (1) figures of the same company prepared in prior years, or (2) figures available for other companies engaged in a similar business. The easiest way to make these comparisons is to reduce the figures to a set of expense and profitability ratios (refer to bottom of page 91.) These can then be analyzed to reveal significant discrepancies, trends, or problem areas.

Never rely on a balance sheet alone when evaluating a company. Only an income statement can tell and give you the results of current operations and help pinpoint possible problem areas. A strong balance sheet is certainly a point in a company's favor, but its income statement is usually much more indicative of its future prospects.

FINANCIAL RATIO ANALYSIS CHECKLIST

Every businessman must be able to check the condition of his business quickly and accurately. Many businessmen, however, examine only raw figures, such as the amount of cash on hand, the dollar amount of accounts payable, and so on. This type of analysis can be highly misleading because it neglects the financial interaction between the various sources and uses of capital. For example, it is of little use to know the amount of your current assets if you do not also examine the level of current liabilities. Ratio analysis provides a number of comparative indicators that you can track from month to month to monitor your company's financial condition, efficiency, and profitability.

1. *Ratios Measuring Liquidity*
   - *Current Assets to Current Liabilities.* The "current ratio" is the most commonly used index of financial strength. It measures the ability of the business to pay its current obligations. A current ratio of at least two is considered prudent in most businesses; less than one is unsound.
   - *Cash, Marketable Securities, and Receivables to Current Liabilities.* Called the "acid test", this is the most severe test of a business's ability to pay its current debts. It eliminates inventory and considers only *liquid* assets whose value is fairly certain. A rule of thumb is to keep this ratio at least one to one.

2. *Debt Ratios.* These ratios consider the ability of the business to meet its long term obligations as well as the current liabilities measured above.

   - *Total Debt to Total Assets.* This ratio measures the relative proportion of the firm's assets that have been contributed from borrowed sources. Certain firms, such as leasing companies, often operate with over 90% borrowed funds. For most businesses, however, a figure from 10% to 40% debt is usually considered a prudent maximum.
   - *Current Debt to Total Debt.* This ratio measures the proportion of the company's debt that matures and must be paid within one year. Undue reliance must never be placed on short term sources of debt, and care must be taken to insure that a disproportionate amount of debt does not come due in any given year.

3. *Turnover Ratios*
   - *Sales to Receivables.* This ratio indicates how well the business is collecting its accounts. In times of tight money, it is a critical ratio to monitor.
   - *Sales to Inventory.* This relationship approximates the number of times inventory "turns over" during the sales period. Because inventory ties up a substantial portion of most companies' funds, it is important to keep this ratio as high as possible, without the danger of running out of stock and losing sales.
   - *Sales to Fixed Assets.* This ratio measures how effectively the existing plant and equipment are being utilized. It should be kept as high as possible.

4. *Profitability Ratios*

- *Profit (before interest and taxes) to Sales.* This common ratio is often called "profit margin". It measures the relative efficiency of operations, although it can be distorted by changes in prices or sales volume.
- *Profit (after tax) to Net Worth.* Normally called "return-on-equity", this ratio measures the return to the owners of the business after all taxes and interest have been paid.

The above represents just a few of many financial ratios that are commonly used. Some businesses also monitor certain physical-financial ratios such as:

- Working capital per unit of product
- Sales volume per unit of product
- Fixed costs per unit of product
- Total capital per unit of product

Try to identify the critical factors that are unique to your particular business. By periodically tracking only a few key ratios, you can have a fail-safe early warning system to spot any deteriorating conditions. If you would like to see how your company compares with others in your industry, Dun & Bradstreet publishes a free, handy booklet called *Key Business Ratios*, which contains statistics from the 1972 Census of Business on 125 lines of business activities. Write, Dun & Bradstreet, 99 Church Street, New York, NY 10007, Attention: Public Relations Department.

ELEMENTS OF COST ACCOUNTING

Almost every manager fears that certain costs may get out of hand without his knowledge. Yet any time a business grows beyond the point where one individual can supervise each and every expenditure, a major element of cost control has been lost. This is why many companies never reach full potential. Management effectively stifles growth by devoting too much time to watching minute expenses and not enough time determining which products are most profitable and promoting their sale. In any business the key to staying on top—and growing—is an effective cost accounting system.

What is meant by cost accounting

When a businessman says something costs him a dollar to produce, what does he really mean? Is he talking about the material cost, the materials plus labor, or all the direct costs to produce the item plus some allocation for overhead? To avoid confusion, it is important to understand how various costs are defined. On the following page is a chart that shows a cost breakdown for a typical manufactured item that has a "full cost" of $1. Similar groupings of costs could be used for service or retail firms.

ELEMENTS OF FULL COST

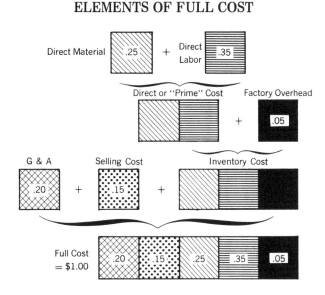

Elements of full cost

As you can see from the chart, costs break down into the general categories of material, labor, and various types of overhead. Here are examples of each:

- *Direct material cost* includes raw materials that become part of the final product. Not included are supplies, such as tool bits and lubricating oil, which are used in production but do not become part of the final product.
- *Direct labor cost* includes those labor costs that can be traced directly to the production of the product. A direct relationship exists between the number of units produced and direct material and direct labor costs.
- *Factory overhead* is all manufacturing costs except direct materials and labor. This includes expenses of the factory, such as janitors, tool room keepers, supplies, heat, water, lights, maintenance, depreciation, taxes, etc. The sum of direct materials and labor and factory overhead yields the cost at which completed goods are carried in inventory. In financial accounting when the items are eventually sold, this amount is called "cost of goods sold".
- *Selling cost* includes the costs incurred to get the goods from the factory to the customer. Included are such expenses as shipping and salesmen's commissions.
- *General and administrative cost* is a catchall category to reflect expenses not covered above. It includes officer's salaries, research and development, accounting, legal, and public relations.

The difference between cost accounting and financial accounting

Although interrelated, cost accounting and financial accounting differ considerably and are used for dissimilar purposes.

Financial accounting. This is the familiar type of accounting that involves an income statement and a balance sheet. As the term financial accounting implies, its primary use is summarizing all the financial information concerning a firm at a particular time. It is based on *rather rigid principles*, relies on *past history* and information, and is of special interest to *outsiders*, such as lenders or investors. Chart 1 (below) shows an example of financial accounting.

Cost accounting. Primarily for *internal* use of a firm, it is not bound by rigid accounting principles, and its main purpose is to help management make decisions about the future. Note on Chart 2 (below) that cost accounting breaks down by product line the aggregate figures provided by Chart 1 so each cost element can be analyzed in detail.

How cost accounting is used

Cost accounting allows management to easily and quickly pinpoint problem areas. Here are several examples:

- *Which product to produce?* The fact that Product C is in trouble is immediately visible from Chart 2. Its manufacturing costs are out of line, and it may have to be dropped. It *is* able to carry $3,000 of factory overhead, and this is a point in its favor. Nevertheless, if some plant capacity devoted to Product C could be diverted to Products A or B, it obviously would be profitable to do so.
- *What price to charge?* Pricing is a crucial management decision based on many factors, such as competition, state of the economy, regulation, or seasonality. However, management must also have accurate knowledge of its costs, or errors can result.

FINANCIAL AND COST ACCOUNTING

Chart 1
FINANCIAL ACCOUNTING SYSTEM

XYZ Company Statement for month ended Nov. 30, 1976		
Sales		$50,000
Cost of goods sold:		
Direct materials	15,000	
Direct labor	10,000	
Factory overhead . . .	10,000	35,000
Gross profit on sales		15,000
Selling expense		5,000
General & administrative		5,000
Net profit before tax		$5,000

Chart 2
COST ACCOUNTING APPROACH

XYZ Company
Statement for month ended Nov. 30, 1976

	Product A	Product B	Product C
Sales	25,000	15,000	10,000
Manufacturing costs			
Direct materials	7,500	3,500	4,000
Direct labor	3,500	3,500	3,000
Factory overhead	4,000 15,000	3,000 10,000	3,000 10,000
Gross profit (loss)	10,000	5,000	0
Selling expense	2,500	1,500	1,000
General & administrative	2,500	1,250	1,250
Net profit (loss)	$5,000	$2250	($2250)
Units completed and sold	1,000	500	500
Selling price per unit	$25.00	$30.00	$20.00
Full cost per unit	20.00	25.50	24.50
Gross profit (loss) per unit	$5.00	$4.50	($4.50)

- *Cost Control.* Once each of the elements of cost to produce an item is known, "standards" can be established. For example, if the average cost of direct materials for Product A is $7.50 per unit, then $7.50 per unit can be set as the direct materials standard. Thereafter, rather than analyze Product A's costs, only deviations from its standard costs would be examined.

Every manager must know the approximate full cost of everything he produces and sells. Without this knowledge, it is impossible to know where money is being made or lost in a business. However, before proceeding further, ask yourself these questions:

- *Do I need a formal system?* If you're right on top of every item of expense in your firm, including close supervision of the labor force, an informal system may be sufficient. If, however, you are at all removed from the productive process, a limited system of cost accounting may be needed to adequately control your business.
- *Is my product (or service) mass produced or custom made?* If your production level is fairly steady and your products are uniform, the simpler "process-costing" system will be more appropriate. Here total costs incurred by the firm in a period are divided by the number of units produced to arrive at the full cost. To keep on top of a custom-made or changing product, you will need a "job-costing" system that accumulates costs for each individual item being produced.
- *What costs should I accumulate and control?* In most businesses, 80% of the costs are caused by only 20% of the expense items. You should worry most about accumulating costs, setting standards, and controlling the crucial 20%.

HOW TO PREPARE A BUDGET

No business action is more fundamental than preparing a budget. Yet a surprisingly small percentage of business managers actually use a budget to help plan and control their operations. They feel that if they know what their sales volume is and if their bank account tells them how much money they have, there is nothing to worry about. Unfortunately, many business people are finding that there is indeed more to worry about. For example, what happens to cash balances if a big order goes out late or raw materials shoot up 15% in price? No business manager will get very far with his banker if he uses a seat-of-the-pants approach to dealing with these working capital problems. Budgets are not simply nice to have anymore—they may be your lifeboat to financial safety.

How to begin

There are many different kinds of budgets, such as sales budgets, production budgets, and expense budgets. The most important one to the average business manager is a *cash* budget. Let's prepare a hypothetical cash budget for the manager of the Wooley Woolen Factory who is considering a new sweater line. First, estimate sales levels from the new line for the next year. Then, the breakdown between cash and credit sales can be estimated and the length of time to collect the receivables computed. For example, January sales are projected at $20,000. Of this amount, $2,000 is expected to be cash sales and the remainder on credit. Fifty percent of the $18,000 accounts receivable ($9,000) is expected to be collected in the current month, 40% in the next month, and the rest in three months. These figures are noted by arrows. The cash and collection figures for subsequent months follow the same general pattern. (See worksheet below.)

Purchases of raw materials are also heavily dependent on sales levels. In the case of Wooley Woolen, raw materials cost about 30% of sales, and suppliers allow Wooley Woolen thirty days payment terms. As a result, although $6,000 of supplies were purchased in January, the cash was not actually disbursed until the following month.

The final cash budget

Now that the major sources and uses of cash are available from the worksheet, Wooley Woolen's manager can prepare his final cash budget.

The basic figures for receipts and purchases were taken from the worksheet. In addition, disbursements for salaries, rent, and other expenses were also accounted for. The result shows the net gain or loss in cash for each month and the cumulative total. (See Final Cash Budget.)

Case history of cash budgeting in action

A small midwestern company was notified that it was the low bidder on a subcontract from an aircraft manufacturer to produce part of an engine assembly. The contract called for initial deliveries of parts in two months, with completion of the contract three months later. To meet the deadline,

WORKSHEET

Wooley Woolen Factory — Preliminary Worksheet for New Sweater Line

	Jan.	Feb.	March	April	May	June	July	Aug.	Sept.	Oct.	Nov.	Dec.
Total Sales	$20,000	$20,000	$10,000	$5000	—	—	$5000	$10,000	$30,000	$20,000	$20,000	$20,000
Cash Sales	2000	2000	1000	500	—	—	500	1000	3000	2000	2000	2000
A/R Collection												
50% (present month)	9000	9000	4500	2250	—	—	2250	4500	13,500	9000	9000	9000
40% (next month)	—	7200	7200	3600	1800	—	—	1800	3600	10,800	7200	7200
10% (third month)	—	—	1800	1800	900	450	—	—	450	900	2700	1800
Total Cash In	$11,000	$18,200	$14,500	$8150	$2700	$450	$2750	$7300	$20,550	$22,700	$20,900	$20,000
Purchases (30% of sales)	6000	6000	3000	1500	—	—	1500	3000	9000	6000	6000	6000
Cash Out for Purchases (Disbursements made 30 days after purchase)	—	6000	6000	3000	1500	—	—	1500	3000	9000	6000	6000

FINAL CASH BUDGET

Wooley Woolen Factory — Final Cash Budget

	Jan.	Feb.	March	April	May	June	July	Aug.	Sept.	Oct.	Nov.	Dec.
Estimated Receipts												
Cash Sales	$2000	$2000	$1000	$500	—	—	$500	$1000	$3000	$2000	$2000	$2000
A/R Collection	9000	16,200	13,500	7650	2700	450	2250	6300	17,550	20,700	18,900	18,000
Total Cash In	$11,000	$18,200	$14,500	$8150	$2700	$450	$2750	$7300	$20,550	$22,700	$20,900	$20,000
Estimated Disbursements												
Purchases	—	6000	6000	3000	1500	—	—	1500	3000	9000	6000	6000
Wages	1500	1500	1500	1500	1500	1500	1500	1500	1500	1500	1500	1500
Rent	1000	1000	1000	1000	1000	1000	1000	1000	1000	1000	1000	1000
Other	500	500	500	500	500	500	500	500	500	500	500	500
Total Cash Out	$3000	$9000	$9000	$6000	$4500	$3000	$3000	$4500	$6000	$12,000	$9000	$9000
Net Gain (loss) In Cash	8000	9200	5500	2150	(1800)	(2550)	(250)	2800	14,550	10,700	11,900	11,000
Cumulative Total	$8000	$17,200	$22,700	$24,850	$23,050	$20,500	$20,250	$23,050	$37,600	$48,300	$60,200	$71,200

the company first thought it would have to borrow $125,000 for extra working capital. However, by preparing and analyzing a cash budget, it was able to reduce working capital needs to $25,000 and successfully complete the contract. (See Cash Budget below.)

Note that in the original plan all inventory was to be purchased and paid for in the first month. But by buying supplies only as needed and negotiating sixty-day terms with suppliers, the company cut the working capital dramatically. The company also negotiated a progress payment of $50,000 from the

CASH BUDGET

Original Estimate of Working Capital Needs

	\#1	2	3	4	5	6
Receipts	—	—	$100,000	$100,000	$100,000	$100,000
Disbursements						
Materials	75,000	—	—	—	—	—
Labor	25,000	25,000	25,000	25,000	25,000	—
Total	100,000	25,000	25,000	25,000	25,000	—
Total Gain (loss) In Cash	(100,000)	(25,000)	75,000	75,000	75,000	100,000
Cumulative Total	$100,000)	($125,000)	($50,000)	$25,000	$100,000	$200,000

(peak working capital requirement under Month 2: ($125,000))

Revised Estimate of Working Capital Needs

	1	2	3	3	5	6
Receipts	—	$50,000	$100,000	$100,000	$100,000	$50,000
Disbursements						
Materials	—	—	25,000	25,000	25,000	—
Labor	25,000	25,000	25,000	25,000	25,000	—
Total	$25,000	$25,000	$50,000	$50,000	$50,000	—
Total Gain (loss) In Cash	(25,000)	25,000	50,000	50,000	50,000	50,000
Cumulative Total	($25,000)	—	$50,000	$100,000	$150,000	$200,000

(peak working capital requirement under Month 1: ($25,000))

aircraft manufacturer, which eased working capital requirements considerably. As a result of both of these actions, working capital requirements were reduced from $125,000 to $25,000—a figure that the company had no difficulty obtaining. Without a careful look at a cash budget and searching for ways to reduce borrowing needs, the company could very easily have been forced to pass up a lucrative contract.

How a cash budget is used

There are two main uses for a budget—for planning and for control.

- *Planning.* Budgeting is the only way that cash requirements can be estimated in advance. For example, your banker will be far more disposed to lend money if you tell him you need $50,000 in two months and show him that the loan will be liquidated three months after that than if you say, "I can't meet Friday's payroll!"
- *Control.* While never 100% accurate, budgets give a standard against which actual performance can be measured and controlled. For example, if cash receipts are below forecast, either sales are off or collections are down, or both. The slippage is immediately apparent and remedial action can be taken. Similarly, disbursements that are out of line will also be readily visible.

Limitations and pitfalls

Like most management techniques, budgets are no panacea, and they can be used improperly. Watch for these points:

1. *Budget period.* Ordinarily, the budget should be prepared for at least as long as the time required to complete the natural cash cycle from purchase of raw materials (cash out) to ultimate collection of money from sale of the finished goods (cash in). In the case of a sweater manufacturer who produces an inventory for sale next winter, the cycle could be as long as a year. In other cases, only a few weeks or months will suffice. Revise budgets periodically and don't budget too far ahead, or the projections become meaningless.
2. *Tyranny.* Budgets are to be used only as guides. They should not be used to tyrannize employees if the fault for shortcomings lies beyond their control.
3. *Flexibility.* Opportunities can arise and conditions change. Budgets are aids to administration, not substitutes for business judgment.
4. *Birth pains.* Anything new can be difficult to introduce. There will be resistance to any attempt to tie things down with a budget. Do not expect the budgeting process to proceed smoothly. Any time an employee must commit him-

self to specifics, such as certain sales levels or holding the line on expenses, he also gives up autonomy. Cooperation will come grudgingly and slowly until the benefits of the system are apparent.

DEPRECIATION METHODS: HOW TO SAVE TAX DOLLARS

What is Depreciation?

With the exception of land, most fixed assets have a limited useful life and "depreciate" or decline in value for one of two reasons: (1) *deterioration*, the physical process of wearing out, and (2) *obsolescence*, the loss of usefulness due to technological change. Depreciation is the *accounting process* of estimating this decline in value and gradually converting an asset's cost into a business expense.

Basic Elements of Depreciation

To calculate the depreciation expense for an accounting period, three factors must be known for each fixed asset:

1. *Cost of the Asset.* Purchase price plus the cost to put the asset in service.
2. *Service Life.* How long the asset is expected to last before it has to be replaced. This means the period of time for which you expect to use the asset. It doesn't have to mean the entire physical life of the asset. You may generally make your own estimate of the asset's useful life based on the circumstances surrounding its use.
3. *Salvage Value.* The estimated value of the asset at the end of its useful life.

Let's take an example that we will use throughout this section to illustrate basic depreciation methods. Suppose that you purchased a piece of equipment for $1,100. You estimate that it will last five years and can then be sold for $100. The total amount that can be depreciated is $1000.

ALLOWABLE DEPRECIATION

Cost of the depreciable asset	$1,100
Less: Estimated salvage value (amount to be realized when asset is retired from use)	100
Total allowable depreciation ("depreciable base")	$1,000

STRAIGHT LINE DEPRECIATION

Year	Calculation	Depreciation Expense
1	(1/5 × $1,000)	$ 200
2	(1/5 × 1,000)	200
3	(1/5 × 1,000)	200
4	(1/5 × 1,000)	200
5	(1/5 × 1,000)	200
	Total allowable depreciation	$1,000

Depreciation Methods

Once total allowable depreciation and estimated life are known, several depreciation methods can be used. Here is an explanation of the three most popular systems:

- *Straight Line.* Straight Line (S.L.) is the simplest and most widely used depreciation method. Under S.L. the depreciable base of the asset is converted to an expense in *equal installments* over the asset's useful life. Unlike other depreciation methods that have certain restrictions, S.L. is acceptable for both financial reporting and tax accounting.
- *Sum-of-Years Digits.* To compute the annual depreciation deduction using this method (S.Y.D.), the sum of the digits is totaled for the number of years of the asset's life. For example, the sum of the digits for an asset with a five-year life would be: (1+2+3+4+5=15). The depreciation for the first year is then computed by taking 5/15 times the depreciable cost. For the second year it is 4/15 times the cost, then 3/15 in the third year, and so on, as shown below. As with S.L., the computations are based on the depreciable base, not full purchase cost.
- *Double Declining Balance.* The depreciation expense for each year using this method (D.D.B.) is found by taking the asset's "book value" as the depreciable base and then applying double the rate allowed under the straight line method. (Book value is the asset's cost less the accumulated

SUM-OF-YEARS DIGITS

Year	Calculation	Depreciation Expense
1	(5/15 × $1,000)	$ 333.33
2	(4/15 × 1,000)	266.67
3	(3/15 × 1,000)	200.00
4	(2/15 × 1,000)	133.33
5	(1/15 × 1,000)	66.67
	Total allowable depreciation	$1,000.00

DOUBLE DECLINING BALANCE

Year	Book Value	Calculation	Depreciation Expense
1	$1,100.00	($1,100.00 × 1/5) × 2	$ 440.00
2	660.00	(660.00 × 1/5) × 2	264.00
3	396.00	(396.00 × 1/5) × 2	158.40
4	237.60	(237.60 × 1/5) × 2	95.04
5	142.56	(142.56 – 100.00)	42.56
		Total allowable depreciation	$1,000.00

depreciation up to that time.) The book value's balance is always declining over time—hence the name, double declining balance. Refer to the example which should make the method clear. Remember, when using D.D.B., the asset's book value cannot fall below its estimated salvage value.

Both S.Y.D. and D.D.B. are called "accelerated" methods and have been widely adopted since their use was authorized for tax purposes. The effect of either of these methods is to write off over two thirds of an asset's depreciable base in the first half of its estimated life. This contrasts with the straight line method under which, of course, only 50% of the depreciable base is written off in the first half of the asset's life. See the graphic comparison of the annual depreciation allowance using each of the three methods for a $1000 asset depreciated over five years.

Class Life System

Probably the most significant development in the depreciation field was the issuance by the IRS of "guideline lives" for about seventy-five different

COMPARISON OF THREE DEPRECIATION METHODS

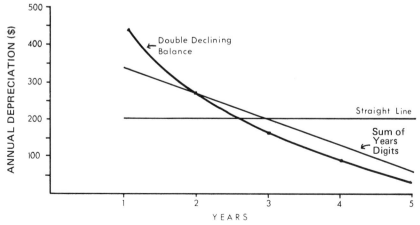

classes of assets. Generally, these guidelines are quite liberal and even allow shortening or lengthening of the recommended life by 20%. These guideline lives are optional, and the class life system, as it is called, is used in conjunction with—not in place of—various standard depreciation methods. If, for example, you elect to shorten the recommended life by 20% in accordance with the class life system, and at the same time you use an accelerated depreciation method, you can dramatically increase early year deductions. On the other hand, if you anticipate a need for deductions in the future, you can lengthen the recommended life by 20% and apply the straight line depreciation method. Class life is explained in detail starting on page 106.

First Year 20% Write-Off

According to Section 179 of the Internal Revenue Code, a special 20% first year depreciation deduction may be taken (in addition to that allowed under the standard methods) for "tangible personal property" with a useful life of at least six years. Treasury regulations define such assets as machinery, printing presses, office equipment, and grocery fixtures, as tangible personal property. This first year depreciation deduction applies only to the first $10,000 of property cost if your firm is a corporation or if you are a proprietor filing a separate return. A proprietor filing jointly with his wife may deduct 20% of $20,000.

There are several important provisions and limitations on the first year 20% depreciation deduction, but one of the most important is the provision that you reduce the basis of the property by the extra first year depreciation. This means that you don't really get any deduction that you would not have gotten otherwise over time, but you do get a substantial chunk of your overall deduction all at one time in the first year. By taking advantage of the extra first year depreciation deduction you speed up the recovery of the cost of the capital investment through depreciation.

If, for example, you happen to be in a high tax bracket in the year you purchase equipment, you may want to use the large immediate deduction afforded you by the extra first year depreciation deduction. And if you anticipate a higher tax rate in the future, you might decline to use the extra year depreciation deduction so that you could utilize the larger, normal deductions later on to save money on taxes.

Choice of a Depreciation Method

When considering depreciation methods, tax considerations should be kept completely separate from financial accounting (e.g., report to stockholders). For tax purposes the best method is that which minimizes taxes—usually one of the accelerated methods. For financial reporting most businesses utilize the straight line method to maximize reported earnings.

How to Change Methods

According to the Tax Reform Act of 1969 and Revenue Procedure 67-40, Form 3115 (Application to Change Accounting Method) should be filed with the IRS within the first ninety days of the tax year in which you want the change to become effective. Unless a letter is received from the IRS denying permission, you may assume the change has been granted. Consider switching to an accelerated method. It could save you considerable money in cash-short times.

Depreciation Recapture

When you depreciate an asset, you lower its cost basis. If you sell that same asset for a price that is higher than the depreciated cost basis, you are considered to have sold it at a gain. Generally, gain that is realized because of depreciation is said to have been "recaptured" and that gain will be taxed as ordinary income. The IRS, however, treats depreciation recapture on the sale of personal property and real estate in different ways. Let's look first at the treatment of personal property using numbers to keep the issue clear.

Personal Property. Gain that represents depreciation is taxed as ordinary income as long as the gain is less than the amount of depreciation. This applies to personal property depreciation taken after 1962 when they amended the depreciation rules. (Prior to 1962 gain on depreciation was taxed at lower capital gains rates.)

Suppose you have a machine that was purchased in 1970 for $8,500 and you took $3,000 depreciation on it before selling it in 1974 for $7,000. The basis at time of sale (purchase price less depreciation) was $5,500 so the gain on the sale was $1,500. Since the gain ($1,500) is less than the depreciation ($3,000) the whole gain is considered recaptured depreciation and is taxed as ordinary income.

But if you sold the same machine for $9,000, the gain would be $3,500 (sales price, $9,000 less basis, $5,500) and the $3,000 attributable to depreciation would be recaptured and taxed as ordinary income but the extra $500 would be taxed as capital gain.

Real Property. The rule in regard to "real property," or real estate, is that all depreciation is recaptured and taxed as ordinary income if the property is held less than one year. The rule for property held more than one year varies depending on the years in which depreciation was taken.

- 1964–1969. Depreciation taken during these years is recaptured according to an IRS schedule that determines the proper taxable part of the excess of accelerated depreciation over straight line depreciation.
- After 1970. If you sell property on which accelerated depreciation was taken during or after 1970, all the excess accelerated depreciation over straight line depreciation is recaptured. For example, suppose you own property three years and take $2,000 accelerated depreciation. Had you elected straight line let us say that the depreciation would have been only $1,200 over those same three years. So, upon sale of the property, $800 in depreciation is recaptured and taxed as ordinary income.

Having depreciation recapture taxed as ordinary income can be a costly experience. Therefore, it would be pleasant to avoid depreciation recapture if possible. Here are a few ways to do it.

1. *Hold onto Real Estate for at Least A Year.* All depreciation is recaptured (be it straight line or accelerated) if the property sold is held less than twelve months. It all gets taxed as ordinary income. But if you hold on for more than one year, you only recapture the difference between straight line and accelerated depreciation. There is an exception to this in the area of residential rental property. Check with your tax man if you need details on this.
2. *Sell the Corporation's Stock, Not the Assets.* Instead of selling a corporation's assets, which would be subject to expensive depreciation recapture, sell the corporation's stock. That way you avoid recapture.
3. *Borrow on the Property Instead of Selling It.* Suppose you need money and you have property to sell. If you sell it, you will get hit by a large depreciation recapture, but if you borrow on the property—refinance it—you will not pay for depreciation recapture.
4. *Giving the Property to a Member of the Family.* If you want to sell a property that will be subject to heavy depreciation recapture, consider giving it to your son or daughter. They will still have to pay the recapture, but their ordinary tax rate is probably considerably less than yours.

These are just a few suggestions for avoiding expensive recapture of depreciation. Whether you or your tax man can find a way to get around depreciation recapture or not, be aware that the effect of recapture can be significant, especially if it catches you unaware.

WHAT EVERY BUSINESSMAN SHOULD KNOW ABOUT THE CLASS LIFE DEPRECIATION SYSTEM

Among the most important tax benefits provided by the 1971 Revenue Act is the new "class life" system of depreciation. It is substantially a codification of the Asset Depreciation Range (ADR) regulations previously adopted by the Treasury.

What is class life?

By using the class life system, a businessman may choose from a range of depreciable lives 20% shorter or longer than the liberal guideline lives previously established by the Treasury for various assets. The depreciable life used by the businessman is not subject to change by the IRS, if the election is properly made. In addition, the taxpayer is granted an annual "repair allowance" that allows deductions for all repair and maintenance expenditures up to certain limits. This allowance assures the taxpayer that the IRS will not argue that certain repairs should have been capitalized and written off over several years.

Both the depreciation ranges and repair allowances for a few selected classes of assets are shown on the chart below. Note, for example, that a businessman in the contract construction industry could depreciate all of his construction machinery and equipment over a period as short as four years or as long as six years. In addition, each year he could deduct as a repair allowance an amount equal to 12½% of the adjusted basis of all assets in that class.

Which assets qualify for class life?

Class life applies to all tangible assets or classes of assets (except buildings and their components) first placed in service after 1970 for which a guideline life has been prescribed by the Treasury. If the class life system for a particular asset category is used, *all* the assets in that class must be placed on the system. There is, however, an exception for used equipment. If the unadjusted basis of used assets placed in service during the year is more than 10% of the unadjusted basis of all assets placed in service that year, then the businessman may elect not to depreciate this used property according to the class life system. This is important because the used equipment may have a shorter economic life than allowed under the class life system.

Depreciation methods

Once the depreciable *life* is decided, either (a) declining-balance, (b) sum-of-years digits, or (c) straight-line depreciation may be used. To use accelerated methods (a or b), the life must be at least three years. For new property, 200% declining-balance may be used; for used property, 150% of the straight-line rate is the maximum allowable. In addition, the 20% first-year allowance is also allowed with class life. Finally, one of the great advantages of class life is that estimated salvage value does not have to be deducted prior to calculating the depreciation allowance.

CLASS LIFE DEPRECIATION ON RANGES

Description of asset	Range (in years)			Annual repair allowance (percentage)
	Lower limit	Guideline life	Upper limit	
Depreciable assets used in general business activities:				
Office furniture, fixtures, and equipment	8	10	12	2.0
Automobiles	2.5	3	3.5	16.5
Light trucks	3	4	5	16.5
Depreciable assets used in following businesses:				
Contract construction	4	5	6	12.5
Manufacture of machinery (except electrical and transportation)	9.5	12	14.5	6.0
Wholesale and retail trade	8	10	12	6.5

How to make the election

The election to use class life is made on IRS Form 4832. Only those assets first placed in service during that year are eligible. Once the election is made, assets subject to the election are required to be kept in separate accounts according to the year placed in service ("vintage accounts"). Normal retirements from such accounts are ignored—no gain or loss is recognized from retirements and the deduction for depreciation is computed as if all assets in the account survived for as long as the period selected.

Advantages of class life

- *Useful life shortened.* Up to 20% shorter than previous guideline lives.
- *Salvage value.* Not taken into account when computing depreciation deduction.
- *Flexibility.* Used property can be excluded and a class life election made at will.
- *Repair allowance.* Expenditures that might otherwise be treated as capital additions are deductible in the year incurred.
- *First-year allowance.* Use of the system does not disallow the 20% first-year allowance.

LIFO VS. FIFO: MANAGING YOUR INVENTORY

How much tax you pay is determined, to a large extent, by the particular inventory valuation method you choose. Unknown to many businessmen, there is considerable latitude to either increase or reduce stated profits by the selection of certain inventory accounting methods—all perfectly acceptable to the IRS and in complete accordance with guidelines known as GAAP (Generally Accepted Accounting Principles).

Cost of Goods Sold

Look at the income statement of almost any business, and you will see that one item usually stands out as a prime determinant of the company's profit —cost of goods sold. See income statement.

As this typical income statement shows, the cost of goods sold figure of $650,000 is by far the most significant expense item. It is computed by taking the inventory on hand at the *beginning* of the year, adding the amount of purchases *during* the year and then subtracting the inventory at the *end* of the year. This yields the amount of inventory that was used up during the year and must, therefore, be subtracted as an expense from the sales revenue figure.

INCOME STATEMENT

XYZ Company — Year Ended 12/31/75

	Sales revenue		$1,000,000
Less:	Cost of goods sold:		
	Inventory, January 1	$400,000	
	Purchases	600,000	
Less:	Inventory, December 31	350,000	650,000
	Gross profit		350,000
Less:	Overhead		225,000
Less:	Interest		25,000
	Profit (before tax)		$ 100,000

Valuation of Inventory

Thus far, everything is quite straightforward. The problem arises, however, when computing two critical factors in the above cost of goods sold formula —the values of the inventory at the beginning and end of the year. Here's why. Many businesses find it impossible or impractical to segregate their inventory, and, as a result, stocks are commingled, regardless of when they were acquired. As an example, a manufacturing business may keep a certain grade of steel on hand. The company uses and replenishes the stock as needed throughout the year without physically identifying which particular lot was used. At the end of the year, however, the accountant has a dilemma —should he assume that the inventory was consumed in the order it was acquired and that what is left is the most recently purchased stock? Or, should he consider that the latest inventory purchased was used first and that it is actually the older stock that is still on hand? Well, in actual fact, the accountant generally doesn't know or care how the inventory was physically used—what he is more concerned about is adopting a bookkeeping convention that will place a reasonably accurate value on the inventory and can be followed consistently from year to year.

LIFO vs. FIFO

In order to value inventory consistently year after year, two main accounting systems are generally used:

- *Last-In, First-Out (LIFO)* assumes that the more recently acquired inventory was used first and that remaining stocks consist of older material.
- *First-In, First-Out (FIFO)* assumes that there is an orderly flow of inventory and that the first material purchased is the first consumed.

Here's the reason for the different systems. When prices are stable, both LIFO and FIFO yield the same results. But in times of inflation or shortages when prices are rising, LIFO yields a lower net profit figure because the cost of goods sold under LIFO assumes that the most recently bought (and most expensive) inventory has been used. FIFO, on the other hand, yields a higher profit since it is assumed that the older stock (bought at lower prices) has been used. Keep in mind, however, that using either LIFO or FIFO, it makes no difference which physical items in inventory are actually consumed. The FIFO and LIFO methods are merely bookkeeping conventions for determining the value of inventory. Let's consider an example that will clarify the situation.

As you can see, all figures to arrive at gross profit (see below) are the same, except for the valuation of the closing inventory. Under the LIFO system it is assumed that the most recently purchased (last-in) inventory was the first to be consumed (first-out). Therefore, what remains as of December 31 is the stock that was on hand at the first of the year valued at $10 per unit times 40,000 units, or $400,000. In contrast, FIFO assumes that the *original inventory* (first-in) was the first consumed (first-out) and that the ending stocks consist of the most recently acquired material valued at $12 per unit or $480,000. Hence, the value placed on the closing inventory is lower under the LIFO system which results in a higher cost of goods sold and lower profit figure than FIFO. The LIFO system, therefore, yields a considerable tax deferment and will continue to do so each succeeding year in which material costs continue to rise, so long as the closing inventory in terms of units doesn't drop below the quantity on hand in the beginning of the year LIFO was adopted.

INCOME STATEMENT—LIFO VS. FIFO

XYZ Company - Year Ended 12/31/75

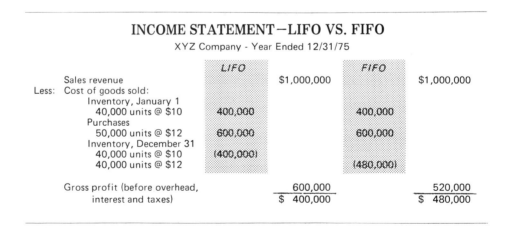

		LIFO		FIFO	
	Sales revenue		$1,000,000		$1,000,000
Less:	Cost of goods sold:				
	Inventory, January 1				
	40,000 units @ $10	400,000		400,000	
	Purchases				
	50,000 units @ $12	600,000		600,000	
	Inventory, December 31				
	40,000 units @ $10	(400,000)			
	40,000 units @ $12			(480,000)	
	Gross profit (before overhead, interest and taxes)		600,000		520,000
			$ 400,000		$ 480,000

Advantages of LIFO

Inflation has a tremendous effect on corporate profits. Every time inflation goes up 1%, the income taxes of some companies potentially go up by nearly one-half that much (assuming a 48% tax bracket). Hence, it can be a large drain on corporate profits. LIFO eliminates these so-called "inventory profits", which can be so deceptive of true performance, *by directly linking the current sales price of merchandise with the current cost to produce it.* Hence, it is the taxpayer's defense against an undeserved tax on "paper profits" as opposed to real ones. Here are several other points to consider:

- If desired, you may designate that only certain raw material items be placed on the LIFO system while others can be left on FIFO.
- Work-in-process, and finished goods inventory (as well as their individual components of materials, labor, and overhead) can be selectively placed on LIFO, if desired.
- Where there is a wide variety of similar products, a "dollar value" method of LIFO can be used whereby inventory value is based on price indices published by the Department of Commerce. In addition, some manufacturers create their own price change index for certain commodities.

How to Adopt the LIFO Method

You do not have to elect the LIFO method until after your tax year is over. You then file for use of LIFO on Treasury Form 970 and once granted, you must continue to use the LIFO system in subsequent years, unless the IRS again authorizes a change. Once LIFO is adopted, the IRS generally requires that it be used for both book as well as tax accounting.

Conclusion

As we have seen, often a company can increase or decrease its taxable profits by selecting an appropriate inventory valuation method. However, both the IRS and accountants insist that you consistently follow whatever method is chosen.

Any company with large inventories should give serious consideration to a switch to LIFO. The only significant disadvantage to LIFO is that if inventory prices fall, profits may be overstated. But, with inflation and the burden of taxes on the inventory profits of companies who do not use LIFO, the switch may not be a choice. It may become a practical necessity.

CHAPTER 8

ALTERNATE SOURCES OF MONEY FOR YOUR BUSINESS

DEBT OR EQUITY: WHICH IS BEST FOR YOU?

The question of whether to finance expansion by selling stock or borrowing is a common one. In general, most businessmen should put off selling equity as long as possible in order to have a better chance of selling shares later at a higher price. However, tight credit conditions plus the insistence of many bankers that more equity funds be put in some company's balance sheets has forced many businessmen to reassess the equity alternative. There are no easy answers to financing problems, but there are certain tools available to help you understand the relative costs of your alternatives. One of the most common techniques is called "EBIT analysis".

Comparative Cost of Debt and Equity

Whenever a business obtains funds from outside sources, there is an explicit cost to the shareholders. If debt is used, the interest charges reduce total earnings and, hence, earnings-per-share (EPS). Selling stock, on the other hand, does not *cost* anything in terms of reducing earnings, but since a larger number of shares become outstanding, the EPS are proportionately reduced. Hence one analytical way to compare debt and equity alternatives is to analyze the impact of each on EPS.

Consider the following example. You wish to expand your plant and need $200,000. The bank has agreed to lend the money, but they insist on a rather exorbitant interest rate of 14% per year. An investor group has also approached you with an offer to buy 4,000 shares at $50.00 per share (about twenty times this year's estimated earnings of $2.50 per share). Which alternative would you choose?

EBIT Analysis

Either way, you will obtain the needed $200,000. But which has a cheaper explicit cost in terms of its impact on EPS? The way to calculate this is by first determining "earnings before interest and taxes" (EBIT). Let's assume that it is $530,000 and that you have present interest charges of $50,000 per year.

As you can see on the EBIT Analysis chart, even though 4,000 more shares are outstanding, the EPS are slightly higher with the equity alternative. You certainly should not decide to sell stock based on this analysis alone, especially since the EPS in both cases are relatively close. It does illustrate, however, that in many cases selling equity can be advantageous to debt, other factors being equal. Before making a final decision, though, consider the following:

1. *Risk.* If you borrow, when must the money be repaid? Don't finance projects with long-term payouts with short-term money. You may be caught by not being able to roll the debt over at maturity. Plus interest rates could rise. With equity you will always have better cash flow since the money does not have to be repaid.

2. *Flexibility.* What are the terms with both debt and equity? Will any restrictive covenants limit your flexibility?

3. *Control.* Is there any chance you might lose control if the company sells stock?

4. *Timing.* Are interest rates expected to rise or fall? Should you finance this project with equity and a later one with debt when interest rates are hopefully lower? Alternatively, could you sell the shares at a higher price by waiting until later?

5. *Leverage.* Most companies should carry only a certain amount of debt. Beyond this point cash flow is constrained, and they become overly susceptible to economic downturns. If your company is leveraged too high, it may be preferable to sell equity even though its explicit cost in terms of EPS is high.

EBIT ANALYSIS

	Debt	Equity
Present earnings before interest and taxes (EBIT)	$530,000	$530,000
Less: Present interest expense	50,000	50,000
Less: New interest on $200,000 @ 14%	28,000	
Earnings before taxes	$452,000	$480,000
Less: Taxes @ 48%	217,000	230,000
Profits after tax	$235,000	$250,000
Common shares outstanding	100,000	104,000
Earnings-per-share (EPS)	$2.35	$2.40

Consider your financing alternatives carefully. With high interest rates, don't lock yourself into an overly expensive debt burden. But don't sell away part of your company unless it can definitely be shown to be the preferred alternative. Try using the EBIT technique to help you avoid a costly mistake.

A BORROWER'S CHECKLIST

Every businessman needs to borrow money from time to time. The key to effortless financing is the old Boy Scout motto—be prepared. Banks are in business to loan money, and there will rarely be any problem if you've done your homework. Carefully consider the following checklist many bankers use in evaluating a loan application:

Why Does the Applicant Need the Money? When your business needs money, it is a sign of one or two things:

- Success and hence the need to finance expansion, seasonal sales, inventory, or increase working capital.
- Failure and losing money due to poor management, production problems, or sales deficiencies.

It is your job to convince the banker that your need for money is based on success, not failure.

What Security Does the Applicant Offer? Banks lose very little in bad loans because of their strict collateral requirements. Here are several ways to assure your banker that the loan is safe:

- *Endorser, Co-Maker,* or *Guarantor.* Someone else liable if you default.
- *Lease Assignment.* Bank holds as collateral a lease you have with a third party on property you own.
- *Warehouse Receipts.* Money is loaned against merchandise kept in a public warehouse.
- *Trust Receipts.* Used as legal document for "floor planning" which applies to serial-numbered merchandise (such as machines, refrigerators, or cars.). You agree to: (1) acknowledge receipt of the merchandise; (2) keep the merchandise in trust for the bank; (3) pay the bank as you sell the merchandise.
- *Stocks, Bonds, or Life Insurance.* Bank holds as collateral and lends against their cash or current market value.
- *Accounts Receivable.* Sometimes called "factoring". You assign accounts receivable to the bank.
- *Real Estate.* Common collateral for longer term loans.
- *Chattel Mortgages.* A direct lien on specified physical assets, such as a machine or vehicle.

What is the Character of the Applicant?   This can be the most important question of all. Collateral is small comfort if the banker questions your integrity. Address this one head on:

- Provide a list of references with whom you've had business dealings.
- Provide a list of any previous borrowings and your payment record.

To protect your good name and make the process easier next time, take these steps:

- If you might be late with a payment, tell the banker ahead of time.
- Once the loan is paid, keep sending periodic financial statements.
- Visit with your banker occasionally. Keep him informed how you are doing.

Key Financial Ratios   Here are a few key ratios that almost every lender will want to see:

- *Current Ratio.* (current assets divided by current liabilities) Ability to repay debt and margin of working capital.
- *Debt to Equity.* (debt divided by shareholders' equity) Shows if the business is already highly leveraged.
- *Sales to Receivables.* (annual sales divided by outstanding receivables) Shows how well receivables are being collected.
- *Operating Ratio* (net income divided by sales) Shows the profit margin of the business.
- *Return on Capital.* (net profit divided by total capital employed) Shows how efficiently the business uses money.
- *Inventory Turnover.* (cost of goods sold divided by inventory at end of period) Shows how fast inventory turns over.

HOW TO OBTAIN A LOAN FROM THE SBA

Many business managers who are refused a business loan by a bank never think of turning to the Small Business Administration (SBA). The fact is that *by law the SBA cannot make a loan until you have been turned down by private sources, such as a bank.* Here are the facts concerning the many types of SBA loans and how you may qualify.

Types of loans
Traditionally, the SBA has made loans directly to small businesses, but the recent demand for financial assistance has seriously depleted SBA loan funds.

As a result, the SBA now emphasizes maximum banking industry participation in each loan. The agency does this by *guaranteeing* loans made by banks to small businesses or by *participating* with banks in such loans. Additionally, in 1971 the SBA introduced a program to help provide a *revolving line of credit* for certain businesses. Here again, the SBA does not actually lend its funds, but guarantees funds extended by banks. Each of these types of loans is explained in the chart. Besides those listed, the agency can also make several special types of loans, such as economic opportunity loans to help disadvantaged persons, disaster loans, and economic displacement loans, to help offset the effects of legislation, such as the Occupational Safety and Health Act.

Who qualifies for SBA loans

For purposes of making loans, the SBA defines a small business as one meeting these general size standards:

- *Wholesale.* Annual sales less than $5 million to $15 million depending on the industry.
- *Retail or service.* Annual sales or receipts less than $1 million to $5 million depending on the industry.
- *Construction.* Annual sales or receipts of not more than $5 million averaged over a three-year period.
- *Manufacturing.* Generally up to 250 employees depending on the industry.

How to proceed

If you wait until you are desperate for funds, chances are you may be unsuccessful in obtaining a loan in time. The key to dealing with the government is to have all the necessary paperwork prepared and to allow enough time.

- Prepare a balance sheet and income statement for the previous year and current period.

TYPES OF SBA LOANS

Types of Loans	Loan Limit	Loan Purpose	Maximum Loan Maturity	Maximum Interest Rates	Maximum SBA Participation	Collateral	Pre-payment Fee
Direct Loan	$350,000*	• Business construction, expansion, or conversion • Purchase of machinery, equipment, facilities, supplies or materials • Working capital	10 years (up to 15 for construction portion)	6¾%	100%	Mortgage on land, buildings, machinery and equipment, automotive equipment, furniture and fixtures, warehouse receipts on inventory, accounts receivable; personal guarantees; assignment of life insurance, etc.	None
Guaranteed Loan	$350,000 (SBA Share)			10¼%	Up to 90% guaranteed		None
Participating Loan	$350,000* (SBA Share)			9¼% on SBA portion. Participating Institution may set higher rate on its portion	75%		None
Revolving Line of Credit (Guaranty Only)	$350,000* (SBA Share)	Finance small construction contractors, manufacturing, or service firms providing a specific product or service under an **assignable** contract	18 months	10¼%	Up to 90% guaranteed	Assignment of proceeds of contract; other similar to regular business loans.	None

*While this limit was set by legislation, federal fiscal constraints have necessitated an administrative limit of $100,000 for direct loans and $150,000 for participation loans.

- Prepare a personal financial statement for any stockholder owning 20% or more of the business.
- State the amount of money needed and explain the purposes of the loan.
- List collateral to be offered for the loan and estimate its current market value.
- Take the above materials to your banker and ask for a direct loan. If denied, ask if the bank will participate with the SBA or make a SBA guaranteed loan. In most cases of participation or guaranteed loans, the bank deals directly with the SBA on your behalf.
- If SBA participation for a guaranteed loan cannot be obtained, write or visit the nearest SBA office. To expedite matters, present your financial information when you first contact the SBA. The administrative process can take as long as several months.

LEASING: ANOTHER FORM OF FINANCING

Leasing is one of the most important sources of long term capital. But surprisingly, leasing is often overlooked entirely as an alternative form of financing.

Types of Leases

There are two general types of leases:

- *Operating: Cancelable* payments for use of an asset or service. An example would be telephone service.
- *Financial: Noncancelable* commitment to make a series of payments over a fixed time period for use of an asset. The sum of the payments is generally sufficient for the lessor to: (1) recover the equipment cost; (2) pay for interest cost on capital involved; (3) compensate for risk of obsolescence; (4) recover administrative expenses and provide a profit.

Financial Leases

Since a financial lease represents a fixed commitment over time, it is, strictly speaking, a form of debt. Because it doesn't usually appear on the balance sheet as a liability, however, it is often referred to as "off the balance sheet financing". This accounts for its enormous growth and popularity since World War II. Literally thousands of companies are involved in leasing everything from cattle and brood sows to computers and complete chemical plants. Financial leases are of two types:

- *Sale-Lease Back.* Used to free up capital invested in fixed assets, such as land or machinery already owned by the business. The assets are sold to a financial institution and then leased back over time. Purely a financial transaction. The asset doesn't move, only its legal title.

- *Direct Acquisition Lease.* Used to acquire specific assets needed in the business. The lessor may be an equipment manufacturer, a leasing specialist, or a financial house.

Advantages of Financial Leases

Leasing offers several advantages to the businessman:

- Frees working capital for more productive use (money not tied up in low yielding fixed assets).
- Finances 100% of the cost of assets involved (versus 75 to 80% through other methods).
- Generally leaves normal bank lines of credit undisturbed.
- Doesn't require pledging other assets as collateral.
- Allows tax write offs of certain assets such as land that normally can't be depreciated.
- Simplifies tax accounting. Entire lease fee generally deductible. Saves the trouble of depreciation calculations, recapture, interest deductions, etc.

Disadvantages of Leasing

- Higher cost. Always more expensive than outright purchase and generally more expensive than any other form of financing.
- Loss of salvage value. At expiration of the lease the residual value of the equipment usually belongs to the lessor. However, some lease agreements allow the leasee to purchase the asset at its market value at the time of lease expiration.
- Capital gain. In a sale-lease back transaction, if the tax basis of the asset is below its sale price, there may be capital gain tax to pay on the difference.

Questions to Ask Before Signing a Lease

Whether it is a sale-lease back or a direct acquisition lease, you should always check the following points before signing:

- Investment credit. Who receives the benefit? (It can be passed on to you for a significant tax savings.)
- Insurance. Who pays?
- Maintenance. Who provides and pays?
- Purchase option at end of lease?
- Repossession. On what basis?
- Restrictive covenants. Check your present lending agreement for prohibition against financial leases.
- Deductibility of lease fees. Check with your accountant or

lawyer to be sure there are no terms in the lease that could jeopardize deductibility.

Personal Tax Breaks—Lease to Your Company

Many businessmen have found it advantageous to lease assets to their companies themselves, either directly or through a sale-lease back arrangement. For example, you may own a valuable piece of property that your business could use. Rather than sell it, you can retain title to the property and lease it to the company. You will still get to take a deduction for the depreciation and interest costs, and the company will be able to deduct the lease payments to you. Be sure, however, to have your accountant check the "preference income" rules of the 1976 Tax Reform Act.

Lease arrangements such as this are not limited to real estate. For example, you can keep patents, equipment, and any other asset you may own outside the business by leasing. It is important, however, to insure that the lease payments hold up as reasonable under IRS scrutiny.

Summary

Leasing can be done through equipment manufacturers, third-party leasing specialists, or financial houses. There are over one thousand leasing companies. Additional information about leasing can be obtained by writing to the Association of Equipment Lessors at 6815 West Capital Drive, Suite 200, Milwaukee, WI 53216. Also, information can be obtained from the National Industrial Conference Board, 845 Third Avenue, New York, NY 10022.

VENTURE CAPITAL

There are three standard ways for a business to obtain funds. For short-term needs, it can *rent* money at a local bank. For longer term requirements, it can *lease* money by issuing bonds. For permanent funds, it can *buy* capital by issuing stock to investors. When the first two debt alternatives are unavailable, "venture capital" financing can often be a solution.

What is venture capital?

Venture capital (V.C.) has traditionally been the seed capital injected into a new company by investors who become part owners in exchange for the risks they assume. In fact, today most venture capital firms prefer to invest in a company once it is off the ground, during its so-called second- or third-round financings. Whenever the investment is made, however, venture capitalists generally take risks and expect returns higher than most other sources of financing.

Where is V.C. obtained?

- *Wealthy individuals.*
  High tax brackets and the opportunity to deduct most losses against ordinary income make wealthy individuals a prime

source of V.C. Generally, these individuals are inclined to take greater risks and desire less involvement in a business than the institutional sources described below.

- *SBICs.*

  Small business investment companies are government-chartered venture capital firms formed specifically to increase the availability of V.C. The over six hundred SBICs break down into those that are controlled by large financial institutions and those that are independent. Many large banks and insurance companies, for example, have captive SBICs that provide equity funds to supplement the debt funds these institutions normally provide. Independent SBICs are sometimes owned by a few individuals or a group of institutions, and some are even publicly held. However, SBICs are normally limited to minority investments and may not take an active role in management unless covenants of the original purchase agreement are violated.

- *Private V.C. Firms.*

  These firms are usually related to family fortunes. Notable examples would be the New Court Securities (Rothchilds), Bessemer Securities (Phipps), and Venrock Associates (Rockefellers). These firms maintain the reputation of the family name and desire to make major contributions to society, technology, or industry. Because they can afford to screen opportunities, these V.C. firms tend to prefer large investments (over $100,000) in highly selective situations.

- *Corporate V.C. activities.*

  Many large corporations engage in V.C. activities. The investments are usually made in related but noncompeting fields to cultivate potential customers or acquisition candidates. This source is generally not well publicized.

What does a V.C. firm look for?

A venture capital firm divides its analysis of any proposed investment into two main categories—management and business proposition. Here is a check list of some of the major points it is looking for:

Management

- Self-discipline and motivation. Ability to work hard and deal with prosperity as well as adversity.
- Management expertise and balance. Venture capitalists have seen too many people more adept at raising money than building a solid business. They shun promoters and look for a management team capable of handling all facets of the proposed business.
- Integrity and reliability. Is there any question?
- Candor and flexibility. Is the candidate realistic about the risks involved? Is he flexible enough to respond to new

situations? Are his goals realistic and compatible with the investors?

- Financial stake. Are the managers staking their financial fortunes on the venture by investing their own funds, however limited?

Business

- Growth potential. Venture capitalists are not interested in static situations. They like to see a tenfold return on their money in five to seven years.
- How can the V.C. liquidate? The venture capitalist is interested in prospects for recovering his investment if he decides to pull out.
- Unique business. A proprietary product or unique service is generally preferred. V.C. firms tend to specialize in certain types of business.
- Probability of success and downside risk. Even after careful analysis, over 50 percent of V.C. investments are often complete losses.
- Size of investment required. Each V.C. firm has certain amounts above and below which they prefer not to invest. Most firms prefer to make larger investments since the investigation for a $10,000 proposed investment can take as long as one for $100,000. Individuals tend toward smaller investments.

How to proceed

The first step to take for V.C. financing is to prepare a business plan. The following is a list of topics that should be covered in the plan.

1. Summary
2. Table of contents
3. Background and history
4. Description of product/service
5. Market
- Who is the customer?
- How large is the market?
- What portion of the market do you hope to penetrate?
6. Competition
- Who are they?
- How does their product/service differ?
7. Marketing strategy
- Price
- Method of promotion
- Channels of distribution

8. Production
   - How will the product/service be produced?
   - How long will production take—one year, three years, five years?

9. Financial
   - Past and present balance sheets and income statements
   - Future cash flow budgets
   - Use of proceeds of the financing

10. Ownership and management
    - Who owns the company?
    - Short resume of each member of management team

Sources for further information

The SBA publishes a complete list of SBICs on a quarterly basis. Write: SBA, Investment Division, 1441 Second Street NW, Washington, DC 20416. Stanley M. Rubel publishes *A Guide To Venture Capital*, as well as newsletters, and other information on V.C. The book is available in many large libraries or write: Capital Publishing Company, 10 South La Salle Street, Chicago, IL 60603. Finally, Leroy W. Sinclair publishes a book entitled *Venture Capital* that offers details on all V.C. firms in the US. In addition, he publishes a practical "how to" spiral bound book entitled *The Business Plan*. Write: Technimetrics, Inc., 919 Third Avenue, New York, NY 10022.

CHAPTER 9

ADDITIONAL FINANCIAL TOPICS

TEN QUESTIONS YOU SHOULD ASK YOUR ACCOUNTANT EACH YEAR

Your outside accountant is much more than an auditor. Besides being a valuable source of information with respect to planning, taxation, and control systems, he can help you with many operational problems. However, your accountant must be asked relevant questions before he can supply the services you need. Here are ten questions you should ask every year:

1. *What will be our need for funds over the coming year?* With tight money and high borrowing costs, it is essential that you know by month, week, and even by day what your cash needs will be.

- Review pro forma cash statements and help assess the impact of unexpected fluctuations in sales, receivables, inventory, and interest rates.
- Outline the pros and cons of such alternate sources of funds as leasing, factoring, debentures, and equity.

2. *Have payroll tax returns and deposits and estimated business income tax deposits been made on time?*

- Payroll. If $200 or more, federal withholding must be deposited at least monthly in a federal depository bank. In addition, the IRS and most states require quarterly informational returns. Failure to file usually results in penalties and interest charges.
- Business income tax. Federal and state governments require deposit of business income taxes throughout the year in anticipation of year-end taxes. Estimates must be paid quarterly and failure to comply results in interest and penalties of up to 25% in the case of the federal government.

3. *Can the state of accounts receivable (A/R) be improved?* It costs money to be a banker for your customers and any excess funds tied up in A/R can be costly.

- Compute average collection period (A/R divided by average daily sales).
- Compare the collection period to normal credit terms and industry norms.
- Set up and/or review collection procedures and files.

4. *Should we adopt a pension plan?* This may be the time to consider a pension or profit-sharing plan. The big advantage of such plans is that pretax dollars go into a fund to be distributed at a future time when, presumably, personal tax brackets will be lower. Also ask about tax-saving features of other plans, such as medical reimbursement, disability insurance, and life insurance.

5. *Are all necessary records required by federal and state governments and other authorities available?* Payroll statements, general ledgers, journals, cash books, and so on— must be kept for varying lengths of time for different authorities.

6. *Can the business be split into two or more taxable entities?* Does the nature of your business allow it to be split into different taxable entities—perhaps a corporation, a partnership, or sole proprietorship? A Subchapter S corporation might also be used. The resulting split in taxable income may result in substantial tax savings.

7. *If incorporated, have all required state annual reports been filed?* All states require that corporations file annual reports in addition to state income tax returns.

- The reports include year-end balance sheet and possibly an income statement, as well as information on capital stock, directors and officers.
- The reports become a part of the public record and are often used by credit agencies.
- If your company does business in other than its state of incorporation, you may be required to file in that state as well.
- Failure to file properly may mean revocation of your corporate charter and possible personal liability for corporate debts.

8. *Are present accounting systems adequate for future growth?* You may wish to revise present accounting procedures and/or investigate minicomputers and time-sharing service bureaus to reduce clerical efforts and obtain:

- Timely information. Statements should be available within ten days of month's end.
- Complete information. Basic financial statements supplemented with aged listing of accounts receivable, accounts payable, and pertinent ratios.
- Flexibility. The accounting systems should be capable of growing with business.

9. *Do we need certified financial statements?* Unless required by lenders, investors, or other outsiders, certified statements can be an unnecessary expense. Your accountant can review your internal controls and furnish unaudited statements that should be just as useful for management purposes.

10. *Are assets being adequately protected?* Be sure your accountant checks:

- Cash control. It is better to have A/R and A/P handled by different people. Also, be sure all receipts are deposited daily to minimize possible juggling of figures.
- Inventory. Any evidence of undue shrinkage?
- Fixed assets. Is full advantage being take of the 10% investment tax credit? Are class life, 20% first-year write-off, and accelerated depreciation being used where possible to minimize taxes?
- Intangibles. Are taxes being minimized by adequate write-off of organizational expenses, R&D, and so on?

FISCAL VS. CALENDAR YEAR

There are actually three types of accounting years from which you can choose:

- *Calendar year.* Required for any taxpayer who does not elect a fiscal year and used by most individuals, partnerships, and corporations.
- *Fiscal Year.* Any twelve-month period ending on the last day of any month except December.
- *52–53 Week Year.* A fiscal year, but varying between 52–53 weeks and always ending on the same day of the week.

The obvious question is why use anything other than a standard calendar year? Here are three reasons a new corporation or partnership should carefully consider its reporting year options:

1. *Subchapter S Corporation.* If you choose to be taxed as a Sub S where the shareholders pay tax by including a pro rata share of the corporation's income in their personal tax return in lieu of paying tax at the corporate level, you have an opportunity to postpone tax for as long as fourteen months. Here is how:

- Assume you report your personal income on a calendar-year basis.
- You are a stockholder of a Sub S corporation that began business February 1, 1976 and will have a fiscal tax ending January 31, 1977.

- On December 31, 1976 your personal tax year ends, but you do not have to assume your portion of the Subchapter S corporation's income because its accounting year does not end for one more month. In other words, you can defer your share of fiscal 1976 corporate income into your 1977 calendar tax year. Actually, since final payment of your 1977 personal taxes is not due until April 15, 1978, you can effectively stay over fourteen months ahead of most of your Sub S tax liabilities! However, check with your accountant to be sure that proper reports are filed with the IRS.

2. *Surcharge Saving.* Ordinary corporations pay only 20% tax on income up to $25,000, 22% for the next $25,000, and 48% thereafter. For a new corporation, you may wish to choose your first fiscal year so that it cuts off as you approach the $50,000 mark.

3. *Budgeting and Control.* Certain businesses wish to budget and measure performance on strict weekly cycles. For example, you may wish to close your books on the last Saturday of May each year. A 52–53 week year will permit this type of accounting.

Remember, however, that once you have chosen your accounting year, you are pretty much locked in. You normally cannot change unless you file Form 1128 with the IRS and state a good business reason for desiring the change (other than tax avoidance).

CASH VS. ACCRUAL ACCOUNTING

Almost every day businessmen run up against accounting problems. Unfortunately, many managers feel that the subject is too technical for them to understand. In actual fact, armed with only a few basic concepts, there is no reason why you shouldn't manage this important function as competently and confidently as any other part of your business.

Choice of Accounting Method

One of the most fundamental decisions a manager must make concerns the choice of an accounting method because it determines *how and when income and expenses will be computed* for his business. Depending on the system you choose, it is often possible to defer certain income items and accelerate expenses in order to reduce taxable income. Here is a list of the eight most common systems:

- Cash
- Accrual

- Hybrid
- Installment
- Long Term Contract
- Completed Contract
- Deferred Payment Sales
- Crop

The two most popular accounting systems used by businesses are the cash and accrual methods.

Cash Method

The cash receipts and disbursements method of accounting is used primarily by businesses where *inventories are not a significant revenue-generating factor.* These would include many professional firms and individuals whose income consists primarily of salaries, fees, or commissions, as well as certain service, financial, and real estate businesses.

- *Recognition of Income.* Under the cash method, a business does not recognize income until the cash or property is *actually received.* Sometimes additional income is said to have been "constructively" received and hence, is taxable. Examples would be interest coupons accrued on bonds that have not been redeemed or checks from customers that have been received but not cashed.
- *Recognition of Expenses.* Deductions for any expenses actually paid are generally allowed *in the year paid,* even though they may actually relate to a different tax year. Hence, under the cash method, expenses can be prepaid or supplies purchased ahead to reduce taxes, so long as they don't materially distort income.

Advantages of the Cash Method

- Income is not taxable until cash is actually (or constructively) received.
- Taxable income can be reduced by prepaying certain expenses.
- Accounting is simplified. Only a cash journal or checkbook is required.

Disadvantages of the Cash Method

- Unless income is carefully managed, it can bunch up and not reflect the true financial condition of the firm.
- If the business is sold or liquidated, careful attention must be given to the accounts receivable and payable to insure that income is not accelerated or deductions lost.

Accrual Method

This method is used by practically all manufacturing, retail, or service businesses where the production, purchase, or sale of merchandise represents a significant portion of income. The accrual method generally provides a more accurate representation of the true condition of a business at any point in time.

- *Recognition of Income.* Under this method of accounting, income is "accrued" and taxed not when actually received, but when one has the *right* to receive it. To illustrate, under the accrual concept, a business realizes taxable income when it sells, ships, or invoices an item. Under the cash concept, income would not be recognized until payment is actually received.
- *Recognition of Expenses.* Expenses are considered accrued and deductible when payable, not when actually paid.

Advantages of Accrual Method

- Income and expenses tend to be more closely matched than in the cash method and more accurately reflect the true financial condition of the firm.
- Taxable income is not subject to gross distortion due to accelerated or lagging payables and receivables.

Hybrid Method

The hybrid method is, as the name implies, a combination of two or more of the other recognized methods. It can be used, for example, by a businessman who would prefer the accuracy of the accrual method, but finds the bookkeeping too burdensome. He can use the accrual method to record such major income and expense items as sales and purchases while keeping the remainder of the business on a cash basis. Chief beneficiaries of the hybrid method are small businessmen.

How to Change Your Accounting Method

To adopt a new method, even when proper and allowed by regulation, you must file Form 3115 with the IRS and obtain approval. Normally, the change must be filed within 180 days after the start of the year for which the change is desired.

Too Important for Accountants Alone

As you can see, accounting policy is not a humdrum science best left to men in green eyeshades. It is a dynamic area of business where decisions can influence the amount of tax you pay as well as have a significant impact on your financial statements and those who read them such as bankers, creditors, stockholders, and suppliers.

DOES YOUR FINANCIAL YEAR FIT YOUR BUSINESS?

With current economic conditions, it is more important than ever to accurately communicate with lenders and outside shareholders concerning your sales and profits. Many businessmen are hampered by accounting years that distort or confuse true financial performance. Here is what you should know to insure that your business is not inadvertently caught up in the crisis of confidence affecting many companies today.

Many businesses are on a January 1 to December 31 calendar year simply because it coincides with the normal tax year. Other companies adopt a fiscal year (any twelve-month period ending the last day of any month but December) for reasons such as conformity with industry practice or because sales are slack and personnel are available to take physical inventory. However, no matter what accounting year is used, it's likely that little thought was given to whether the year accurately reflects the company's profits from quarter to quarter. (Refer to charts below and on page 132.)

A business can have sales that rise and fall according to a seasonal pattern. Profits can also vary. As shown on the charts, cumulative earnings are sub-

QUARTERLY SALES AND CUMULATIVE EARNINGS

These comparisons are for one company with the same quarterly sales and quarterly earnings but different starting dates for the fiscal year. Quarterly Sales and Cumulative Earnings are in thousands of dollars.

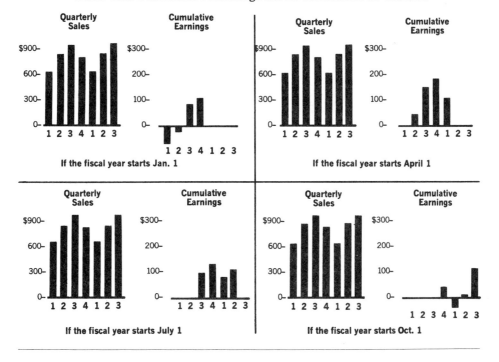

PROFITS FOR YEAR

1st calendar quarter	$-63,000
2nd calendar quarter	+46,000
3rd calendar quarter	+89,000
4th calendar quarter	+28,000
Total profit per year	$100,000

stantially different, depending on when the company starts its accounting year. If, for example, it opens its books January 1, the company will show two quarters when cumulative earnings are negative. A fiscal year beginning in April or July would be far more appropriate.

How to change your financial year

It is permissible to change your business calendar under existing federal tax law. However, a tax return covering the fractional year between the close of the old period and the beginning of the new is required. Application to change is made on IRS Form 1128 on or before the fifteenth day of the second calendar month following the close of the short tax year. The change will normally be approved if it does not distort income and reduce taxes.

Special rule

Corporations need no approval if: (1) the corporation has not changed its accounting year for ten years, (2) the short tax year shows no operating loss, or (3) taxable income is at least 80% of the taxable income for the previous full tax year.

HOW TO INVEST EXCESS CASH AT MAXIMUM RETURN—MONEY MARKET INSTRUMENTS

Many companies occasionally have more cash than they need in the near future. For convenience and security these idle funds are often put to work in short-term investments, such as Treasury bills. You should be aware, however, the several other money-market instruments also exist—most offering sound security and considerably higher yields than Treasury bills. Here is an explanation and summary chart of the ones of most importance to the businessman.

Treasury Bills. "T-bills" constitute direct obligations of the US government and are the safest and most liquid investment available. These and other government securities can be bought from commercial banks and brokerage firms for a slight fee or directly from the Federal Reserve.

Negotiable Time Certificates of Deposit. Introduced by commercial banks in 1960 to lure back corporate funds that had disappeared into other short-term securities, CDs represent the second most important money-market

MONEY MARKET SECURITIES

	Description	Denominations	Maturity	Security	Secondary Market
United States Treasury Bills	Direct obligations of U.S. Government 3 & 6 months bills auctioned weekly; 6 months & 1 year bills auctioned monthly	$10,000 to $1 million	Up to one year	Excellent	Excellent
Negotiable Time Certificates of Deposit	Negotiable time deposits in a commercial bank	$100,000 to $1 million	30 days to one year	Dependent on Issuer	Good if well known issuer
Commercial Paper	Promissory notes of industrial and finance institutions	$25,000 to $5 million	5 to 270 days	Dependent on Issuer	Limited
Bankers' Acceptances	Time drafts drawn on and "accepted" by a banking institution	$25,000 to $1 million	Up to 6 months	Good	Fair
Federal Agency Issues	Obligations of federal agencies but not government guaranteed	$1,000 to $1 million	Variable to one year and beyond	Good	Good
Short-Term Tax Exempts	Notes of local municipalities or states, some federally guaranteed	$25,000 to $100,000	Variable usually 3 months to one year	Dependent on Issuer	Good

instrument. Basically, a CD is a bank's IOU for a time deposit but with the distinction of being negotiable (i.e., it can be bought and sold before maturity). This gives the corporate treasurer the advantage of somewhat higher yields than T-bills along with good liquidity.

Commercial Paper. Unsecured promissory notes issued by industrial and finance companies. Commercial paper has proved a highly popular outlet for short-term funds for many companies.

Bankers' Acceptances. A negotiable draft drawn on a commercial bank used to finance commercial transactions. It offers the credit worthiness of the bank creating the acceptance, fair liquidity, and usually a higher yield than T-bills and commercial paper.

Federal Agency Issues. Several US government agencies are allowed to borrow directly from the public. Although these securities are not guaranteed by the federal government, it is considered highly unlikely that they would be permitted to default on an obligation. Because of the slightly higher risk, these securities carry higher yields than T-bills. There are five federally sponsored agencies whose securities make excellent short-term investments: Federal Home Loan Bank, Federal Land Banks, Federal Intermediate Credit Bank, Federal National Mortgage Association (Fannie Mae), and Bank for Cooperatives.

Short-Term Tax-Exempts. Obligations of states and municipalities as well as of local branches of such federal agencies as the Public Housing Authority and the Housing and Home Finance Agency.

Taxation

Before deciding whether a particular investment provides a good yield, be sure to check its tax status. T-bills and all federal agency issues except securities of the Federal National Mortgage Association are subject to federal taxes but exempt from state and local taxes. "Fannie Mae" issues are taxed at all three levels of government while tax-exempts are normally free from such taxes. A word of warning about tax-free securities: If a corporation buys tax-exempt securities rather than paying off its interest-bearing debt, interest on an equivalent amount of the interest-bearing debt may be disallowed.

COST-CUTTING CHECKLIST

Sales are necessary for business; profits are necessary for survival. What keeps a sales dollar from becoming a profit dollar? One thing—expenses. In tough times most businessmen concentrate on increasing sales when it might be more productive to concentrate on cutting costs. A $100 increase in sales may increase profits by $10, *but only a $10 decrease in costs is equivalent to a $100 increase in sales, since reduced costs flow directly to the "bottom line" as additional profits.* Put your effort where you get the most profit leverage—in cutting costs. Here are some ways to reduce expenses in your company:

Productivity. More output per employee and per dollar invested means lower costs. To remain competitive, start programs now for higher productivity.

- *Upgrade employees.* The government will pick up much of the tab to train and upgrade skills of your employees. For more information, contact your state employment office.
- *Solicit ideas.* No one can save you more money than your employees if the proper incentive and recognition is given by top management.

Payroll.

- *Overtime.* Slash overtime by: (1) adding shifts, (2) staggering working hours, (3) hiring part-timers for peak loads, (4) personally inspecting all overtime records to be sure the the work was necessary. Also, cut mandatory overtime payments under the Wage Hour Law by qualifying supervisors and foremen as "exempt" employees with varying workweeks on a guaranteed wage plan and granting compensatory time off in slack periods in lieu of cash overtime payments.
- *Special employees.* Whenever possible, hire employees who are less expensive in terms of salary, benefits, recruitment, and payroll taxes than your regular work force. Also, keep close track of everyone who performs services for you. Many may be classified as "independent contractors," which means you avoid needless payroll taxes.

- *Unemployment taxes.* To successfully cut expenses in this area: (1) learn how the "experience rating" works in your state. There are four types of plans: reserve ratio, benefit wage ratio, benefit ratio, and payroll stabilization; (2) if at all possible, avoid layoffs that will increase your rating; (3) be sure your experience rating is correct. A small error could cost hundreds or thousands of dollars; and (4) take aggressive action to insure that all claims paid from your account are fully justified. Appeal any that are questionable.
- *Workmen's compensation.* Take the following steps: (1) review your policy and compare it to several other insurers (there are both mutual and stock companies as well as state-run funds) to determine the lowest net premium; (2) insist on preemployment physicals to avoid undetected disabilities; (3) use the insurance company's safety engineers. They are experienced, expert, and usually free; and (4) review your experience rating to be sure it is correct.

Purchasing.

- *Discounts.* Take advantage whenever possible. For example, if you pass up "2/10 net 30" terms, you are paying 36.5% per year for use of a supplier's money! Use blanket orders. Buy everything you need in one bulk discount but have it delivered and pay for it only as you need it.
- *Economic Order Quantity.* See page 137 to determine the proper EOQ for major inventory items. Also, conduct a "make or buy" analysis on purchased items to see if you can possibly make them cheaper.
- *Suppliers fair.* Advertise what you want to *buy* rather than sell, or even set up a suppliers fair where potential vendors can come to see what you need. It is convenient to go to a known vendor, but he could be considerably more expensive.

Advertising. Find some way to key media to tell which types are most effective—eliminate the least effective. Drop some of the out-of-town Yellow Pages listings if they have not been productive. Test the pulling power of slightly smaller newspaper ads.

Accounts receivable. Take an aggressive stance with late payers. Being a banker to your customers means you have to borrow more at your bank and pay high interest charges.

Production. "Value analysis" looks for new techniques, materials, and procedures to do the same job at a significant cost savings. Ask the following value analysis questions about everything you make, buy, or sell: What does it do? What does it cost? What else would do the job cheaper but as efficiently?

CHAPTER 10

INVENTORY CONTROL

THE EOQ CONCEPT—HOW TO MANAGE YOUR INVENTORY

One basic problem in almost every business is inventory. Small wonder so many businessmen find themselves asking, "Why the devil are we always out of stock on this item?" or, the other extreme, "What happens if we get stuck with all this inventory?" So go the laments and frustrations of trying to simultaneously maintain a steady work flow, provide customers with adequate service, and still keep investment in inventory stocks down to reasonable levels. Whether you are a restauranteur buying lettuce or a manufacturer ordering component parts, there is a technique you should understand. It is called "economic order quality" (EOQ) analysis, and it will help you determine: (1) *when* an inventory item should be ordered and (2) *how large* the order should be.

Elements of Inventory Cost

There are two cost factors that affect the decision of how much inventory to order. The first is the cost of *investment* in the inventory ("carrying cost"). The second is the cost of placing inventory *replenishment orders* ("ordering cost"). The economic order quantity is that order quantity that *minimizes the combined cost of ordering and carrying any inventory item.*

Let's take a simplified example: The Ace Manufacturing Company purchases a certain metal flange at $10 apiece. Expected usage of the flange is 6,000 a year, with 1,500 purchased every three months. With some help from its accountant, the company can determine its inventory cost as follows:

- *Carrying cost* By determining an annual carrying cost (as a percentage of total dollars invested in inventory), Ace management can quickly determine the total carrying cost for this item based on different order levels. (See the Annual Carrying Cost computation on the next page.) For example, if orders are placed for 1,000 units, there will be an average inventory on hand of $5,000 (500 units times $10 per unit). Based on the 25% annual carrying cost, this amounts to $1,250. When the annual carrying cost is

ANNUAL CARRYING COST

Spoilage and theft	2%	
Obsolescence	3	(risk of product or design obsolescence)
Storage and insurance	8	
Opportunity cost	12	(the amount that could be earned if the cash invested in inventory were to be put to work elsewhere)
Total annual carrying cost	25%	(Note: US Department of Commerce studies estimate that a 25 percent annual carrying cost is typical for small manufacturers.)

computed at other order sizes and plotted graphically, management can see that it is a straight-line function of order size. (See the chart at the top of page 139.)

- *Ordering cost.* The management of Ace estimates that the paperwork, handling, inspection, and other costs associated with placing an order for flanges comes to about $30 per order. They can now determine the annual cost of ordering associated with different order sizes as follows:

ANNUAL ORDERING COST

		100	500	1,000	1,500
	Order size (units)	100	500	1,000	1,500
	Number of orders placed per year	60	12	6	4
times:	Cost per order	$30	$30	$30	$30
equals:	Annual ordering cost	$1,800	$360	$180	$120

When each of these annual ordering costs is plotted at the different volume levels, the second graph shown at the top of page 139 results.

The Economic Order Quantity

The total inventory cost to Ace for the flanges can now be determined by graphically adding the carrying and ordering cost charts. The resultant chart is shown at the bottom of page 139. The low point of the total inventory cost curve occurs where the carrying cost and ordering cost lines intersect. By visual inspection, we can determine that the EOQ is approximately 400 units. In other words, if Ace changes its order quantity for flanges from 1,500 to 400, it could save about $1,000 per year in total expenses on this one inventory item.

Mathematical Technique

You can eliminate the graph and determine the EOQ on any inventory item by a simple formula.

$$EOQ = \sqrt{\frac{2 \times \text{(expected annual usage in units)} \times \text{(ordering cost per order in dollars)}}{\text{(cost per unit of material)} \times \text{(annual carrying cost percentage} \div 100)}}$$

ANNUAL CARRYING AND ORDERING COST

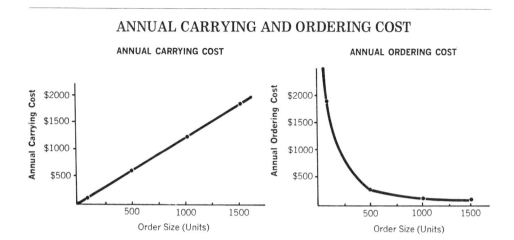

ANNUAL CARRYING COST

ANNUAL ORDERING COST

In this example where annual usage is 6,000 units, ordering cost is $30, cost per unit is $10, and the annual carrying cost is 25 percent, the exact EOQ would be 380 units. The EOQ can be off by a factor of two and still cause only a 6% change in total cost. So as long as Ace orders somewhere between $1/2 \times 380$ units = 190 units and 2×380 units = 760 units, they will be within the EOQ ballpark.

Quantity Discounts

Some businessmen fear losing volume discounts if they reduce the size of their orders. The chart on the top of page 140 compares the incremental cost advantage of purchasing at the EOQ lot size as compared to large orders at a 2% price discount. Even though larger orders would yield a discount, it is more economical to purchase the small quantity. In times of material shortage and rising prices, it may be safer to hold larger stocks and avoid paying higher prices later. But prices can sometimes fall dramatically after an inflationary period—don't be caught with excess inventory and high carrying costs.

TOTAL ANNUAL COST OF
ORDERING AND CARRYING INVENTORY

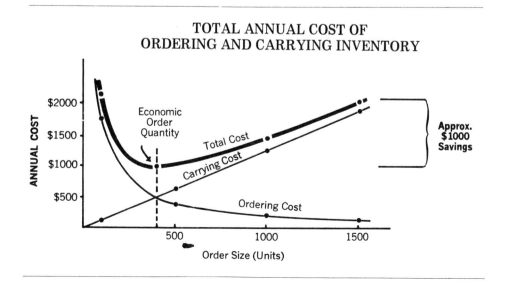

Incremental Cost Analysis to Determine Net Advantage
When 2% Price Discount for 2000 or More Units is Offered

	Lots of 380, price $10.00 per unit	Lots of 2,000, price $9.80 per unit (2% discount)
Purchase cost one year's supply (6,000 units)	$60,000	$58,800
Ordering cost	480	90
Inventory carrying cost (average inventory × unit cost × 25%)	475	2,450
	$60,955	$61,340

Can your Company Use EOQ?

Not all inventory items lend themselves to using the EOQ formula. Use this checklist to determine if EOQ is appropriate:

- The inventory item should be periodically replenished in batches, either purchased from outside vendors or manufactured internally.
- Sale or usage rates should be fairly steady and predictable.
- Inventory of the item should represent a significant dollar investment to make it worth the analysis. It is estimated, for example, that less than 20% of the items inventoried by the average company represents over 80% of their total inventory investment. Concentrate on the 20% first. This is often accomplished by using the so-called ABC technique.

ABC ANALYSIS: SAVE MORE BY FOCUSING INVENTORY CONTROLS

Inventory controls are vital. But they can be expensive—often meaning more paperwork, more formal procedures, and more overhead cost. ABC analysis lets you save more on your inventory controls by focusing them where they will do the most good—on the few items that probably make up most of your inventory costs.

Using the ABC system

Split your inventory items into three broad groups. The chart on the top of page 141 shows how the breakdown worked for one typical company.

How to classify your inventory

The exact method you use to classify your inventory depends on the nature of your business, but most manufacturing businesses use the following method:

- Determine the cost of each part in inventory. For parts you produce, charge materials, labor, and overhead.

ABC SYSTEM

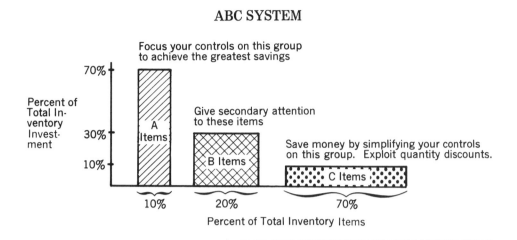

- Estimate the average number of each part you need to inventory. Multiply the cost for each part by this number. Add all the figures to get your total inventory investment, and find what share each part has.

A sample ABC Analysis worksheet is shown below. The two columns on the right have been used to classify the full list of parts into the A, B, and C categories. These three items are typical of the relationships between the number of items and investment levels for a typical company's inventory.

Controlling the A items. Achieve the smallest reasonable stock level of these items by:

- Rechecking your estimates of usage of these parts. Overestimates waste money.
- Reducing the size of your buffer stocks by having more frequent checks on usage and stock levels.
- Trying to negotiate faster delivery times in order to reduce the stock cover needed for reorder time.

ABC ANALYSIS

Part Number	Cost per Part	Average Number in Inventory	Total Investment in this Part	% of Total Inventory Items	% of Total Inventory Investment	Category
258: Motor	$20.00	50	$1000	1%	10%	A
1091: Bearing	$ 1.60	250	$ 400	5%	4%	B
3372: 5/8 Screws (in gross)	$ 0.20	500 gross	$ 100	10%	1%	C
Totals:		5000 items		5000 items	$10,000	

- Insuring that their receiving and their flow through the factory is as fast as possible.

Special handling for C items.   Because C items represent only a small portion of your investment, it's generally better to place just a few big orders for these items during the year. This way you can obtain quantity discounts, reduce your order-processing costs, and save clerical costs by looser control.

Getting the most from the ABC system

ABC analysis makes a great partner with the EOQ method of inventory management. The ABC method will show you the items to focus on when applying control techniques like EOQ. ABC works best if everyone helps. Your employees will probably be as interested as you to find how much money is tied up in a few items. Get them to help in controlling A items. Publicize the method. Let them know which items you are trying to control. It's a good way to get your employees involved in the vital problem of inventory control.

CHAPTER 11

INTRODUCTION TO MARKETING AND MARKET RESEARCH

INTRODUCTION: MARKETING MYTHS*

Fifty years ago, a Boston millionaire unintentionally sentenced his heirs to poverty by stipulating that his entire estate be invested exclusively in electric streetcar utilities.

Like the electric streetcar business, every major company was once a growth company. But where growth slowed or stopped, it did so not because the market became saturated, but because there was some lack of management foresight.

- The *railroads* are in trouble because they limited their business to the rails rather than "transportation," ignoring a need for expanded freight haulage by truck and air.
- *Hollywood* barely escaped total devastation from television; it thought it was in the movie business rather than entertainment.
- *Dry cleaning*, a growth industry in an age of wool garments, now faces decline because of synthetic fibers.
- The *corner grocery store*, well established in the 1930s, never recovered from the competition of the supermarket.
- *Electric utilities* are supposedly a "no-substitute" industry. Yet solar energy and chemical fuel cells may spell their end.

In each case, the industry's strength lay in the apparently unchallenged superiority of its product; it was a runaway substitute for the product it replaced.

Warning signals

There is really no such thing as a growth industry—only companies organized and operated to create and capitalize on *growth opportunities*. Do you

---

*Portions of this section were condensed from: Theodore Levitt, "Marketing Myopia," *Harvard Business Review*, September–October 1975.

wonder what you can do to keep your company growing, even after the obvious opportunities have been exhausted? Here are four basic assumptions that can lead you astray:

1. *Population myth.* Every manager likes to believe that profits are assured by an expanding and more affluent population. If consumers are multiplying and also buying more of your product or service, you don't have to think very hard or imaginatively. As a result, you will not give much thought to how to expand your market. For example, the oil industry has done little to create a demand for its product since John D. Rockefeller sent free kerosene lamps to China. That industry's efforts have focused on improving production efficiency, rather than on improving the generic product or its marketing. Thus, the oil industry is asking for trouble from outsiders who might come out with a solar energy system that is more ecologically sound and more reliable.

2. *No competition.* There is no guarantee against product obsolescence. If your company's own research does not make it obsolete, another's will. Unless your company is especially lucky, it can easily go down in a sea of red figures—just as many of the railroads and the corner grocery stores have. The best way for your company to be lucky is for you to know what makes it successful.

3. *Mass production.* In some respects, Ford was the most brilliant marketer in American history. He fashioned a production system designed to fit market needs. However, his real genius was not in production but in marketing. He actually invented the assembly line because he had concluded that he could sell millions of cars at $500. Mass production was the *result*, not the cause of his low prices. You can take a lesson from this approach: you are not in business to create a better production line but to satisfy customer needs.

4. *Scientific improvements.* Top management can become transfixed by the profit possibilities of technical research and development. The greatest danger facing the glamorous new electronics companies is not that they do not pay enough attention to R&D but that they pay too much attention to it. Their success has been shaped in the virtually guaranteed market of military subsidies. Consequently, their expansion has been almost totally devoid of marketing effort.

These managements have developed the philosophy that continued growth is a matter of continued product innovation and improvement; the company grows under the illusion that a superior product will sell itself. Once its management has created a superior product, it continues to be oriented toward the product rather than toward the people who consume it.

What gets shortchanged are the realities of the market. Consumers are unpredictable, varied, fickle, shortsighted, stubborn, and generally bothersome. The engineers/managers don't say this, but deep down, it's what they believe.

Produce consumer services, not things

What can be learned from these four warnings? *An industry is a customer-satisfying process, not a goods-producing process.* There is a crucial difference between marketing and selling. *Selling* focuses on the needs of the seller to convert the product into cash, and *marketing* focuses on satisfying the needs of the buyer through the product and through everything associated with creating, delivering, and finally consuming it.

A company begins with the customer and his needs, not with a patent, a raw material, or a selling skill. Given the customer's needs, the industry develops backwards, from the physical *delivery* of customer satisfactions, to *creating* the things by which these satisfactions are achieved, to *finding* the raw materials necessary for making those products. To be successful, a company must concentrate on its customers. Customer orientation involves the following:

- The entire corporation must view itself as a customer-creating, customer-satisfying organism.
- Your industry must be customer oriented, not product oriented.
- The company should not produce products, but provide customer-creating value satisfactions.
- This idea must pervade every aspect of the organization.
- You must set your company's style, its direction, and its goals.

PREVENTING MARKETING DISASTERS*

Reliance upon marketing myths and wives tales can mean your undoing, but sometimes even the experts can lead you astray. These days instead of gypsies and tea-leaf readers, we now have "futurologists"—experts in predicting what is going to happen in the future. Overreliance on these contemporary soothsayers, who often combine computers with their crystal balls, can lead to modern marketing disasters.

Every business manager is concerned about the future. Whenever a supposed expert predicts that certain markets will open up, we all take note.

*Portions of this section were condensed from: Theodore Levitt, "The New Markets—Think Before You Leap," *Harvard Business Review*, May–June 1969.

However, forecasts based on technology must be tempered with common sense. Too often there can be a need, but no market, or a market, but no customer, or a customer, but no salesman available to sell the product.

Market forecasters frequently fail to understand these miscalculations about such highly publicized opportunities as pollution control, educational technology, urban transportation, and the leisure market.

A need, but no market

A popular prescription for guaranteed success in business is "find a need and then fill it". However, prospective caterers to an obvious need may find the road to commercial success blocked by custom, tradition, or just plain stubbornness.

Before any business manager hurries to satisfy an obvious need, he should first consider that accustomed habits can be difficult to change. For example, in a world of starving people, we are told that the sea can provide 30% of our nutritional needs. Yet food habits are among the most difficult to change, and there are numerous discouraging examples of companies that created new, low-priced, high-protein foods for the undernourished masses of India and South America who refused to abandon their traditional diets. Thousands continue to starve in India amid a large roving supply of edible beef.

Thirty years ago smoke from the steel mills of Pittsburgh blotted out the sun. The need for pollution control was obvious, but there was no market even though means to control the smog were available. Numerous examples of a need, but no market abounds in today's business world.

A market, but no customer

There are many exciting prospects in such fields as education, mass transit, and medical care, but the existence of a market does not mean that anyone can afford to buy the product. For example, General Electric and Time teamed up and spent $10 million to develop electronic teaching materials only to discover that no school system was affluent enough to afford them. Similarly, there is a huge market for pollution control equipment, but the difficulty has been to persuade various towns and cities along a river bank or a shoreline to share the cost of buying it. Before any business manager commits resources to a new market, he should first assure himself that there is someone on the receiving end willing—and able—to buy the product or service.

A customer, but no salesman

Few problems in business get so much attention as the salesman problem—how to recruit, train, pay, evaluate, and retain them. The simple fact is that although your product may be excellent and the customer willing to buy, if you cannot get enough effective salesmen into the field, the product may flop.

In these cases, you may need to attack the problem from the other end. Instead of spending more money hiring and training salesmen, you need to use a "controlled sales proposition"—a fully controlled, carefully executed, standard sales pitch. For example, instead of using a highly paid super-talker, try a salesman of lesser skills who uses an attache case-sized projector to show slides or a movie to clearly and effectively explain the details of what is being offered. Similarly, telephones can be used to give the customer a prerecorded explanation of an item that interests him. Just be sure that before gearing up to produce a new product or service the people and the means are available to sell it.

Case example of a potential disaster—the illusory leisure market

Few markets have been more confidently anticipated by futurologists than the so-called leisure market. Certainly sales of skis, boats, and camping equipment have grown at a rapid rate for the past few years. With the four-day/forty-hour work week, Monday holidays, and rising income, the trend toward increased recreation time and bigger leisure markets seemed assured. Business managers everywhere climbed on this safe and growing bandwagon. Yet it now appears that the experts were predicting the wrong actions for the wrong reasons:

- The U.S. population actually works more today than it did in the 1930s. In 1939 the average factory worker was on the job 37.7 hours per week; in 1967 the figure was 40.6 hours.
- Less time at work does not mean more leisure time. It may take an hour to get to work today from the suburbs as opposed to ten minutes in a streetcar in the 1930s.
- Spending on leisure goods and services is more dependent on affluence than free time. As inflation cuts into disposable income, leisure-related spending is quickly cut back. During the Great Depression there were twelve million unemployed who had plenty of free time, but they were certainly no market for leisure goods. If real incomes decline, there may be no need and few salesmen necessary to serve this market that so recently was described by experts as a solid growth area of the future.

Conclusion

We generalize to simplify our business life. Similarly, we are drawn to experts who seem to have clear answers and strategies for the future. However, today more than ever, it is apparent that the essential difference between those who get to the top and those who don't is not the ability to expound management principles and textbook formulas, but the ability to determine what the problem *really* is. Intuition and common sense are generally of more use to the average business manager than reliance on supposed experts and their forecasts of the future.

PRODUCTS—LIKE PEOPLE—HAVE LIFE CYCLES

We can all think of industries that qualify for that mythical title "growth industry". And, of course, within those industries there are numerous growth products. But, products really have life cycles. From introduction to demise, a product exists in different stages and changing competitive environments. Unless management recognizes and responds to its products' evolutionary cycles, the shadow of market decline and obsolescence is never far away.

Life Cycle Stages

A product's life cycle can normally be divided into six stages: introduction, growth, maturity, saturation, decline, obsolescence. The time required to go from introduction to obsolescence can vary considerably among products. A fashion or apparel fad may last only a few weeks from start to finish while other products, such as the automobile or telephone, may continue for several decades before they become obsolete. Even the duration between each stage can vary considerably. But, inevitably decline and abandonment set in for one or more reasons:

- *Superior marketing by a competitor.* A good example would be Proctor & Gamble's coup when the American Dental Association endorsed the decay-prevention claims of Crest toothpaste.
- *Superior or less expensive product introduced.* For example, transistor radio for tube type, or plastic substituted for wood or metal parts.
- *Lack of need.* Such as coal stokers for indoor furnaces.

It is important for management to analyze the life cycle stages of each of its products. This is because the competitive environment and resultant marketing strategies necessary to prolong "life" and profitability will normally vary depending on the stage. A brief summary of each stage is given below:

1. *Introduction.* During the first stage of a product's life cycle, demand must normally be "created" and the consumer educated as to the superior merits of the product. As a result, this stage is characterized by high prices, high promotional costs, low sales volume, and minimal profits. In general there are few competitors at this point, and the key success factors are: (1) accurate market research to pinpoint probable consumers; (2) product design and adaptation; and (3) promotional expertise.
2. *Growth.* Because of the high risk of failure in the introductory phase, many companies have a conscious "second bite" strategy. They will settle for their piece of the apple after someone else has taken the risk and proven the viability of the product. Hence, this stage is characterized by the entry of

LIFE CYCLE STAGES

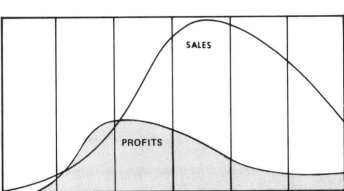

competitors and a scramble for competitive position. Advertising shifts to "buy my brand" rather than "try this product." Sales and profit increase rapidly, but prices and margin per unit begin to decline. Distribution and promotional support to lock up market shares are essential during this phase.

3. *Maturity.* At this point, marginal competitors are shaken out, and a highly volatile competitive situation emerges between the survivors. While sales continue to rise, competition is so intense that overall profits begin to decline. The ability to adapt to the volatile competitive situation and to innovate with new uses or models of the product is essential during this phase.

4. *Saturation.* During this phase total sales peak and replacement sales become a significant factor. Automobiles are still considered to be in this stage. Sales begin to be more responsive to basic economic forces such as recession or inflation than to promotional expenditures. With sales peaking and profits dropping further, production efficiencies become a vital competitive factor.

5. *Decline and Obsolescence.* It now becomes a question of how long to "milk" the product before dropping it completely. Although margins are lowest during this phase, competition has lessened and promotional expenditures can be reduced or eliminated. With proper management, this phase can be highly profitable, although perhaps short-lived.

A Classic Example—Electronic Calculators

In 1971 the first hand-held models were introduced, costing over $200 each. Several Japanese companies captured an estimated 65% of the US market. However, once the market potential had been demonstrated, many American manufacturers decided to enter the market themselves. Sales prices dropped to an average of $100 per unit. Numerous assemblers and marginal producers were forced out of the market. Fully integrated American companies moved ahead to become the dominant forces. A fierce competitive battle is now raging between these companies and prices have continued to drop, approaching $5.00 to $10.00 per unit. A proliferation of features and models are now being developed for specific users.

How to Manage Your Product's Life Cycle

How do your products fit the life cycle model? Don't be overly concerned if they appear fairly mature, because a product's life can be extended by revitalizing it through new packaging, repricing, or design modifications. For example, Jell-O and Scotch tape—two classically mature products—have extended their lives by constantly innovating with new uses and applications. If you have a sick product, however, don't invest scarce money and management time in it if those resources could be devoted to a healthy one. Often, knowing when to abandon old products is as important as introducing new ones. We will return to product life cycle considerations numerous times in following sections.

BASIC OVERVIEW OF MARKET RESEARCH

Product life cycle isn't just some isolated and abstract business concept. Customer buying patterns are the primary determinants of the product life cycle. Thus the life cycle helps you to keep in touch with your market—the people "out there" who pay real cash for your product. But life cycle is only a reflection of market conditions. A good manager's essential market information comes from market research.

What is market research?

Market research is a methodical search for a comprehensive, accurate, and useful description of your market. It should help you to answer any of the following questions:

1. *Market Potential and Characteristics. How large* is the estimated market in terms of units and dollars? What *growth rate* can be expected? What are the *potential profits* in the market? What *share of the market* can be expected? *Where* are potential customers located (industries, geography, etc.)?
2. *Consumer Attitudes and Needs. Who* will buy this product? *Why?* What are the main perceived advantages and disadvantages of the product? *How often* will the product be bought?
3. *Price Information.* At what *price* are *competitive* products being offered? At what *price* should *our* product be sold?
4. *Product Information.* What are the prime *characteristics* of

competitive products? *How* will our product be *perceived* by the consumer?

5. *Promotion.* What *media* should be used to help sell the product (i.e., radio, TV, print, etc.)? *What points* should be *stressed* that will be most effective in selling the product?

6. *Place* (channels of distribution). What *distribution channels* should be used to sell the product? *How* can the product be *moved* most efficiently from the producer to the consumer?

You may not need the answers to all of these questions, so be clear about what you *do* want before the research gets underway. You save time and money by knowing what you want before you go after it.

Why Should You Do Market Research?

There are three outstanding reasons for investing time and resources in marketing research:

- The information you get back helps you to perceive, evaluate and hopefully profit from new money making opportunities.
- The information aids in spotting problems in current programs and in determining whether previous goals are being met.
- Marketing research provides information that must be used in making vital decisions and in formulating alternative action plans.

When Should You Do Marketing Research?

Countless variables will determine the proper timing for a given individual's need for market research, but it would not be facetious to say that you'll use it when you need it. Marketing research takes time and it can be expensive. But how much more is risked when important corporate decisions are made without access to vital information? Chances are good that you will call for market research when you can't afford to risk making a decision without it.

MARKET RESEARCH TECHNIQUES

Segmentation Analyses

One technique used to obtain a useful picture of your market is market segmentation. Whatever your business, from plumbing to politics, chances are that you have assorted customers who subscribe to your particular product or service for a variety of different reasons. This is the key to successful marketing—identify the particular characteristics or "consumer profile" of every conceivable customer and then to the extent economically feasible, mount a market campaign tailored to his specific needs.

Market segmentation is a relatively recent and revolutionary concept.

Traditionally, American business saw the keys to profit based on a single uniform product, massed produced, and mass distributed. As Henry Ford once put it: "They can buy any color automobile they want—as long as it is black." But as competition increased and consumer tastes proliferated, the key to profit shifted from mass production skills to the skill of determining exactly what the customer wanted—and then giving it to him. Companies such as General Motors and Procter & Gamble have followed this credo and profited immensely. They introduced quality, style, and image in their products, and this has led to the profusion of brands, models, colors, and options that distinguish today's marketplace.

Segmentation Categories

How do you start this process of splitting up your market into manageable pieces? The traditional variables of market segmentation fall into two main categories: demographic and geographic. In recent years, however, two additional methods of segmentation have proven successful: psychographic and consumer-behavioral. (See chart below.)

Examples of Segmentation

We can best illustrate the use of these variables by taking a number of examples.

Demographic. Everyday, whether we realize it or not, we are barraged with advertisements focused at a certain age group, sex, or occupation. However, sometimes demographic segmentation can backfire as Rheingold Beer found out in New York. Rheingold promoted the fact that Puerto Ricans, Italians, Greeks, Poles, and other ethnic groups drank Rheingold more than any other beer. It did not work, and subsequent research revealed the problem—no one ethnic group wanted to be identified so closely with the other. Creative segmentation is fine, but back it up with market research *before*, not after the fact.

Geographic. Different areas of the country have different tastes. And, of course, the consumption characteristics of city dwellers can be distinguished from country folk. A small grocer knows his primary trading area to

SEGMENTATION CATEGORIES

DEMOGRAPHIC	*GEOGRAPHIC*	*PSYCHOGRAPHIC*	*CONSUMER-BEHAVIORAL*
Age	Country	Leader or follower	Rate of usage
Sex	Region	High or low achiever	Benefits sought:
Income	State	Extrovert or introvert	(i.e., economy,
Occupation	Size of population	Compulsive or placid	reliability,
Religion	Climate	Independent or dependent	comfort, etc.)
Race	Density of	Conservative or liberal	Method of usage
Education	population	Dominant or submissive	Frequency of usage
Social Class			

be perhaps only a few blocks, while a national manufacturer may classify his customers by region of the country or by state, county, or township. For example, few people would want to invest heavily in a scheme to sell cowboy hats to the general population of New York City.

Psychographic. This is a relatively recent and highly interesting market classification method. One of the most famous studies was of the psychological characteristics of Chevrolet versus Ford owners. It was found that the Ford owners were independent, impulsive, and masculine, while Chevrolet owners were conservative, thrifty, and prestige-conscious. No doubt these particular labels have shifted today, but the entire range of American cars can be segmented according to the dominant psychographic characteristic to which each one appeals. Knowledge of these factors is crucial to successful styling and effective advertising. And, of course, the cigarette companies are masters at psychographic segmentation. Who really *is* the Marlboro Man?

Consumer-Behavioral. Another relatively recent entrant, behavioral segmentation, has proven successful for a large number of companies. The key here is to know *why* the customer bought and how he *uses* your product. For example, we find Shaefer going after the "more-than-one" beer drinker, Ultra-Brite after those who need sex appeal, and the soap companies after so many behavioral segments in the laundry room that there can't be any more left. But excessive segmentation can be dangerous too. With a neat bit of unsegmenting, the Gillette Company sensed in the mid-1960s that in spite of being distinctively designed and promoted, men's and women's deodorants were often being used by the whole family. Right Guard quickly became the leading *family* deodorant! The same is true of Johnson's baby shampoo which is now being pitched to Dad, Mom, and the teens.

Can you begin to conceive of various market segments for your product you have not previously considered? Remember, however, that creating different versions of a product does not constitute market segmentation. *Marketing starts with the customer and his constantly shifting needs, not what you have on hand and would like to sell.*

Sources of Market Research Information.

Market research information comes from two types of sources, primary and secondary. A primary source would be a direct survey or interview with consumers. Secondary sources are usually printed sources of information, such as books, surveys, catalogues, or trade magazines, that have been prepared for reasons other than your specific marketing problem.

Secondary Sources

Odd as it may sound, you begin your market research with the secondary sources. The main reason is that it's generally more efficient to consult already published data in order to gather as much information as possible before you conduct any special field studies or interviews. Other reasons are it: is usually easier and less expensive; is usually quicker; may be all you need to solve your problem; should help clarify your problem; and helps in planning for primary research.

Basic Secondary Sources.   Secondary sources are vital. Too often business and marketing judgments are made in the dark or on the basis of intuition simply because the decision maker doesn't know where—and how—to quickly obtain relevant facts and figures. Remember: *An important difference between business managers who make good decisions and those who don't is the quality of their information.* You don't have to be a part of a large company with a market research staff to have the information you need.

Here is a basic list of reference sources, available at any city library. This list is by no means complete, but it should indicate that no business manager need make ill-considered decisions for lack of information.

Business bibliographies
   Sources of Business Information. (Edwin T. Coman, 1964) This is the basic reference guide to all types of business information.
   Business Reference Sources. (Lorna M. Daniells, 1971) A compact working guide, this booklet was originally intended for students at the Harvard Business School but is an excellent reference source for most business people. It is available for $3.00 from Baker Library, Harvard Business School, Boston, MA 02163.
Directories
   Guide to American Directories. (Bernard Klein & Co., 1968) This guide provides an annotated listing of over 5,000 major industrial, business, and professional directories.
   Middle Market Directory. (Dun & Bradstreet, annual) This directory lists over 33,000 US companies with net worths from $500,000 to $1 million. Gives officers, products, sales figures, and number of employees. Standard and Poor also publishes a similar directory, *Poor's Register of Corporations, Directors and Executives.*
   Thomas Register of American Manufacturers. (annual) This standard reference of ten volumes lists manufacturers by specific product, and two volumes are devoted to selected company catalogues.
   Guide to Venture Capital Sources. (Stanley M. Rubel, biannual) This directory lists over 600 venture capital firms and indicates how to deal with them.
   American Guide to Business Directories. (Public Affairs Press), 419 New Jersey Ave. SE, Washington, DC 20003
   Trade Directories of the World. (Croner Publications) This one offers a list of business directories for trades in the US and abroad.
   American Guide to Directories (Prentice-Hall, Inc.) This guide has 400 categories containing 2,200 titles.

Data on specific industries

Trade associations. There are over 4,300 national trade and professional associations that compile innumerable statistics and reports. For addresses of associations and a listing of their publications, consult the *Directory of National Trade and Professional Associations* (Columbia Books, Inc.). Also useful are the *Encyclopedia of Associations* (Gale Research Co.) and the *National Trade and Professional Associations of the United States* (Bernard Klein Publishers Inc.).

Trade journals. Most trade publications have special editions containing specialized information. Consult the *F & S Index to Corporations and Industries* (Predicasts, Inc., weekly), which lists by specific company and SIC code articles and reports in all major trade journals and business periodicals. For a list of trade journals and their addresses, see the *Standard Periodical Directory* (Oxbridge Publishing Company).

Market Information

A Guide to Consumer Markets. (Conference Board, annual) This excellent source contains statistics and graphs on population, employment, income, expenditures, production, and prices.

Marketing Information Guide. (US Department of Commerce, monthly) This guide is probably the most useful source of studies and statistics for market research.

Market Guide. (Editor & Publisher Co., Inc., annual) This compendium of marketing information covers every city and large community in the US and Canada.

Survey of Buying Power. (Published in the July issue of *Sales Management* magazine, annual). This survey estimates population, retail sales, and buying income for each city, county, and state in the US.

Government Sources

Statistical Abstract of the United States (US Census Bureau.) This comprehensive compilation includes US industrial, social, and economic statistics.

Census statistics. Of most interest to the business manager are the censuses of: population (1970), business (1972), manufacturers (1972), *County and City Data Book*, and *County Business Patterns.*

Monthly periodicals. For an excellent source of basic tables and charts on the US economy, consult *Economic Indicators* (published by the President's Council of Economic Advisors).

Facts for Marketers. This is a series of market studies encompassing the one hundred largest standard metropolitan statistical areas (SMSAs) in the US. It covers population, housing, employment, income, and industry sales.

US Census Data—Free Market Research Some of the most important secondary sources for market information listed above are publications from the US Bureau of the Census. You can obtain and use this vital and free source of information at almost all larger public libraries.

In order to efficiently utilize Census Bureau statistics it is important to understand the basic definitions of market classifications. Generally, all products fall into two broad categories. The distinction between the two is the use to which the product is put:

Consumer goods are manufactured products used by individuals and families. They are generally broken down into two further subgroupings: (1) "durables", such as passenger cars and appliances, and (2) "non-durables", such as food, clothing, and tobacco.

Industrial goods are products used in manufacturing consumer goods and other industrial goods, in supplying services, or in facilitating the operation of a business.

The marketer of consumer goods is primarily interested in population and income characteristics of individuals and families. In contrast, the marketer of industrial goods is more interested in sales and employment statistics of business firms that might use his product. In some instances, however, certain products have both a consumer and industrial use (e.g., electric light bulbs), in which case both the consumer and industrial market may be of interest to a manufacturer and/or distributor. Now that we have an idea what type of information we're seeking, let's find out where to find this information in the census data.

US Census Data The census of the United States actually incorporates over eight different censuses. Together with other bulletins and reports issued by the Census Bureau, they constitute the single most fruitful source of data useful for market research. Here are some of the censuses of most importance to the businessman:

1. *Census of Population.* This census reports the count of population by state, county, city, metropolitan area, and, in large cities, by census tract. Census tracts are fixed geographical areas of about 4,000 residents that were established with the intention of being maintained over a long period of time—very convenient in marketing surveys as constant indices from one census to another. The 1970 Census of Population covers such population characteristics as age, sex, race, mother tongue, citizenship, education, families and their composition, employment status, place of work, occupation, and income.

2. *Census of Housing.* Made in conjunction with the Census of Population, this census enumerates types of structure, year built, equipment (for example, clothes washer or air conditioners), water source, sewage disposal, fuel used, rent paid, value, number of persons per room, occupancy and tenure, race of occupants, conditions of dwelling, size, and mortgage status. The 1970 census gives reports by city block for those cities with over 50,000 population.

3. *Census of Business.* This census was last taken in 1972 and is divided into three parts: retail trade; wholesale trade; and

selected services. The statistics cover total sales, number of employees, payrolls, and number of establishments for each principal type of business. The enumerations are made by state, county, metropolitan area, and city.

4. *Census of Manufacturers.* This census gives data on the number and size of establishments, the legal form of ownership, payrolls, manhours, sales by customer class, inventories, selected costs and book value of assets, capital expenditures, metal working operations, fuels and electric energy consumed, and value added by manufacturer. The census covers all establishments in over 430 manufacturing industries.

Write to the Government Printing Office, Washington, DC 20402, and ask for the *Bureau of Census Catalog* ($2.25 postpaid). It lists a potpourri of current reports you can order.

Primary Research

Secondary sources are invaluable for calculations that are based on broad statistics, but there are some things that secondary sources simply cannot provide. For example, a secondary source may be able to tell you how many tons of soap were produced last year, but it cannot tell you why Mrs. Johnson bought brand X instead of brand Y. To understand Mrs. Johnson's reasoning or to find out how many bars of brand X she bought this week, you have to ask her. When you ask the consumer directly, you are doing primary research.

How To Do Your Own Consumer Surveys. The key to successful marketing is learning why customers are (or are not) satisfied with what you sell. Remember, customers don't buy products, they buy satisfaction. If you hesitate to make decisions because buyers seem illogical and unpredictable, remember that their *actions would be logical if you knew their real needs.* Here are some research-it-yourself methods so you can get the kind of primary information you need without paying high prices for it:

1. *Interviews.* Use interviews when you have relatively complex questions you need answered, when the type of people you want to question are easy for an interviewer to meet, and when an interviewer's assessment of the respondent (e.g., his age, social class, or income) is important. Suppose you are a supermarket operator who wants to increase business. You must decide four things before you begin your interview research:

- *Who to ask.* If you feel your store is doing pretty well and you just want more of the same type of customer, you'll probably want to interview existing customers. But if you have a small slice of the market and want new customers, you face the larger task of researching consumers in general. You might do this by interviewing customers who shop at one or two of your main competitors. If you are a manufacturer, you must choose between asking immediate buyers (the distributors) and ultimate buyers (the consumers or end-users).

- *How to ask.* You should begin with a statement of why you are conducting the study (for example, to improve service). Be careful not to offend people. Open-ended questions are best, like "What line of goods do you normally buy?" rather than "Do you always buy the cheapest lines?" You should probably keep the total number of questions below thirty, and you shouldn't have more than ten items on a checklist. Accurate research only comes from a fairly large sample (over one hundred people) that is representative of all the people you wish to interview.

- *What to ask.* It is vital to define what you want to learn from your research. Typically, you will want to know the motives of the people who buy your product. For example, you'll want to know if attitudes depend on such buyer characteristics as income, sex, or social level. You may want to know how much television they watch or how long they've used your product. The motives of people who have just switched can also be very significant. Here are some useful questions to consider for our supermarket example: Which supermarket does the person regularly patronize? How long has he used it? Why did he first use it (e.g., advertising, location, friend recommended it). Why is it his regular store? You could show him a checklist of reasons to place in order of importance (e.g., prices, opening hours, quality of meat and dairy goods). What other supermarkets has he tried? What did he like or dislike about them? What is the range of age, income, and family size of the respondent? This information will help you define your market segment.

- *How to interpret the data.* It's best to look at answers as a percentage of people answering the question. Looking at answers within subgroups or segments is useful, too. With small numbers in the sample, only differences greater than 15 percentage points will mean much, and you should treat interview research as a broad guide only, to be used along with your intuition.

2. *Questionnaires.* There are two good uses for questionnaires that are generally less costly than interview research: when you want relatively simple answers from a large number of people or when you need answers from a small number of specialists who wouldn't have time to see an interviewer and who are scattered geographically. You can regard questionnaires as postal interviews and apply most of the rules given above. However, a big problem with questionnaires is that the rate of response is often quite low, and those who reply may not be typical.

3. *Panel tests.* For some products you can get useful data
by testing with a small panel of potential users. Ask them to
use the product and note their reactions to whatever features
they feel are important (appearance, ease of operation,
flavor, and so on). Ask them to guess the price. Two or three
panels of three to seven people each will often provide much
useful information. Sometimes you can recruit panel members from among your employees, their families, or customers you know well. However, because they may be biased
in your favor, it is usually better to use outsiders, if possible.

CHAPTER 12

THE MARKETING MIX

Having looked at how to get basic information on your market from primary and secondary sources, you're now in a better position to decide how to sell your product or service most effectively by using what is called the "marketing mix."

The marketing mix is the interplay of the four basic and interrelated elements of a marketing program, the four P's: product, price, promotion, and place. They will be examined, one at a time, but it is of primary importance that you realize that they are interdependent. A change in one usually brings on a change in the other elements. Proper orchestration of these elements is the key to developing a sound marketing program.

PRODUCT

The product you sell is the very heart of your business so you must be clear in your mind about what it is you are really selling. The best way to define your product is to define it from the point of view of the consumer. Suppose you sell lamps. Are you selling a necessity, i.e., a light producing device to prevent your customer from stumbling in the dark, or are you selling economic status symbols for your customer's living room?

The customer's perception (which you can control to a degree) determines the true nature of your product and you must be sensitive to his perception when you define your "product policy"—the degree of quality you will build into the product, its appearance, and its physical characteristics. But the needs of the marketplace often change, so in addition to defining your product (or service) as it exists now, you should periodically reassess the product to see if you need to update what you sell or reposition it in the marketplace.

Positioning Your Product
> "A rose by another name smells different."—Anon

Positioning a product is a matter of aiming it at a particular segment of a market. You promote your product with a different image to differentiate it from the competition. For example, there are many soaps on the market today, but they all seem to have a slightly different position. Lava is a tough soap; Camay is a gentle, feminine soap. Lux promises to make you look like a bathing movie star; Dial will allow you to get into a crowded elevator with confidence; and Tone will moisturize your skin. Each product occupies a different "position" and each appeals to a different segment of the market. You distinguish your product by promotion rather than by its inherent characteristics. While this concept is controversial (and some feel overrated), its skillful use has allowed an impressive number of relatively small companies to successfully outspecialize many industrial giants. To understand what positioning is all about, a look back in time will be helpful:

The 1950s was the *product* era. All you needed was a superior product and enough money to tell people about it. However, the late 1950s brought a technological revolution, and manufacturers found that as soon as a new product was introduced, a "new and improved" competitor followed immediately behind. So marketing strategies that stressed a product's superior attributes declined in effectiveness.

Next came the 1960s, the *image* era. Successful companies found that reputation and image could be more important in selling their product than specific product features. Classic examples of successful images are the Hathaway man, the Cadillac purchaser, or the Marlboro man. But just as the differences between products became confused in the consumer's mind in the 1950s, competing images soon became confused and ineffective as well.

The *positioning* era officially began in the 1970s when Avis boldly announced that it was only number two in the car rental industry. Prior to that time it was considered bad taste (and poor strategy) to mention competitive products. However, in desperation after thirteen straight years of losses, Avis took the chance and acknowledged that Hertz was ahead but stressed that "Avis tries harder." By admitting its shortcomings but stressing its strengths, Avis soon moved into the black.

The Need for a Position. It is estimated that today's average person receives well over two hundred commercial stimuli per day. As a defense mechanism against this volume of advertising, the human mind screens and rejects much of the information it receives. In general, it tends to filter out all information that does not match its prior knowledge. For example, when an advertisement says, "NCR means computers," the mind rejects it. IBM means computers; NCR means cash registers. For a competitor to somehow gain a foothold in this market, he has to relate to IBM's dominant position—for example, Honeywell's strategy of describing itself as "the other computer company." The attempt by RCA and GE to compete head-on with IBM was doomed to failure. When there is a dominant force in a business, a competitor is often far better off relating his product to the industry leader rather than trying to establish his own independent beachhead.

The Seven-Up theme is a good case in point. Colas are the dominant force in the soft drink industry. There's not much room left for competing brands. But no product is invincible—consider the "Un-Cola" theme for Seven-Up. This reverse twist may seem silly—until you take a closer look. "Wet and Wild" was fine for the image era, but the Un-Cola is more appropriate for the positioning era. Sales jumped 10% in the first year of the campaign. The brilliance of the theme can be understood when you realize that two out of three soft drinks consumed in this country are cola beverages. By linking itself to the dominant position of cola drinks and at the same time stressing its difference, Un-Cola firmly established its identity in the consumer's mind as an alternative to cola drinks (and hence most of its competition).

It is sometimes possible to undercut the competition by taking a niche that no one else wants. Probably the best example is Volkswagen's positioning against sleek, good-looking cars with its "ugly but reliable bug" theme. Like Avis, admitting to a shortcoming often stimulates a positive reaction. Another example is Smuckers—"with a name like Smuckers, it has to be good."

Most businessmen think their product (or service) is superior to their competitors' and promote it as such. However, the din from so many rivals all claiming to be the best only serves to confuse and make the customer skeptical. Rather than being drowned out by the competition, you may be able to reposition your product to fill a specific need other competitors don't emphasize. What is required is to forget the literal definition of your product and focus on what it *does* for the customer. You will probably discover numerous niches that can be both secure and profitable.

Positioning can be a powerful marketing tool. Although for clarity we've used well-known consumer products as examples, the same principles apply to any business. You don't necessarily have to crash head-on with a competitor to compete effectively. A slight shift in your product's position might make a dramatic difference in sales and profits.

How to Analyze Ideas for New Products

When existing products are reaching the maturity stage of their life cycles, you should be thinking of new products to introduce into your line. The chart beginning on page 164, "Factor and Subfactor Ratings for a New Product," illustrates some criteria with which you can analyze your ideas for new products and rank them in order of priority.

PRICING

Once you decide that a new product is viable you must still decide how much you are going to charge for it. Ford automobiles are good products and they have a definite share of the market, but they wouldn't sell at $20,000 each and Ford would collapse at $100 each. The optimal price for long term profits generally requires careful analysis.

Certainly, pricing strategy isn't just the province of huge corporations. Every business manager from a hardware dealer to a beauty parlor operator faces the problem of how to price his product or service. Of course, there are rules of thumb in every industry, and certainly there is always the old stand-by—charge what the market will bear. Pricing is one of the most important

FACTOR AND SUBFACTOR RATINGS FOR A NEW PRODUCT*

	Very good	Good	Average	Poor	Very poor
I. MARKETABILITY					
A. *Relation to present distribution channels*	Can reach major markets by distributing through present channels.	Can reach major markets by distributing mostly through present channels, partly through new channels.	Will have to distribute equally between new and present channels, in order to reach major markets.	Will have to distribute mostly through new channels in order to reach major markets.	Will have to distribute entirely through new channels in order to reach major markets.
B. *Relation to present product lines*	Complements a present line which needs more products to fill it.	Complements a present line that does not need, but can handle, another product.	Can be fitted into a present line.	Can be fitted into a present line but does not fit entirely.	Does not fit in with any present product line.
C. *Quality/price relationship*	Priced below all competing products of similar quality.	Priced below most competing products of similar quality.	Approximately the same price as competing products of similar quality.	Priced above many competing products of similar quality.	Priced above all competing products of similar quality.
D. *Number of sizes and grades*	Few staple sizes and grades.	Several sizes and grades, but customers will be satisfied with few staples.	Several sizes and grades, but can satisfy customer wants with small inventory of nonstaples.	Several sizes and grades, each of which will have to be stocked in equal amounts.	Many sizes and grades which will necessitate heavy inventories.
E. *Merchandisability*	Has product characteristics over and above those of competing products that lend themselves to the kind of promotion, advertising, and display that	Has promotable characteristics that will compare favorably with the characteristics of competing products.	Has promotable characteristics that are equal to those of other products.	Has a few characteristics that are promotable, but generally does not measure up to characteristics of competing products.	Has no characteristics at all that are equal to competitors' or that lend themselves to imaginative promotion.

	Should aid in sales of present products. (the given company does best.)	May help sales of present products; definitely will not be harmful to present sales.	Should have no effect on present sales.	May hinder present sales some; definitely will not aid present sales.	Will reduce sales of presently profitable products.
F. *Effects on sales of present products*	Should aid in sales of present products.	May help sales of present products; definitely will not be harmful to present sales.	Should have no effect on present sales.	May hinder present sales some; definitely will not aid present sales.	Will reduce sales of presently profitable products.
II. DURABILITY					
A. *Stability*	Basic product which can always expect to have uses.	Product which will have uses long enough to earn back initial investment, plus at least 10 years of additional profits.	Product which will have uses long enough to earn back initial investment, plus several (from 5 to 10) years of additional profits.	Product which will have uses long enough to earn back initial investment, plus 1 to 5 years of additional profits.	Product which will probably be obsolete in near future.
B. *Breadth of market*	A national market, a wide variety of consumers, and a potential foreign market.	A national market and a wide variety of consumers.	Either a national market or a wide variety of consumers.	A regional market and a restricted variety of consumers.	A specialized market in a small marketing area.
C. *Resistance to cyclical fluctuations*	Will sell readily in inflation or depression.	Effects of cyclical changes will be *moderate*, and will be felt *after* changes in economic outlook.	Sales will rise and fall with the economy.	Effects of cyclical changes will be *heavy*, and will be felt *before* changes in economic outlook.	Cyclical changes will cause extreme fluctuations in demand.
D. *Resistance to seasonal fluctuations*	Steady sales throughout the year.	Steady sales — except under unusual circumstances.	Seasonal fluctuations, but inventory and personnel problems can be absorbed.	Heavy seasonal fluctuations that will cause considerable inventory and personnel problems.	Severe seasonal fluctuations that will necessitate layoffs and heavy inventories.
E. *Exclusiveness of design*	Can be protected by a patent with no loopholes.	Can be patented, but the patent might be circumvented.	Cannot be patented, but has certain salient characteristics that cannot be copied very well.	Cannot be patented, and can be copied by larger, more knowledgeable companies.	Cannot be patented, and can be copied by anyone.

(continued)

165

FACTOR AND SUBFACTOR RATINGS FOR A NEW PRODUCT (Continued)

	Very good	Good	Average	Poor	Very poor
III. PRODUCTIVE ABILITY					
A. *Equipment necessary*	Can be produced with equipment that is presently idle.	Can be produced with present equipment, but production will have to be scheduled with other products.	Can be produced largely with present equipment, but the company will have to purchase some additional equipment.	Company will have to buy a good deal of new equipment, but some present equipment can be used.	Company will have to buy all new equipment.
B. *Production knowledge and personnel necessary*	Present knowledge and personnel will be able to produce new product.	With very few minor exceptions, present knowledge and personnel will be able to produce new product.	With some exceptions, present knowledge and personnel will be able to produce new product.	A ratio of approximately 50–50 will prevail between the needs for new knowledge and personnel and for present knowledge and personnel.	Mostly new knowledge and personnel are needed to produce the new product.
C. *Raw materials' availability*	Company can purchase raw materials from its best supplier(s) exclusively.	Company can purchase major portion of raw materials from its best supplier(s), and remainder from any one of a number of companies.	Company can purchase approximately half of raw materials from its best supplier(s), and other half from any one of a number of companies.	Company must purchase most of raw materials from any one of a number of companies other than its best supplier(s).	Company must purchase most or all of raw materials from a certain few companies other than its best supplier(s).
IV. GROWTH POTENTIAL					
A. *Place in market*	New type of product that will fill a need presently not being filled.	Product that will substantially improve on products presently on the market.	Product that will have certain new characteristics that will appeal to a substantial segment of the market.	Product that will have minor improvements over products presently on the market.	Product similar to those presently on the market and which adds nothing new.

B. *Expected competitive situation — value added*	Very high value added so as to substantially restrict number of competitors.	High enough value added so that, unless product is extremely well suited to other firms, they will not want to invest in additional facilities.	High enough value added so that, unless other companies are as strong in market as this firm, it will not be profitable for them to compete.	Lower value added so as to allow large, medium, and some smaller companies to compete.	Very low value added so that all companies can profitably enter market.
C. *Expected availability of end users*	Number of end users will increase substantially.	Number of end users will increase moderately.	Number of end users will increase slightly, if at all.	Number of end users will decrease moderately.	Number of end users will decrease substantially.

*From John T. O'Meara, Jr., "Selecting Profitable Products," *Harvard Business Review* January–February, 1961.

strategic decisions a business person can make, and if arbitrary criteria are used, there may be undesirable results. Here is how to approach this difficult problem.

Cost structure of the business

Before an effective pricing strategy can be devised, every manager must know his firm's cost structure. One useful way to determine a cost structure is to classify costs as variable or fixed. Variable costs change almost in direct relation to changes in sales or output. These include direct labor costs and most materials. Fixed costs, such as rent or administrative expenses, tend to remain constant, regardless of output.

Once the costs have been segregated, a breakeven chart (see p. 67) can be prepared and the impact of various selling prices on profits can be easily calculated. Firms with high fixed costs and low variable costs, such as the airlines or oil refineries, are highly *volume sensitive*. A 1% change in an airline's passenger load factor, for example, can make a 25% difference in overall profits. Therefore, whenever demand falls off, these types of firms are willing to cut prices just to keep their planes (or pipelines) full.

Firms with low fixed costs and high variable costs, such as supermarkets, guard service companies, or fuel oil distributors, are highly *price sensitive*. For these types of firms, a 1% change in price can make a 10% or 20% change in their profits. As you can see, it is very important to understand your cost structure and how your company's profits vary at different sales volumes.

The Nature of the Product

The type of product you are trying to sell also influences the price you will charge. For example, a man who makes steel cable may stockpile his product for a while and wait for an improved market, but a man who produces avocados cannot. The avocado farmer may charge a stiff price when the season opens and his particular produce is a novelty. Later, he must settle for what he can on the matter of price when his product threatens to rot in the sun. There is also a difference between products that are easy to imitate and those that are virtually unique. If your product is easily imitated, you will have only a short introductory stage in which you can extract large profit margins. If it is difficult to copy, you may have more latitude in setting your price. These kinds of considerations must be recognized as you look for the right pricing strategy.

Price Life Cycle

You will recall that products have a predictable life cycle. Well, prices go through a life cycle too. In a product's introductory stage, the price is usually higher because there is less competition and the consumer is often willing to pay more for a novelty. For example, when the digital wristwatches or the hand calculators first came on the market, they were novelties and sold for a high price. Later, when the product had reached maturity and many companies were manufacturing them, the prices fell drastically. The same item (or an improved model for that matter) now sells at a significantly lower price. The point taken here is that you should be sure you know where a given product is in its life cycle when you determine the price.

Competitive situation

Competition obviously affects a pricing strategy. The question, however, is why some products have high profit margins while others have low profit margins. The answer hinges on the "differentiation" of the product. If the product is nondifferentiated (i.e., all products are similar), the market is generally highly competitive and profit margins are low. In some cases, the prices even have to be supported by government subsidies. Some examples of nondifferentiated products would be gasoline, lumber, and agricultural products, such as milk and eggs.

At the other extreme are highly differentiated products, such as Polaroid film and cameras, the latest style of clothing, and many drugs. In fact, the drug companies are in a desperate battle to try to prevent their differentiated (and high profit margin) name-brand drugs from becoming generic or nondifferentiated.

If you have a product that tends to be difficult to differentiate, try to reposition it away from immediate competition. One classic solution is to rename it (Excedrin instead of aspirin); another is to emphasize some particular feature (the little nose bridge, rather than what Ocusol does for your eyes). You should be able to think of many ways to differentiate your product to lessen competition and successfully allow its profit margin to be maintained or even raised.

Without a degree of differentiation between your product and its competitors you lose a good deal of price flexibility. Without differentiation you dare not raise your price for fear of being abandoned by the consumer. You're locked into what is called an elastic market.

Price Elasticity

Price elasticity of demand is a high sounding economic term used to describe a very simple concept—how sales of an item respond to a small change in price. If a big price increase results in only a small decrease in unit sales, the market is said to be "inelastic." Conversely, where sales drop significantly as a result of a price increase, the market is termed "elastic."

Clearly, the object of raising prices is to increase dollar sales volume and profits by holding unit sales relatively stable at the increased price. But you must avoid a price raise that will drop sales volume below the point where the price rise compensates for the loss. Two illustrations may be helpful here.

The Ajax Jewelry Company increased its retail prices by 20% across the board and discovered that unit sales only dropped by 1% as a direct result. Actual sales revenue and income increased substantially. Here, the market was relatively inelastic, the customers were not price sensitive, and the small loss in unit sales was more than offset by the 99% of stable business paying 20% more for the same items.

The Morning Fresh Bakery, Inc., raised bread prices by 5% only to discover that unit sales rapidly dropped off by 30%. The result was obviously disastrous. The market was highly elastic, and the consumer was clearly price sensitive.

If you belong to an industry association, consult them. They may have made recent elasticity studies on your products or product lines that could be helpful. In any case, before finalizing a price adjustment, you should consider the following points in relation to your particular product and business and the price sensitivity of your particular customers.

- How strong is the competition? Would a price hike put you out on a limb or bring you more in line with competitors' price levels?
- Is your product intended for a luxury, high-price market (not generally sensitive to price) or intended for a standard product or "commodity" market (highly price sensitive)?
- Do you compete primarily on the basis of price or on other marketing aspects, such as promotion, advertising, location, reputation, innovation, or quality?
- Is there anything distinctive or unique about your product that reduces competition or the importance of price competition?

Legal Considerations

Naturally, there are limits to the ways in which you may seek to increase profit margins through pricing. For example, you can't sell you product to Smith's Department Store down the block for $5.00 and then turn around and sell the same product to Jones' Department store around the corner for $7.00. This kind of price discrimination is out because the Robinson-Patman Act forbids the selling of the same product at different prices to different buyers who compete with each other, except in certain limited situations. Although the law is gradually changing, many states still have fair trade laws that limit pricing flexibility. Finally, according to the Sherman Act, no producers or sellers may conspire to maintain or fix prices except in fair trade situations.

Strategic goals for the firm

Every firm should have specific short-term and long-term goals. To become quickly established in the market, for example, one company may choose to charge extremely low prices in the hopes that large sales volume plus gradual price rises over a period of time will be the most profitable long-term strategy. Other companies may choose to charge high prices initially and "milk" the product. Over a period of time they might gradually lower prices. Study the "Pricing Strategy Checklist" on the following pages and choose the strategy most appropriate for your product or service.

PROMOTION

You have now got a feel for what it is you want to sell and at what price you want to sell it, but how are you going to promote the product? In the broadest sense, promotion is the communication between the producer and the consumer.

PRICING STRATEGY CHECK LIST

STRATEGY/OBJECTIVE	WHEN GENERALLY USED	PROCEDURE	ADVANTAGES	DISADVANTAGES
Skim the cream of the market for high short-term profit (without regard for long term)	No comparable competitive products Dramatically improved product or new product innovation Large number of buyers Little danger of competitor entry due to high price, patent control, high R&D costs, high promotion costs, and/or raw material control Uncertain costs Short life cycle Inelastic demand	Determine preliminary customer reaction. Charge premium price for product distinctiveness in short run, without considering long-run position. Some buyers will pay more because of higher present value to them. Then, gradually reduce price to tap successive market levels (i.e., skimming the cream of a market that is relatively insensitive to price. Finally, tap more sensitive segments).	Cushions against cost over-runs Requires smaller investment Provides funds quickly to cover new product promotions, and initial development costs Limits demand until production is ready Suggests higher value in buyer's mind Emphasizes value rather than cost as a guide to pricing Allows initial feeling out of demand before full-scale production	Assumes that a market exists at high price Results in ill will in early buyers when price is reduced Attracts competition Likely to underestimate ability of competitors to copy product Discourages some buyers from trying the product (connotes high profits) May cause long-run inefficiencies
Slide down demand curve to become established as efficient manufacturer at optimum volume before competitors become entrenched, without sacrificing long-term objectives (e.g., obtain	By established companies launching innovations Durable goods Slight barriers to entry by competition Medium life span	Tap successive layers of demand at highest prices possible. Then slide down demand curve faster and further than forced to in view of potential competition. Rate of price change is slow enough to add significant volume at each successive	Emphasizes value rather than cost as a guide to pricing Provides rapid return on investment Provides slight cushion against cost overruns	Requires broad knowledge of competitive product developments Requires much documented experience Results in ill will in early buyers when price is reduced Discourages some buyers from buying at initial high price

(continued)

PRICING STRATEGY CHECK LIST (Continued)

STRATEGY/OBJECTIVE	WHEN GENERALLY USED	PROCEDURE	ADVANTAGES	DISADVANTAGES
satisfactory share of market)		price level, but fast enough to prevent large competitor from becoming established on a low-cost volume basis.		
Compete at the market price to encourage others to produce and promote the product to stimulate primary demand	Several comparable products Growing market Medium to long product life span Known costs	Start with final price and work back to cost. Use customer surveys and studies of competitors' prices to approximate final price. Deduct selling margins. Adjust product, production, and selling methods to sell at this price and still make necessary profit margins.	Requires less analysis and research Existing market requires less promotion efforts Causes no ill will in early buyers since price will not be lowered soon	Limited flexibility Limited cushion for error Slower recovery of investment Must rely on other differentiating tools
Market penetration to stimulate market growth and capture and hold a satisfactory market share at a profit through low prices. Become strongly entrenched to generate profits over long term.	Long product life span Mass market Easy market entry Demand is highly sensitive to price Unit costs of production and distribution decrease rapidly as quantity of output increases	Charge low prices to create a mass market resulting in cost advantages derived from larger volume. Look at lower end of demand curve to get price low enough to attract a large customer base. Also review past and competitor prices.	Discourages actual and potential competitor inroads because of apparent low profit margins Emphasizes value more than cost in pricing Allows maximum exposure and penetration in minimum time	Assumes volume is always responsive to price reductions, which isn't always true Relies somewhat on glamour and psychological pricing, which doesn't always work May create more business than production capacity available Requires significant investment

Strategy	Characteristics	Method	Advantages	Disadvantages
Newer product	No "elite" market willing to pay premium for newest and best		May maximize long-term profits if competition is minimized	Small errors often result in large losses
Preemptive pricing, to keep competitors out of market or eliminate existing ones	Used more often in consumer markets. Manufacturers may use this approach on one or two products, with other prices meeting or higher than those of competitors	Price at low levels so that market is unattractive to possible competitors. Set prices as close as possible to total unit cost. As increased volume allows lower cost, pass advantage to buyers via lower prices. If costs decline rapidly with increases in volume, can start price below cost. (Can use price approaching variable costs.)	Discourages potential competitors because of apparent low profit margins. Limits competitive activity and expensive requirements to meet them	Must offer other policies which permit lower price (limited credit, delivery, or promotions). Small errors can result in large losses. Long-term payback period

Portions of chart adopted from The Marketing Problem Solver by Cochrane Chase and Company, Inc., Newport Beach, California.

First you must decide what it is you intend to tell the consumer about your product (i.e., different, less expensive, better). Second, you must decide how to get the message across and then finally you might want to find out if the promotion worked by checking results through surveys and other established means.

Most businessmen are experts when it comes to *producing* the goods, but companies fail to reach their full potential when it comes to the *marketing* side—selling the goods.

Why is this so? Well, one major reason is that production is "in here" while marketing is "out there." It's relatively easy to control the production process. You can literally see what's gone wrong. Marketing is another matter entirely. As a result, few companies are selective or systematic in their marketing approach—they tend to see many markets and want to sell to all of them—often with disastrous results!

Differentiation

As discussed earlier one of the first steps in understanding your competitive situation and formulating an effective marketing strategy is to determine how your product is differentiated. By this we mean does the consumer see your brand as significantly *different* from other similar or competing products. For example, at one extreme, milk, meat, or eggs are prime examples of almost completely nondifferentiated products. Eggs are eggs. They come bigger and smaller, but they're still eggs. Thanks to strict government regulations and cooperative chickens, one carton of eggs is about the same as another. Many other commodity products, such as lumber, metal, and gasoline also fall in this nondifferentiated category.

It is possible, however, to take a relatively nondifferentiated product and make it differentiated (in the consumer's mind) through massive doses of advertising. "All aspirin is *not* alike. Bayer is different—it's purer". Hundreds of millions of dollars are spent trying to make us think Brand X really is different (and therefore better) than Brand Y. You may be able through skillful advertising to differentiate your product if it tends to be nondifferentiated.

At the opposite extreme, we have products that are highly differentiated. Good examples would be Rolls Royce or Cadillac automobiles, the skills of a specialized brain surgeon, or a rare French perfume.

Push or Pull

Once you have a rough idea where your product falls on the differentiation spectrum, we are ready to consider the next question—would it be more efficient to "push" or "pull" your product through the distribution channels? By push we mean using a direct marketing method to literally push your product toward the customer. Examples of this would be all forms of direct sales, such as door-to-door salesmen, insurance agents, securities brokers, or manufacturer's representatives. By pull we mean advertising or other forms of promotion to literally pull the customer to your product. Examples of this would be promotional flyers, television advertising, leaflets, or brochures.

Generally speaking, the pull approach is more efficient than push simply because of the high cost associated with using direct salesmen. As a result, companies who use push are constantly seeking ways to supplement it with pull. For example, rather than have an agent "cold call" from door-to-door (push), insurance companies constantly advertise and send out promotion pieces (pull), often offering free gifts, just to find who might be interested in buying insurance. The agent then has a better chance of success when he calls on a customer who has already expressed some interest.

The final decision of whether to use push or pull is dependent on two additional factors: product and pricing.

Certain products must be pushed or pulled. A complicated and specialized machine requiring a skilled salesman cannot be sold on television (pull). Likewise, it would be economically impossible to sell Band-Aids from door to door (push). Consequently, before deciding on your marketing strategy, you must consider the product itself. Must it, because of its very nature, be sold one way or the other? Also, what is the price margin of the product? If you don't have a high dollar contribution from the item, it will not financially support the services of a direct sales force.

Thus far, we have considered the nature of the product, its profit margin, and differentiation. If you sell a relatively nondifferentiated, low margin product, would you advertise it heavily or not?

The answer is no. It would be wasteful and perhaps disastrous financially. Let's go back to our egg example. Since eggs are basically a commodity, it would do little good to advertise because the consumer wouldn't take much notice. But, even more important, there is extreme price competition in selling a commodity simply because the consumer won't pay more to get a different type of egg (because there aren't different types). As a result, there is relatively little profit margin to allow for advertising.

But when you do have a product that merits some advertising, be sure you are clear about what you would like the advertising to do for you. It isn't good enough to say that you would like your advertising dollar to increase profits, bring more people into the store, or convey what good guys you are in the community. You want to be more specific.

What Advertising Can Do

1. *Raise Immediate Sales*
- By announcing special promotions like sales.
- Dispensing coupons that may be redeemed with purchases.
- By urging people to come into your store.
- By alerting people who might be interested in distributing your product.

2. *Increase Consumer Awareness of Your Company through:*
- Telling people where you are located.
- Extolling special product features.
- Listing new products.
- Publicizing special changes like price or packaging.

- Emphasizing the company's service record.
- Demonstrating the proper use of the product.
- Comparison with competing products.

Advertising is designed to convey these messages. Just be sure you're communicating the information you want and to the right people. In order to further specify what you want your advertising dollar to accomplish, you might say that you would like to see 40% more children aware of new speed wheels bicycle tires within the next nine months. This is what you're after. After the advertising campaign you could use a survey to see if you accomplished your goal.

Media Choice

Assuming you know what you want to say and to whom you want to say it, you are then faced with the choice of medium. Of all the media available, which one suits your market best? To help you evaluate the various media, here is a list of their various characteristics.

1. *Newspapers*
- Eight out of ten Americans read them.
- They lend a factual air to your advertisement due to their overall news.
- They are local and allow you to hit specific geographic targets.
- You can change your ads easily or submit them on relatively short notice.
- They are good for dispensing discount coupons.

2. *Magazines*
- They allow you to reach select audiences because they are often specialty magazines.
- Can be even more select with special geographic or demographic editions.
- High quality of printing from your advertisement.
- They are read more carefully and are kept around the house longer than most newspapers.

3. *Television*
- Has enormous mass coverage. Over 95% of Americans own a TV
- Filmed ads may have greater impact and are good for demonstrating the operation of your product.
- Production and air time costs can be high.
- Not easy to change ads and rarely can ads be done on short notice.

4. *Radio*
- Since most stations have special listeners, you can reach specialty groups.
- Messages can be changed on short notice.
- Relatively low cost advertising.

5. *Trade Publications*

- The main advantage of this print medium is that you can reach a very special market (i.e., golfers, Teamsters, or restauranteurs.)
- Good for industrial advertising.

6. *Outdoor Advertising*

- Best used as a supplement to advertising in other media.
- Good technique for reminding consumer of your product but not so good for explanations.
- Obviously good for ground transportation user market.

7. *Direct Mail*

- This gives you maximum selectivity of audience since each ad is mailed to an individual.
- It is generally costly in relation to other means.
- It has low prestige because of popular displeasure with junk mail.

This list does not pretend to give you definitive answers about the advantages and disadvantages of each major medium. Talk to an advertising agency for further details.

PLACE (CHANNELS OF DISTRIBUTION)

The fourth key element of the marketing mix is "place", i.e. where your product has to go to get to market. This element of channels of distribution is a vital part of the overall marketing mix. Clearly, even if you have the world's greatest product on sale at a low price and you're spending millions to promote it, you'll be out of business unless you can get that product to the consumer in an efficient manner.

What is a Distribution Channel?

A channel of distribution is a link between the manufacturer and the consumer. It is the means by which the product gets to the buyer. Often the product is channeled through middlemen (wholesalers, retailers, and so on) and these middlemen take over control of, or title to, the product. It is this transfer of control or ownership—more than the physical transfer from a plant to a warehouse—that defines a distribution channel.

Preliminary Considerations

Before you choose a distribution system, be clear in your mind about these three things:

1. What exactly must be done to get your product to your buyer? (Transportation, storage, speed, etc.)
2. What channels of distribution can do this for you and how well can each one do it?

3. How much will each distribution system cost in the long run? Be sure to calculate long run costs because it isn't often easy to switch distribution methods. Check with your legal advisor and accountant before taking action on a distribution plan.

Basic Alternatives

Since the selling of industrial goods can differ significantly from the selling of consumer goods, we will divide our discussion of channels between the two types of goods. However, this distinction is not always so clear in the real world.

Industrial   Industrial goods are those goods that are manufactured to aid in the production of other goods or services. For example, turbine generators, belts, machine lathes, and kilns are industrial goods. Industrial firms usually use one or the following distribution methods:

- *Direct Sales.* Company employees sell directly to the buyer. The producer must have a sales staff.
- *Manufacturer's Representatives* (agents). These agents are independent of the company and may supply many different products within a defined market.
- *Distributors.* Generally, a distributor is an independent company offering a whole line of related products.

Which Method is Best?   Generally, situations that would call for the use of a *direct* sales force are:

- Established firms with funds to support sales staff.
- The product demands a high level of technical skill in sales effort, installation, or maintenance.

THE THREE CLASSIC SYSTEMS OF INDUSTRIAL DISTRIBUTION

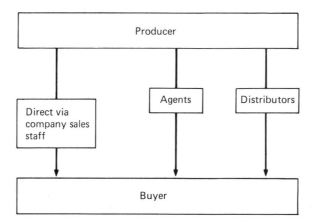

- Sales territories are already stable. The market is already established.

Conditions usually associated with the use of *manufacturer's representatives* are:

- Company lacks funds for its own sales force.
- Company is limited to a single product line.
- Unknown company
- Regular sales force is otherwise occupied.

Distributors are necessary in industrial sales when:

- Customers are accustomed to dealing with distributors.
- Little known company needs the use of the reputation of an established distributor.
- New territory
- Company cannot meet the needs of the buyer without the distributor.

A chart summarizing the advantages and disadvantages of the three basic industrial channels of distribution is found on page 180.

Non-Industrial Distribution   The three principal means of nonindustrial distribution are: direct to consumer; manufacturer to retailer to consumer; and manufacturer to wholesaler to retailer to consumer.

1. *Direct.* If you intend to sell directly to the end user of your product, you may need to set up, for example, a mail order

THREE PRINCIPAL MEANS OF NONINDUSTRIAL DISTRIBUTION

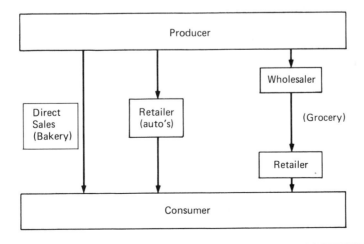

ADVANTAGES AND DISADVANTAGES OF THE THREE BASIC INDUSTRIAL CHANNELS OF DISTRIBUTION

	Advantages	*Disadvantages*
Direct Sales	• Your own salesmen sell only your product. • Good control of prices. • You control level of service to your buyers. • Good feedback from your market. • Possibility of giving discounts for dealing direct.	• High cost of retaining a sales force. • More effort needed to open new territories. • Takes time to build sales force and train personnel. • Must add specialists for delivery, credit management, etc.
Manufacturer's Representatives	• Lowers cost of sales personnel. • Lowers time spent on training and recruiting salesmen. • Rep is already established in his territory. • Good price control.	• May represent other as well. • May purposely restrict your contact with your buyer. • Minimum feedback on your market. • Less control over sales end.
Distributors	• Little cost incurred until sales are made. • Localized warehousing of stock. • Already has an established sales force. • Can handle complaints • Good knowledge of local market.	• Less enthusiasm about selling your product. • May have to grant special discounts to keep him happy. • Less control of pricing. • Insulates you from your customers & the end-user. • Increased advertising obligations.

system that will ensure that your product goes directly from you to the consumer's home. Or else you set up a door-to-door sales force ("Avon calling") and deal one-to-one with your consumer. This cuts out the middleman and offers good customer contact, but it only works for certain products. It does not, for example, lend itself to selling sofas for obvious reasons.

2. *Retailers.* If your own salesmen will not be dealing directly with the consumer, you may find that your consumer is best served by a retailer. Retailing is the most common distribution channel used in the US today. But before you pick the needed retailer(s), consider the following:

• Do you want a discount house, a department store or a high class specialty house?

- Will your retailers be ten miles away or one thousand?
- Will your product sell best in a city, suburb, or a rural area?
- Would you prefer to have your retailers located near schools, shopping centers, office buildings, sports arenas, or some other specific area?
- How many stores will be selling your product in a given area? Even if you can envision the perfect retail conditions for your product, you still have to find out which of them are possible and which are not possible. Finding the right retail distribution channel may boil down to finding the most advantageous compromise on a number of factors.

3. *Wholesalers.* Once you establish the appropriate retail conditions for your product, you must decide if you want to deal with retailers through a wholesaler. Now, to recapitulate, the idea behind your distribution strategy is to meet the needs of the consumer most effectively. If retailers seem to do it best, fine, but now how can you keep the retailers interested in selling your product? In choosing a wholesaler, the overall question is, can he meet the needs of your retailer(s)?

Type of Distribution

1. *Intensive Distribution.* Do you want your product to be sold in every store possible? Dropping your product in every available store front window is called "intensive distribution." This kind of distribution works well for low priced, high volume items like fingernail clippers, razor blades, and chewing gum. Generally, the profit margin on intense distribution items is small.
2. *Selective Distribution.* In this case you elect to have your product available only in certain "select" outlets. This system of distribution usually works best for products of high perceived value. In other words, the customer will go out of his way to buy them. The following must be considered in the area of selective distribution: store location; reputation of the store; clientele; and other products on sale in the store.

   Selective distribution works well when the customer needs more than the simple exchange of cash for goods. He selects the store and the product because of: wide selection; informed and reassuring sales staff; credit arrangements; delivery capacity; and warranty and repair service.

   Examples of product that should be distributed on a selective basis are music equipment, dresses, and cameras.
3. *Exclusive Distribution.* Sometimes high priced and high quality products are distributed "exclusively" to one store in an area. Often these products have a small market (for example, Rolls Royce cars, pianos, or imported crystal) but

the buyers will go to considerable trouble to make their purchases.

To meet the needs of your retailers, the wholesaler must: be close enough to the retailer to allow for ease and speed of resupply; have acceptable space for inventory; a good reputation for reliability; and have reasonable prices.

Generally, the number of wholesalers will depend on your production capabilities and your type of distribution effort. If you intend an intensive distribution, you will need more wholesalers to supply all your retailers. Similarly, a selective and exclusive distribution effort will require fewer wholesalers.

What Needs are Being Met by Your Distribution Channels?

Your very first consideration in the area of distribution should be for the end user of your product, the person (or company) who will finally lay out the cash. Most consumers, be they individuals or companies, will only buy your product under certain conditions, even if they want it and can use it to their advantage. The middleman you want is the one who can best answer these consumer questions.

What does the buyer want?
- Is the price right?
- Can it be obtained easily?
- Is there a guarantee?
- Can it be fixed if it breaks?
- Is this the right product for me?

What does the middleman want?
- A good profit margin on his resale.
- Reliability from the producer.
- Some promotion of the product.
- Easy system of supply.

What do you want from the middleman?
- Good coverage of your potential market.
- Assumption of maximum distribution responsibilities.
- Good service to the buyer.
- Good information about buyer satisfaction, market conditions, and so on.

Criteria for Choosing Individual Outlets.

Assuming you already know the number, type, and location of the outlets you will need for your product, there still remains the problem of picking the specific retailers or wholesalers you wish to do business with. Here are some points you should consider in choosing your individual outlets.

- Credit. Can the outlet pay for what you sell them? Most

businessmen agree that this is the most important consideration in choosing your specific channels of distribution.

- Service available to buyers.
- Facilities (especially important for retailers).
- Percent of market outlet can cover.
- Quality of management.
- Level of inventory carried.
- Degree of adherance to manufacturer's suggested price.
- Skill and quality of sales force.
- Other products carried that might influence the sale of your products.

Your Relationship With Your Distributor

Your business relationship with your distributor can be based on a hand-shake or on a carefully worded written contract. It can be as detailed or as general and liberal as you like, but it should include some understanding of these four areas:

- Territorial rights
- Specific obligations of each party
- Terms of sales
- Price and discount structure

Of course, you should consult your attorney before finalizing any written agreements with your channels of distribution.

CHAPTER 13

LEGAL FUNDAMENTALS

ANNUAL LEGAL CHECKLIST

You may become so preoccupied with the specific details of running your business that you put off touching base with your attorney. To be sure the legal affairs of your business are in order, you should check these points at least once a year:

1. *Corporate housekeeping*
   - *State of incorporation.* State corporation laws are constantly changing, and the business climate of another state may be better. Also check the tax advantages of Delaware's new General Corporate Law.
   - *Purposes and bylaws.* There may be changes in your business that necessitate a revision of your corporate charter and its bylaws. You may wish to change your fiscal year, indemnify officers and directors, or call stockholders meetings out of state. In a close company you may wish to operate by consent rather than by holding director's meetings.
   - *Capitalization.* Stock splits, acquisitions, need for new capital, and stock options are several factors that could result in a need to revise your capital structure. Consider issuing a preferred stock instead of common stock or straight debt. If lenders desire equity participation, debentures with warrants can offer tax advantages over convertibles.
   - *Records and meetings.* Minutes of shareholders and directors meetings can have important tax and legal consequences. Be sure they are in order, and be sure that an annual meeting is held and that all officers and directors are duly elected.
2. *Tax law changes*
   - *Legal organizational form.* Is your present form of doing business appropriate?

- *Personal holding company.* If more than 50% of the stock of your corporation is held by five or fewer individuals and 60% or more of corporate income is from passive sources, such as rents, dividends, or interest, you could be classified as a personal holding company and be taxed at a 70% rate on all undistributed income.
- *Sale-leaseback.* If you are contemplating a personal sale-leaseback with your corporation, watch that you don't receive unexpected dividends, ordinary income instead of capital gains, and that losses are not disallowed. Any transaction between a corporation and its stockholders must always be closely checked for the "form versus substance" rule and tax technicalities. Sections 1239 and 267, among others, of the Internal Revenue Code must be consulted.

3. *Employment laws and requirements.* Review your employment policies to be sure they comply with federal and state statutes concerning wages, working conditions, hours, and nondiscrimination. Be sure any covenants not to compete are properly drawn and valid.

4. *State laws.* Be sure you are validly registered in all states where you do business or certain contracts may be invalid. Check to see if doing business under a "multistate tax compact" could save you money. Compile a list and review the expiration dates of all local licenses and permits.

5. *Liability exposure*

- *Directors and officers.* Review indemnification agreements and their enforceability in view of recent developments. See if "D&O" insurance is needed.
- *Corporate.* If you are considering a private placement, check that the provisions of Rule 144 and other securities regulations are met. Also recent changes in product liability laws should be reviewed.

6. *Benefits and compensation.* Review stock option, bonus, pension, and profit-sharing plans to be sure they conform to the law. All pension plans must be amended to conform to the recently enacted pension law. Be sure that the coverage and dollar limits of your insurance are adequate. Also check that salaries to stockholder-employees are reasonable to avoid double taxation.

7. *Continuity of business*

- *Buy-sell agreements.* Check if stockholders should enter either a buy-sell or redemption agreement. Be sure that any formula valuation is up to date.
- *Control.* If appropriate, review shareholder control devices, such as restrictions on stock transfers, voting trusts, and deadlock provisions.

ANTITRUST LAWS AND THE AVERAGE BUSINESS

Does antitrust legislation have any relevance to the average business? You probably feel that it doesn't if your company is not a huge conglomerate and doesn't engage in monopolistic practices. But you may be surprised to learn that you probably come in contact with antitrust questions more often than you realize—not that your business will ever violate the statutes, but there are numerous situations where unfair pressure can be placed on you by a competitor or supplier. A basic knowledge of what is—and is not—allowed is essential to recognizing an unlawful situation and taking action to protect your company. Know your legal rights and obligations to avoid difficulty and to protect yourself from unfair practices.

The case of enforced price levels

Almost every business manager is familiar with the following situation: John Jones runs a small company and occasionally drops the prices on certain items to generate extra business. Several of his competitors have complained that he is hurting their sales, but Jones continues this practice. Finally, his major supplier tells him, "John, we've been doing business for a long time, but if you don't quit cutting prices, I'm afraid we'll have to drop your account. Too many of our other customers have complained. I'm sure you understand our position." Jones is obviously perplexed and concerned, but he also resents the intrusion into running his business. In fact, he even suspects that it is illegal. Is it? Let's take a look at the basic antitrust statutes.

The antitrust laws in perspective

- *The Sherman Act.* In broadest terms, this 1890 statute forbids any contract, combination, or conspiracy that restrains trade. This includes "horizontal" arrangements (i.e., between competitors) such as fixing prices or allocating territories and customers and "vertical" relationships (i.e., between a seller and his customer). Except for fair trade laws in certain states which involve only brand name products, any resale price maintenance agreement is illegal. Although a supplier may *suggest* resale prices, it is illegal to solicit promises or demand that the prices be maintained.
- *The Clayton Act and Robinson-Patman Amendment.* In 1914 the Clayton Act was passed to restrict tie-ins and exclusive dealing arrangements as well as to clarify the legality of certain types of mergers and acquisitions. A portion of the Clayton Act concerning pricing was later amended in 1936 by the Robinson-Patman Amendment. These laws attempt to insure that costs of supplies are the same for every competitor at a given distribution level, regardless of his size or affiliation. In other words, General Motors must

normally sell its AC spark plugs at the same price to a small gasoline station as to a large discounter or to one of its own dealers.

- *The Federal Trade Commission Act.* This act created the Federal Trade Commission and gave it exceptionally broad authority to stop all unfair competitive methods and deceptive trade practices. The Department of Justice usually enforces the Clayton Act, which can involve criminal penalties, and the FTC enforces the Clayton Act, the Robinson-Patman Amendment, and the FTC Act, which involve civil penalties.

Specific illegal antitrust actions

- *Price fixing.* Horizontal price fixing is *always* illegal. Vertical price maintenance is illegal unless condoned by state fair trade law.
- *Noncompetition.* It is illegal for competitors to apportion customers or markets or to agree to limit production.
- *Exclusive dealing.* A supplier may not require a customer to agree not to buy from a competitive supplier.
- *Tie-in sales.* It is illegal for a supplier to sell one product on the basis that other products must also be bought from the same supplier.
- *Price discrimination.* It is illegal to sell the same product at different prices to two buyers who compete with each other *unless* lower prices to one can be justified in terms of lower costs of delivery or changing market conditions.

John Jones' problem

As you can see, the action by John Jones' supplier is definitely illegal. If the supplier carries through with the threat to drop his account and if Jones can prove that he lost money as a result, he can sue for treble damages. However, a brief letter from Jones' attorney citing the violation would probably straighten out the situation very quickly. But what if deliveries from the supplier mysteriously become delayed? Again, Jones can sue for treble damages if he can prove injury and that the delays are a reprisal for price cutting.

BASIC SECURITIES LAWS

Certain common business activities are covered by various federal and state laws concerning securities. If you sell stock, issue debentures, or even buy out another shareholder's interest, various federal and state securities laws come into play.

The economic disaster of the early 1930s prompted Congress to take a close look at the securities industry. Its study, which uncovered numerous abuses, resulted in the Securities Act of 1933. This act requires adequate disclosure of securities sold to the public to insure that the purchaser has full knowledge to determine for himself how good (or bad) the investment might be. One year later, the Securities Exchange Act of 1934 set up the Securities and Exchange Commission (SEC). In addition to these federal statutes, every state has now enacted its own securities laws, the so-called "blue sky" laws.

Specific aspects of securities laws important to business managers

The securities laws are highly complex, but there are certain aspects of particular importance to business managers that can be broken down into these categories:

Antifraud. Suppose that you make a deal to buy out your partner knowing that you can sell the business to a third party at a handsome gain. This could be a violation of the antifraud provisions of federal and blue sky statutes. Specifically, Rule 10b of the 1934 act requires disclosure of any material information before the purchase or sale of any stock—even of a closely-held company!

Exempted securities. In order to be sold, most securities have to be registered with the SEC—a complicated, expensive process. But there are three important exceptions:

1. *Private offering exemption.* The basic intent of Congress in the 1933 act was to protect the general public from unscrupulous operators. Congress did not intend to encumber legitimate fund-raising transactions involving investors who could decide for themselves whether or not an investment has merit. Recently, the SEC adopted Rule 146 which helps to define the private offering exemption. It provides that a company can sell its securities without registering with the SEC if the following tests are met:

   - *Type of investors.* Only investors who are experienced and sophisticated in business matters and who can bear the economic risk of loss may be approached to purchase the securities.
   - *Manner of offering.* All transactions must be by "direct communications." The purchaser must be able to ask questions about the securities and receive answers from the offerer.
   - *Number of purchasers.* There can be no more than thirty-five purchasers. If one person buys more than $150,000 of the securities, he will not be included in the thirty-five.

2. *Intrastate exemption.* Congress did not intend to regulate local financing when securities were sold entirely within

one state. The mechanics of the intrastate exemption are governed by SEC Rule 147 which stipulates the following:

- *Doing business within the state.* To qualify for an exemption, the issuer must be organized and have its principal office in the state of the offering, must have at least 80% of its assets and revenues within the state, and must use at least 80% of the net proceeds of the offering for operations in the state.
- *Residency of purchasers.* All purchasers must be resident in the state of the offering, and for nine months any resale of the securities may be made only to other state residents. Any violation of this provision, however slight, nullifies the entire exemption and opens the door to liability for failure to register.

3. *Small offering exemption.* According to SEC Rule 240, an offering of up to $100,000 of corporate stock may be made without registration as long as certain conditions are met:

- *Manner of offering.* No securities may be offered through advertising or general solicitation, and no agent may be paid to find prospective buyers.
- *Number of stockholders.* Immediately before and after the sale, there can be no more than 100 owners of the stock. Also, resale of the stock is restricted.

Regulation A. Congress did not want the 1933 act to unduly hamper smaller businesses, so the SEC adopted Regulation A which permits a company to raise up to $500,000 without going through the full SEC registration process. This allows a small company to go public and have a traded stock without much of the elaborate documentation and paperwork of a regular public offering.

Remember that the antifraud provisions *always* apply whether or not the offering is exempt from SEC registration. Never approach unsophisticated investors to buy your stock unless you have an intrastate or Rule 240 exemption. Always retain a competent attorney to advise you.

WHAT YOU SHOULD KNOW ABOUT PRODUCT LIABILITY

Product liability is the liability that a manufacturer and seller have to the user of a product for personal injury or property damage resulting from use of the goods. The evolution and application of product liability law has changed dramatically in the last decade and today represents one of the least understood and potentially most severe of all business liabilities.

Historical Context

Early business transactions usually involved buyers and sellers dealing face to face and bargaining for advantage. As a result, the concept of *caveat emptor* (buyer beware) developed where the buyer purchased at his own peril and the seller rejected responsibility for his product.

As social attitudes changed, manufacturers began to be held responsible for injury caused by goods they sold. Today, whether you are a manufacturer, processor, distributor, or merchant, you now face unprecedented questions of product liability.

Sources of Liability

There are several ways in which a seller can become liable for the goods he sells:

- *Statute.* Where any statutes regulating the production or sale of a product can be shown to have been violated, the offender can be held legally accountable for any injury caused. A well-known statute would be the Pure Food and Drug Act.
- *Negligence.* The seller can be held liable for injuries if there was failure to properly design, inspect, test, disclose known defects or risks, or properly instruct in the use of a product. Automobile manufacturers and dealers have faced numerous suits on grounds of negligence.
- *Misrepresentation.* If the seller advertises a product and makes misrepresentations concerning its character or quality, he can be held liable for any injury caused as a result of the misrepresentation.

Warranty Liability

In addition to the above sources of liability, there is a fourth broad category known as "warranty" liability. In the broadest sense, a warranty is the legal assumption of responsibility by the seller for the quality, character, and suitability of the goods sold. There are two main types of warranties—express and implied.

- *Express warranty.* Any oral or written representation on the part of the seller, which is accepted by the buyer and relied upon by him in purchasing, becomes a part of the sales contract and is known as an "express" warranty. For example, such statements as "100% pure" or "safe for indoor use" constitute legally binding express warranties by the seller. Descriptions, such as diagrams, pictures, blueprints, and technical specifications also constitute warranties where they form a part of the basis of the sales transactions.
- *Implied warranties.* Two warranties are imposed by the Uniform Commercial Code, irrespective of the seller's inten-

tions and regardless of the fact that he has made no promises
or representations concerning the product.

   Merchantability. This warranty is the implied assurance of every seller that his product is of reasonable
   quality and fit for the usual and *ordinary* purpose
   for which the goods are intended.
   Particular purpose. This warranty arises when a
   product is used for a special purpose, and the buyer
   relies upon the manufacturer's skill and judgment in
   furnishing or selecting the product.

Disclaimers

A seller can attempt to restrict or eliminate warranty liabilities, but strict
rules apply to all disclaimers. It is not sufficient to state that "no warranties
are made, either express or implied." Conspicuous and precise language must
be used. Even with proper language and format, however, the courts often
look askance at warranty limitations, especially in cases of injuries to users.

Strict Liability

This is the most controversial and recently developed theory of recovery in
product liability. In many states anyone who sells a product in a defective
condition (including such things as improper packaging, warnings, or directions) or one which is considered "unreasonably dangerous" is liable for any
physical harm caused to the ultimate user or to his property. The theory is
that the manufacturer is better able than the consumer to bear any burden
of injury. *Strict liability applies even though the manufacturer exercised all
possible care in the production, and no warranties were made.* Lack of
privity or warranty disclaimers are not available as defenses.

What Should You Do?

- Make sure products conform to all trade and legal standards.
- Have potentially dangerous products safety tested by an
  independent agency.
- Identify and label all dangerous parts of a product.
- Check that all instructions and manuals give clear directions
  and warnings.
- Review advertising and sales literature for unintended warranties.
- Consider product liability insurance and "hold harmless"
  agreements between yourself and others in your chain of
  distribution.

In 1960 there were fewer than 50,000 product liability suits in the courts.
By 1970 the number had jumped to 500,000 and is soon expected to pass
1,000,000. For more information, contact the Commerce Clearing House,

Inc., 4025 W. Peterson Ave., Chicago, IL 60646. Ask for booklet No. 4992, *Consumer Product Safety Act—Law and Explanation* ($2.50). Also, contact the US Consumer Product Safety Commission, 5401 Westwood Ave., Bethesda, MD 20207, or one of its many regional offices.

HOW TO AVOID TROUBLE WITH THE ANTIDISCRIMINATION LAWS

Business people often unknowingly engage in discriminatory practices. Court interpretations have gone considerably beyond the letter of the original Civil Rights Act, and many states have new, stiff employment practice laws. To avoid a compliance suit and possible penalties, review each of these potential problems.

1. *Employment application.* The law states that you cannot discriminate on the basis of race, color, religion, national origin, sex, or age. Here is what you can—and cannot—ask on the employment application and interview:

    -   *Name.* You may, of course, ask an applicant's name including maiden name, but you may not ask an applicant's original name if changed with court approval.
    -   *Native tongue.* You cannot ask the applicant's native language, but you may ask if the applicant speaks any foreign languages.
    -   *Nationality.* You may ask if the applicant is a US citizen. However, you cannot ask whether he or she is native born or a naturalized citizen or the applicant's country of origin.
    -   *Age.* You may not require the applicant to state his or her age or submit a birth certificate.
    -   *Race and religion.* You may not ask an applicant's religion or require the applicant to provide a photograph before hiring.
    -   *Clubs and military service.* You may ask an applicant only about those clubs and organizations that would not reveal race, color, creed, sex, or country of origin. You may ask about former military service as long as the questions are fairly general.

2. *Testing.* A second broad area of difficulty concerns preemployment and prepromotion tests. The overall requirement as stated by the Equal Employment Opportunity Commission (EEOC) and the Supreme Court is that any employment test *must predict potential job performance* and success. You may wish to review the criteria issued by the American

Psychological Association, 1200 17th Street NW, Washington, DC 20026.

3. *Personnel policies.* Although your application blank and testing procedures may be nondiscriminatory, certain personnel policies could cause you trouble. Here are the most common problems and how to avoid them.

- *Age.* It is illegal to run a help wanted ad stipulating that a job is open to a young lady or a man "age twenty-two to thirty," and you cannot refuse to hire an older person just because he may have only a few years of potential service remaining. However, you may require an applicant to pass a medical examination to be sure he or she is fit for the job.

- *Sex.* Both male and female employees must receive equal pay if they do equal work, and policies such as double pay on Sundays and holidays must apply across the board. Be sure that equal pay includes benefits. The law says you cannot refuse to hire a woman just because most women wouldn't like or couldn't do the job. You must consider the individual applicant on his or her merits alone. However, you can stipulate that certain job-related standards be met, such as education, weight, or height, even if these standards exclude most members of one sex.

State laws and formal reporting requirements

Even though you comply with a state requirement, the EEOC may rule that you violate a federal law. This is especially true concerning equal rights for women where the laws of some states have not kept up with recent amendments to the federal Civil Rights Act. To be safe, check both the state and federal requirements. If your business does work for the federal government or works on a government subcontract, you may have to make a formal nondiscrimination report if: (1) your contract is over $50,000 and (2) you have fifty or more employees. For further information, contact the US Department of Labor, Office of Federal Contract Compliance, 711 14th Street NW, Washington, DC 20210.

If you run into a problem

If you find that one of your practices is discriminatory, correct it immediately and announce the change to employees. Keep a record of all changes you make to document your intent to comply if questioned by the EEOC. If you are faced with a suit and the plaintiff has a strong case, try to settle out of court as rapidly as possible. Go to court as a last resort and retain a specialist in these matters to represent you. Discrimination suits are often emotional, and a substantial judgment could be awarded if you lose. Finally, encourage minority employees to apply for higher jobs.

HOW TO SAVE UNDER THE
WAGE HOUR LAW

In most companies there are busy periods when employees must work more than forty hours per week and other slack times when a full work week is not required. When faced with this situation, business managers would prefer to even out these hours or give compensatory time off, but the Fair Labor Standards ("Wage Hour") Act is very specific—all work over forty hours per week must be paid at time-and-a-half rates. However, certain employees on *salary* can be exempt from overtime provisions of the law. The key to saving payroll dollars is to know which employees can be switched to salary and whether a switch would be profitable. Most employees appreciate the change because of the security of earning a fixed amount.

Employees may be exempted from the overtime provisions of the law if they: (1) are classified as executives, administrators, or professionals, (2) perform certain duties, and (3) are paid a minimum salary. The requirements are outlined in the chart of guidelines and all must be met to receive the exemption.

How to decide whether to change an employee's status

By examining the chart above, you may discover that several of your employees could be salaried and exempt from the Wage Hour Law. Or you may find that with a slight shift in duties they will qualify. The question is whether it is worth raising their salaries to the minimum required for exemption. Here's how to examine each employee's status:

- Estimate the amount of overtime you will probably have to pay the employee over the next year.
- Compare this figure with the increase in wages that you would have to pay as salary to bring the employee up to the required level for exemption.

GUIDELINE TO EXEMPTION UNDER WAGE-HOUR ACT

REQUIREMENTS	EXECUTIVE	ADMINISTRATIVE	PROFESSIONAL
Minimum salary per week	$155	$155	$170
Types of duties	1. Managerial. 2. Directs the work of two of more employees. 3. May hire and fire, or recommendations carry weight. 4. Exercises discretionary powers.	1. Primary duty is office or non-manual work directly related to general business operations. 2. Exercises discretion and judgment. 3. Directly assists owner, executive, or other administrative employees, or performs technical work requiring special training, experience, or knowledge.	1. Primary duty requires advanced knowledge customarily acquired by advanced study. 2. Work requires discretion and judgment. 3. Work is intellectual, varied, and results not standardized.
Restrictions	May not work more than 20% of time (40% if retail or service establishment) on tasks not directly related to executive duties. (Does not apply if paid $200 or more per week, in sole charge of an independent establishment, or own 20% or more interest in business.)	May not work more than 20% of time (40% if retail or service establishment) on tasks not directly related to executive duties. (Does not apply if paid $200 or more per week.)	May not work more than 20% of time on tasks not directly related to professional duties. (Does not apply if paid $200 or more per week.)

Besides the economics of whether it makes sense to change an employee's status, you should also consider the possible effect of any special increase on the other employees and customary wage differentials you may wish to maintain.

How salary is handled

An employee is considered salaried if he receives a certain amount each pay period which is not subject to reduction based on the number of hours worked. In other words, a salaried employee must receive a full wage for any week he or she works. But there are important exceptions to this rule. If an exempt employee takes off for a full day on personal business, you are not required to pay for that day. If an exempt employee is sick for a full week, you don't have to pay unless you have a sick pay plan. You only pay if *part* of a week is worked.

Because you pay a salary does not mean you cannot also use a commission, percent of profit, or other similar method of payment as long as the salary portion of the compensation meets the minimum requirements. For example, if you pay a store manager a weekly salary of $140 plus 3% of sales, the salary would not meet the requirement of $155 per week, even if the manager actually makes much more than that as a result of the bonus scheme.

Conclusion

For more information, obtain a copy of the booklet, *Executive, Administrative, Professional, and Outside Salesmen Exemptions under the Fair Labor Standards Act* from the Wage Hour Division of your local Department of Labor. Or write the Government Printing Office, Washington, DC 20402 and ask for Wage Hour Publication 1363 (Rev.). If you question whether or not an employee is exempt, protect yourself from the cost of back pay and overtime by obtaining a written ruling. Send full particulars to the Department of Labor, Wage Hour Division, 14th and Constitution Avenue NW, Washington, DC 20210.

ANNUAL MEETING CHECKLIST

Most companies, whether large or small, are required to hold an annual meeting to report to stockholders. Here is a checklist you should consult before your next stockholder meeting.

Preparation for the Meeting

While some of these points may not be applicable to your particular situation, you should consider:

- *Agenda*
  Prepare all items to be discussed and resolutions to be ratified, including the proposed slate of directors.

- *Stockholders of Record*
  Prepare a list of stockholders. Usually, the record date of
  the stockholder list cannot be more than sixty days prior
  to the annual meeting.
- *Notice of Meeting*
  Generally, the directors must call the meeting if a time and
  date are not listed in the bylaws or certificate of incorpora-
  tion. Notify all stockholders of the date, time, and place.
- *Proxy Statement*
  Prepare all proxies and proxy statements and distribute to
  stockholders in accordance with notice provisions.
- *Annual Report*
  Usually, the annual report is presented at the time of the
  annual meeting.
- *Corporate Records*
  Gather all documents (bylaws, certificate of incorporation,
  financial records, etc.) necessary to answer any stockholder's
  inquiry. In addition, it is usually advisable to have the company's counsel and accountant present to answer any questions that may arise.

Actions Requiring Stockholder Approval

The annual meeting gives stockholders the opportunity to ratify certain
actions requiring their approval. While the exact requirements vary by state,
here is a list of corporate undertakings generally requiring such approval:

- *Corporate Charter and Bylaws*
  Almost all states require stockholder approval to amend the
  certificate of incorporation. Unless otherwise provided,
  similar approval is also needed for changes in the bylaws.
- *No-Par Value Shares*
  No-par value shares may be issued in most states. However,
  stockholder approval is often required to set a price for such
  shares and to allocate the proceeds between the "paid in
  capital" and the "surplus" accounts.
- *Stock Options*
  Favorable stock options may normally be given to *outsiders*
  in the normal course of business, without specific stockholders approval. (An example would be an equity kicker
  in connection with a debt issue.) When the option is to *existing* officers or employees, however, many states require
  stockholders to approve the details to prevent inside dealings
  and corporate abuse.
- *Officers and Directors*
  In some states, loans may be made by the corporation to
  officers and directors only when approved by the stockholders. Also, many states require stockholder approval before the corporation can grant indemnification to officers
  and directors for mismanagement, conflict of interest, etc.

- *Merger or Disposal of Major Assets*
  Most states require stockholder approval for such actions, often by more than a simple majority vote. In addition, certain large acquisitions must be approved in some states.
- *Guarantees*
  Normally, if the corporation makes any guarantee "not in the furtherance of normal business" (such as guaranteeing a debt of a director or officer), stockholder approval is required.
- *Elections*
  The directors must generally be elected by the stockholders. In addition, ratification of accountants is usually considered a stockholder prerogative.

After the Meeting

- *Minutes*
  Prepare minutes for corporate records and stockholders.
- *Press Releases*
  Usually distributed after the meeting.
- *Amendments*
  Follow up on filing all appropriate amendments (contracts, bylaws, charter, etc.) with the appropriate authorities.

APPRAISAL RIGHTS

Many businessmen do not realize that the laws of every state provide that whenever a corporation makes a major change in its business, nonassenting shareholders have the right to sell their shares back to the corporation. If a price cannot be agreed upon, the dissenters can generally insist on an objective appraisal of the fair market value of the shares — hence the term, appraisal rights.

The theory behind appraisal rights is that a person buys stock in a company with the anticipation that it will be operated as it was in the past. If the company subsequently decides to make major changes in its operation and organization, shareholders who disagree with the changes should have the right to recover their money. The exact definition of which changes are major varies widely by state. However, any action involving a merger, consolidation, sale of a major asset, dissolution, or in some cases, change in corporate charter, generally involves appraisal rights.

How do appraisal rights work?

Because the purchase of their shares may impose a severe burden on the corporation, the nonassenting stockholders must adhere to the letter of the law in exercising their right to sell. For example, most state statutes provide that the dissenter must notify the company prior to the meeting when the proposed change will be voted on. As a result, the corporation is aware of its repurchase obligation in the event that the proposed change is adopted. After the dissent has been filed, but before the shares are finally sold, the stockholder normally has no further right to vote on corporate affairs. Most statutes also provide that if the corporation subsequently decides to abandon the proposed action, the dissenters lose their right to "put" their stock to the company.

What should the businessman do?

Appraisal rights are something most executives don't think about until confronted by a block of stock that will have to be purchased if a proposed change is approved. While minority shareholders may lack the votes to affect company policy, they can be a formidable force in certain important situations. As a first step, every businessman should ask his attorney to summarize the appraisal rights laws of his state of incorporation. And equally important, you should be aware that even though you may own only a small percentage of some other company, you have the right to sell your shares at fair market value if its management makes certain major changes that you feel are unwarranted.

BUY-SELL AGREEMENTS

Most close companies want to avoid shares falling into unwanted hands. To prevent this, participants in any new venture generally have an agreement that sets forth how a shareholder's stock will be handled should he die or wish to depart the business. This is commonly called a buy-sell agreement— it states how the shares will be bought and sold if certain events happen. Here are the major points to understand:

Redemption vs. Cross-Purchase

The first decision when setting up a buy-sell arrangement is whether the shares should be purchased either by the corporation (called a "redemption" agreement) or the remaining shareholders ("cross-purchase" agreement). To make this important decision, these factors should be considered:

1. *Source of Funds.* Under redemption agreement the shares are purchased with *corporate* money, whereas cross-purchase involves the use of the shareholders' personal funds. In certain states a corporation may not be allowed to purchase shares under a redemption agreement if it does not have sufficient capital surplus at the time.
2. *Cost Basis.* When the corporation redeems the stock of a deceased shareholder, the cost basis of the remaining shareholders' stock remains the same while its value increases. Hence, a latent capital gain liability is built up. With cross-purchase the basis of the stock is stepped up to the purchase price, and no tax liability is incurred.

3. *Control.* With redemption the proportionate interests of each remaining shareholder remain the same. With cross-purchase the number of shares that each survivor can or must buy can be varied as desired.

4. *Attribution.* When only a *portion* of a deceased shareholder's stock is redeemed by the corporation, the proceeds may be treated as a taxable dividend to the estate instead of a purchase. With cross-purchase this is no problem since the corporation is not a party to the transaction.

Funding

To assure that enough money will be available to purchase the shares, buy-sell agreements are often funded by life insurance. If a redemption agreement is used, the corporation takes out a policy on each shareholder and names itself as beneficiary. With cross-purchase each shareholder carries life insurance on every other shareholder. With more than three or four major shareholders, cross-purchase can become unwieldy to fund with insurance.

Setting the Price

This is the final trouble spot—how to set the price at which the shares will be bought and sold. There are four alternatives:

- *Fixed Price.* With this most common method, a fixed price is set and periodically changed to reflect the current status of the business.
- *Appraisal.* Price of the stock is set by independent appraisal at the time of sale.
- *Earnings.* A multiple of net profits is set that determines the share price.
- *Book Value.* The price is based on some multiple of the net worth of the company.

THE BASICS OF BANKRUPTCY

History

Bankruptcy has its roots in the law of the Roman Empire and has been a part of English jurisprudence since 1542. Laws relating to bankruptcy have been enacted or amended in the United States after every major economic depression. The current statute was originally enacted in 1938 and had its last major revision in 1952. The statute provides various methods to accomplish three things: relieve debtors of their debts entirely; postpone the time debtors have to pay creditors; and protect some rights of creditors.

Proceedings

Bankruptcy proceedings are based on federal laws and therefore conducted in federal courts. Of the two general types of bankruptcy, "voluntary" (instigated by the debtor) is usually called "Chapter XI" bankruptcy, and "involuntary" (instigated at request of creditors) is known as "Chapter X." The Roman numerals refer to the particular sections of the Bankruptcy Act.

To initiate bankruptcy is a relatively simple procedure. A petition is filed with the local federal court on standard forms and the schedules must be sworn to under oath. If filed by the debtor (voluntary), it must contain four items:

1. List of creditors, secured and unsecured.
2. List of property claimed to be "exempt."
3. Statement of affairs of the bankrupt.
4. List of assets.

Involuntary petitions filed by creditors seek to have the *court* adjudge the debtor bankrupt. In particular, the petition must allege that the debtor committed at least one of the following "acts of bankruptcy" within the past four months:

1. Attempted to sell, hide, or remove any property with intent to defraud creditors.
2. Made a preferential payment to a particular creditor while insolvent.
3. Allowed, while insolvent, any creditor to obtain a lien on his property and didn't discharge it within thirty days or five days before any sale of his property.
4. Made a general assignment for benefit of creditors.
5. Appointed a receiver to administer property and debts.
6. Admitted in writing inability to pay debts and willingness to be judged bankrupt.

Referee in Bankruptcy

Because of the large volume of cases, bankruptcies are generally conducted by an officer of the court called a "referee." The referee acts for the court; while subject to review, his powers are, for all intents and purposes, those of the court.

Judgement of Bankruptcy

After the debtor is judged bankrupt, the procedure is the same whether the petition was voluntary or involuntary. The referee notifies each creditor of the judgement, the date of filing claims, and the date of the first meeting of the creditors with the debtor. If it appears to the referee that it is necessary to control the debtor's property prior to the first meeting, he will appoint a "receiver" to take charge of the assets and run the debtor's business, if necessary.

Trustee in Bankruptcy

At the first meeting, a "trustee" is elected by a majority in number and amount of the claims. The trustee, under supervision of the court, then disposes of all nonexempt property for the benefit of the creditors.

Who May File for Bankruptcy

Any person, partnership, or corporation may file a voluntary bankruptcy, except railroads, banks, insurance companies, municipalities, and savings and loan associations. Farmers, wage earners who make less than $1,500 per year, and nonbusiness corporations may not be forced into involuntary bankruptcy by creditors.

Importance to the Businessman

Too often the first notice that a businessman has that a certain debtor may be in trouble is when notified by the court of bankruptcy proceedings. At the time of notice it is important that the businessman determine his "provable claim" and whether he is entitled to any "dividend" (payment by trustee to creditors). Otherwise, his claim may be counted as "dischargeable" and nothing will be received.

Provable Claims

To qualify as a provable claim, it must be filed with the court within six months of the date first set by the referee for the first meeting of creditors. Most such claims are for ordinary trade credit or instruments in writing such as contracts or rental agreements.

Nondischargeable Claims

Certain claims cannot be discharged in bankruptcy, such as taxes due any governmental body, claim by employees under employment contracts, debts created by fraud, and wages earned within three months of filing the bankruptcy petition.

Priority of Claims

The first priority of claims is to secured creditors who collect their debts to the extent of the security interest they hold. Note, however, that unsecured creditors are last on the list of persons to be paid. They don't get their money until the attorney and receiver fees, taxes, and court costs have been paid. In short, they get what's left, if anything.

Summary

Tens of thousands of bankruptcies occur each year, and it is inevitable that every businessman will eventually confront the terminology, procedure, and priority of claims of a bankruptcy proceeding.

HOW TO AVOID LOSSES IN CHAPTER XI BANKRUPTCY

Imagine that you recently sold several thousands of dollars' worth of merchandise on account. Today you learn that the debtor has filed for bankruptcy. What steps should you take? The situation is not far-fetched—it happens every day and often when it can least be afforded.

What is Chapter XI bankruptcy?

There are fourteen chapters to the Bankruptcy Act. Some deal with railroads, agricultural reorganizations, and Maritime Commission liens. The one of most interest to the average business manager, however, is Chapter XI, which deals in "corporate reorganizations." Here the *debtor* petitions the court to protect him from creditors and allow him to stay in business until a plan of settlement can be worked out with creditors. Strictly speaking, therefore, Chapter XI is not a true bankruptcy proceeding because the business is not liquidated. In fact, the person or corporation seeking court relief is called the "debtor in possession" (of the business) instead of a "bankrupt."

What to do upon receiving notice of a debtor's bankruptcy

Once you learn of a debtor's bankruptcy under Chapter XI, the first step is to form a "creditors committee." This committee will elect officers to represent it and will eventually be recognized by the court as the bargaining agent for all creditors. One of the first documents this committee will issue to all creditors is a "proof of claim" form, which is a standard form showing the obligations owed the creditor and requesting power of attorney to represent the creditor before the court. *You must file a proof of claim form within the allocated time, or you will forfeit later rights to any settlement.*

Should you extend further credit?

Since the debtor in Chapter XI continues to do business, it is likely that you will be asked to extend further credit. You should not do so unless you ascertain that the debtor in possession has obtained a court order allowing him to stay in business and deal on credit terms with outsiders such as yourself. If he has such an order, your new credit extension will rank as an "administrative expense" in terms of payment priority—second only to any taxes due. Check with the creditors committee and proceed with caution in these circumstances.

The "plan of arrangement"

It is incumbent upon the debtor to propose a settlement arrangement and have it accepted by a majority in terms of number and dollar amount of creditors who have filed proofs of claim. If a suitable arrangement cannot be reached, the debtor can be judged a bankrupt, and a trustee will be appointed by the court to liquidate the assets. As you can see, therefore, the decision of the creditors must be whether they stand to get more by accepting the debtor's proposed plan of settlement (sometimes 5¢ on the dollar) or by having the business liquidated.

Confirmation of the plan of arrangement

Once the debtor and creditors acting through their creditors committee agree on a settlement, the Chapter XI proceeding is ended by the court which signs approval to the plan. All unsecured debts, other than those settled in the plan of arrangement, and any tax obligations are wiped off the debtor's books. He is free to continue his business with no harrassment from old creditors as long as he meets his obligations under the plan of settlement.

How to minimize losses in a Chapter XI

1. *Good offense is best defense.* Keep close watch on all delinquent accounts. Bankruptcies don't just happen—they are caused.
2. *Obtain a list of creditors.* If you learn that a major account has filed for bankruptcy, immediately contact the debtor or federal court where the proceeding was filed to obtain a full list of creditors.
3. *Form a committee.* Contact the other major creditors and form an informal creditors committee. Appoint an attorney to represent you as a committee.
4. *Proof of claim.* Be sure all proof of claim forms are correct and promptly filed.
5. *Work together.* One of the toughest jobs is to get major creditors to work collectively. Together you must agree whether to accept a proposed settlement or to ask that the business be liquidated. No plan of settlement will be fully equitable to all parties, but the court cannot confirm a plan unless it is approved by the majority of creditors (and dollar claims).

HOW TO MAINTAIN CONTROL OF YOUR COMPANY

Most businessmen associate 51 percent stock ownership with "control" of a company. As a successful business grows, however, major amounts of equity capital must sometimes be raised with the result that the original founders are often diluted below 51 percent. As shown in this article, this need be no cause for alarm. There are numerous ways to exercise rock-solid control of a company with substantially less than majority stock ownership. It does require, however, careful and deliberate planning.

Two situations affect corporate control that every businessman should recognize: sale of new stock by the *company;* and sale by a *stockholder* of stock already issued.

In the former case, the company has several options since new stock being issued can be restricted to the extent allowed by statute. In the latter case, however, where the stock has already been sold, unless the company exercised its prerogative to restrict the stock in some way at the time of sale, there is little the company can later say about the disposition of the stock.

Hence, it is vital to plan *before* shares are sold. Otherwise, you may literally lose control of your destiny.

Sale of New Stock by the Company

As mentioned, here you have quite a bit of latitude to protect yourself. Long before you might fall below 51% ownership of the common shares, here are several alternatives you should consider:

- *Different Classes of Stock*
  By far the simplest and most popular method is to segregate the classes of stock. For example, certain stock may be sold as "nonvoting" shares, while you keep control of the majority of voting stock. Another possibility is to designate the shares as Class A, Class B, and so on, with each class having the right to elect a certain number of directors. If you control the Class A stock, you take care to have Class A entitled to elect the majority of directors.
- *Voting Agreements*
  Although you must be mindful of applicable state statutes, it is often possible to sell stock with the stipulation that the new shareholders agree to certain conditions, such as voting only for certain directors. In other cases the company can require an "irrevocable proxy" from new shareholders and have it so legended on the face of the share certificates.
- *Staggered Elections*
  One very popular control technique is to amend the bylaws to require that the election of directors be staggered over time. This obviates the threat of a takeover, since only a limited number of directors may be elected at any one time.
- *Veto Power*
  Although it might stifle certain corporate actions, many states will allow bylaws requiring all fundamental corporate acts to be unanimous. In effect, even as a minority shareholding director, you would still have veto power over any undesired changes.

Sale by Shareholders

The second broad area of concern regarding corporate control is what happens to shares *after* they are issued. Most owners of somewhat closely held firms do not want shares to be freely transferable for two main reasons:

- To avoid purchase of shares by certain individuals or groups (such as competitors) who might grant them certain rights (such as inspecting corporate records).
- To insure that the new shareholders and present owners have compatible interests (for example, outside shareholders might wish low salaries and high dividends as opposed to a policy

of high salaries, maximum depreciation rates, and low dividends by shareholders who are also members of management).

There are a number of ways to impose restrictions on transfer of securities. Here are the main ones:

- *Right of First Refusal*
  The corporation or any of its officers and directors may be given refusal rights on all shares available for sale. This method is generally the simplest and most popular way to prevent shares from falling into undesirable hands.
- *Restricted Transferees*
  The stock may be restricted so that it can be sold only to certain persons or classes of individuals, such as family, back to the corporation or other employees.
- *Option to Buy Out*
  Upon certain events (such as the death or incapacity of a shareholder), the corporation, officers, directors, or other shareholders may exercise an option to buy out the shares in question.

Legal Note

Two points should be observed:

- It is difficult to generalize concerning corporate control because the statutes of each state vary widely in this area. We have tried to give you some guidelines, but, of course, you should check specifics with your attorney.
- Some measures restricting control may invalidate a Sub S election. Remember, Sub S corporations can have only one class of stock outstanding.

ANNUAL REPORT CHECKLIST

Almost every business has some outside investors. For some companies, they are the shareholders who own part of the equity of the business. Other companies, even if they are 100% owned by management, also have interested "investors"—usually the local commercial bank. But whoever your investors are, they can be instrumental to growth and sometimes even to survival. Keep them informed at least once a year of the following points via an informal chat with your banker or a written report to stockholders.

1. *Business activity*
   - *Products and/or services.* Describe each in as much detail as possible and try to include photographs or samples. Note

how the products and/or services have changed over the past year.

- *Organization.* Illustrate how the company is organized. List where subsidiaries or divisions operate and what they produce. Also, note major properties owned and important lease arrangements.
- *Success factors.* What does it take to be successful in your business—production expertise, marketing abilities, ability to motivate people, or some other special competence? Without releasing confidential information, discuss the keys to success and how you plan to improve your company's capabilities.

2. *Management.* Note who runs the firm. Name each officer and director and list his background, age, length of service, outside relationships, if any, and duties in the firm.

3. *Financial.* The financial highlights should always include an easy-to-read, one-page summary. Use charts or graphs to make trends easier to interpret. Always compare present results with past performance, if possible. When practical, statements should be audited. Be sure to address the following:

- *Sales and profits.* Show absolute figures and percent of change over past few years.
- *Retained earnings.* Show what proportion of profits is retained in the business and what part is paid as dividends.
- *Accounting conventions.* Discuss depreciation, capitalization, bad debt write-offs, and other financial policies that can significantly affect performance.

4. *Marketing*

- *Pricing.* Discuss the impact of inflation on pricing policies. Have higher product prices resulted in customer resistance and loss of sales?
- *Advertising.* Show how the various media (TV, radio, newspapers, direct mail, etc.) are being used for promotion. Discuss their effectiveness and your future plans.
- *Distribution.* Describe how your products and/or services are delivered to the consumer. Have there been changes? Are you investigating more efficient distribution methods?

5. *Employees.* Discuss the number of employees, their efficiency, morale, and the situation concerning a union. In particular, list:

- *Employee plans.* Briefly outline any pension, stock option, or profit-sharing plans the company has.
- *Health and safety.* What has been the effect of OSHA requirements? Has the business been inspected? Were there any violations? What is being done to remedy the situation?

6. *Future prospects and objectives.* Future goals should seem aggressive, yet they must be credible. If possible, show last

year's projections and how well (or poorly) they were met. Address such important points as:

- Expected sales and earnings.
- New products to be developed and marketed.
- Growth in number of employees and size of facilities.
- Expected market share and position in the industry.
- Pending legal proceedings that may materially affect the company.

Final notes

Always discuss the bad with the good. Rosy forecasts alone can only damage your credibility. When possible, show how *outside* factors in the local and national economy have affected your business. Finally, always disclose as much as possible without jeopardizing your competitive situation. The more your investors can understand the business and its problems and prospects, the more they will be able to assist you.

CORPORATE DIRECTOR'S LIABILITY CHECKLIST

If you are now a director, or you are considering becoming a director of a corporation, know your responsibilities. Ignorance of the law could prove disastrous.

Don't Confuse Your Loyalties

Corporations are creatures of the state. As a director, you have a fiduciary responsibility *not* as an agent for the stockholders as commonly supposed but to the corporation as an *entity* (and to the state that sanctioned it).

Ultra Vires Acts

To insure that you do not participate in any acts beyond the corporation's power (ultra vires acts) for which you could be personally responsible, consult with your attorney concerning applicable state statutes. In addition, check the certificate of incorporation and the bylaws of the corporation to be sure you understand your rights and responsibilities. In particular, check these points:

- *Dividends.* In most states you can legally pay a dividend only after certain conditions are met. Be sure to check the statutes.
- *Compensation.* If possible, all matters of compensation where the board may benefit (such as salary, bonus, pension, profit sharing plans, and stock options) should be ratified by the majority of shareholders. As long as you adhere to reasonable guidelines, you should incur no liability.
- *Employees.* Directors can be personally liable if they indiscriminately fire any employees who have contracts, such as

an officer with a management contract or certain union workers.

- *Taxes.* A critical item. If you are a director as well as a "responsible officer," you are *personally* liable for any payroll deductions either not withheld or used for any other purpose. You may be personally liable for a 100% penalty because you have *no discretion* to use such funds for corporate purposes.

- *Annual Reports.* Even if you are the sole stockholder, you must still file an annual report in most states. Not doing so can involve personal liability.

- *Signature.* If you have signature authority, always sign the name of the corporation, then the word "by", and put your name and title. If you leave out the word "by", you may have *personally* bound yourself.

Corporate Opportunity Doctrine

- *Conflict of Interest.* If there is any possibility that you might personally profit from a corporate action to which you are a party, make full disclosure and get the facts into the record. Then make sure that the matter was supported by a sufficient vote of the disinterested directors. Also, be sure the bylaws contain an "exculpatory" clause permitting such transactions.

- *Inside Information.* According to a recent court ruling, inside information belongs to the *corporation*, not to its officers or directors. Remember your fiduciary responsibilities to all shareholders, and there will be no problems.

Outside Dealings

- *Personal Loans to the Corporation.* Although usury laws do not apply in many states, you should take care that the interest rate charged is considered reasonable by the stockholders.

- *Borrowing from the Corporation.* May be hazardous. In the event of default, you may be personally liable if you voted funds for a loan to a fellow director.

Don't Be a Dummy Director

- *"See no evil . . .".* It used to be if you saw no evil, you couldn't be held responsible. No more. If you accept the responsibility of being a director, you may be personally liable for corporate acts, even if you were absent from a director's meeting. Don't lend your good name to a corporation as director unless you plan to actually participate in corporate affairs.

- *Professional Advice.* Always insist on qualified outside advice to insure "due care" whenever you feel a professional opinion is needed.
- *Dissent.* If you object to a corporate action, your dissent should be carefully noted in the corporate minutes. To minimize your liability, you should continue to exert influence on the corporation to change its course.

EMPLOYEE VS. INDEPENDENT CONTRACTOR

Many businesspeople are fed up with the ever rising costs of employee benefits, taxes, and so on and have considered the possibility of firing certain employees and hiring them back as independent contractors. Quite often you can do just that and save a lot of money in the process—but there are also pitfalls to avoid. Here's the law:

Who is an Employee

If the employer has the right to control an individual's work not only as to *what* is done but also *how* it is done, that person is an employee. It doesn't matter that the employee has considerable freedom of action and discretion, as long as the employer has right of control.

Who is an Independent Contractor

If the employer has the right to control the *final result* but *not the means or methods* for doing it, then the worker is an independent contractor. See the chart on the next page for a summary analysis of employee vs. independent contractor.

WHAT TO DO IF FACED WITH UNIONIZATION

At some point, most business managers will face the prospect of having their work forces unionized. Many managers will react by firing union leaders and sympathizers, but this can be dangerous. If unfair labor practices can be proved against you, the National Labor Relations Board (NLRB) can certify a union as the workers' exclusive bargaining agent, *even though* an election was not held or a majority vote obtained. Here is what you may—and may not—do when dealing with this delicate situation.

May Do

● Tell employees that if a majority of them select the union, the company will have to deal with it on all their daily problems involving wages, hours, and other conditions of employment.

EMPLOYEE VS. INDEPENDENT CONTRACTOR

	Employee	Independent Contractor
Employer's right to dismiss individual	Free right to discharge.	Right to discharge limited by contractual relationship, written or implied.
Payment	Periodically or by the hour.	By the job.
Tenure	Permanent relationship intended.	More limited relationship intended.
Employment conditions	Employee furnishes place to work, tools, and equipment.	Substantial investment by the worker in tools, equipment, etc., giving opportunity for profit or loss.
	Work done personally. May not employ assistants without permission from employer.	Worker has right to employ others to assist him.
Employment restrictions	Outside employment by worker may be restricted.	None. Services offered to the general public. Recognized trade or calling.

Some operations in your business could possibly be turned over to outsiders at a lower net cost. Examples would be delivery services, building and equipment maintenance, office cleaning, and bookkeeping services. Or you might wish to set up certain existing employees in business for themselves and give them a long-term contract to handle these services. The possibilities are numerous, but before making a change, consider two points: (1) A worker may be classified as an independent contractor for federal purposes but as an employee under state law. Check with your local employment office. (2) The IRS is alert to any change in a worker's status. Substantial potential liabilities for FICA and withholding can build up unless you get an advanced ruling than an individual is actually an independent contractor. To avoid problems, apply for a ruling on Form SS-8.

• Tell employees that you and other members of management are always willing to discuss with them any subject of interest to them.

• Tell the employees about the benefits they presently enjoy—all of which may have been obtained without union representation. Avoid promises or threats, either direct or veiled.

• Tell employees how their wages, benefits, and working conditions compare favorably with other companies in the area, whether unionized or not.

• Tell employees some of the disadvantages of belonging to a union—such as, the expense of initiation fees, monthly dues, fines, strike assessments, and membership rules. Quote from the specific union's constitution and bylaws granting the union power to impose punishment and discipline on its members.

• Tell employees that there is a possibility that a union will call a strike or work stoppage even though many employees may not want to strike and even though the employer is willing to bargain or has been bargaining with the union. Inform employees that any strike will cost them money in lost wages.

• Tell employees that in negotiating with the union the company does not have to agree to all the union's terms and certainly not to any terms that are not in the economic interest of the business.

• Tell employees that merely signing a union authorization card or application for membership does not mean that they must vote for the union in an election. If the situation warrants, advise employees that the union may use the signed authorization cards to obtain bargaining rights without an NLRB election.

• Enforce rules that solicitation of membership or discussion of union affairs must be outside working time so that it will not interfere with work. However, an employee can solicit and discuss the union on his own time, even on company premises, when it does not interrupt work.

• If two or more unions are organizing, you may express your personal preference of one union over the other.

• Lay off, discipline, and discharge for cause so long as such action follows customary practice and is not done with regard to union membership.

May Not Do

• Don't promise or grant employees a pay increase, promotion, betterment, benefit, or special favor if they stay out of the union or vote against it. Customary wage increases must be granted as scheduled.

• Don't threaten loss of jobs, reduction of income, discontinuance of privileges or benefits presently enjoyed, or use intimidating language that may be designed to influence an employee in the exercise of his right to belong to a union. Don't threaten or actually discharge, discipline, or lay off an employee because of his activities in behalf of a union. And don't discriminate against employees actively supporting the union by intentionally assigning undesirable work to the union employee or transfer employees prejudicially because of union affiliation.

• Don't threaten to close or move the plant or to drastically reduce operations if a union is selected as a representative.

• Don't spy on union meetings. (Parking across the street from a union hall to watch employees entering the hall would be suspect.) Don't ask employees about the internal affairs of unions, such as meetings. (Some employees may, of their own accord, tell you of such matters. It is not an unfair labor practice to listen, but you must not ask questions to obtain additional information.)

• Don't engage in any partiality favoring nonunion employees over employees active in behalf of the union or discipline or penalize employees actively supporting a union for an infraction that nonunion employees are permitted to commit without being similarly disciplined.

• Don't intentionally assign work or transfer employees so that those active in behalf of the union are separated from those you believe are not interested in supporting a union.

• Don't ask employees for an expression of their thoughts about a union or its officers, and don't ask employees how they intend to vote in a union election or ask them the identity of the instigator or leader of employees favoring the union.

• Don't ask employees at time of hiring or thereafter whether they belong to a union or have signed a union application or authorization card.

• Don't make a statement that you will not deal with a union.

• Don't make speeches to massed assemblies of employees on company time within the 24-hour period before the opening of polls for a representation election. And do not speak to an employee or small group of employees in your office about the union campaign. The best place to talk to them about the union is at their work stations where other employees are present.

RECORDS RETENTION CHECKLIST

Business records, especially those that are voluminous and bulky, should be disposed of as soon as they outlive their usefulness. In fact, of the staggering volume of paper kept by business firms, it is estimated that the majority could be destroyed after just three or four years. By systematically following the checklist below of many common business documents, you should be able to reduce unnecessary records to a minimum. Developed from the requirements specified in over 900 federal and state regulations, the list summarizes the practices of a large number of companies.

RECORDS RETENTION CHECKLIST

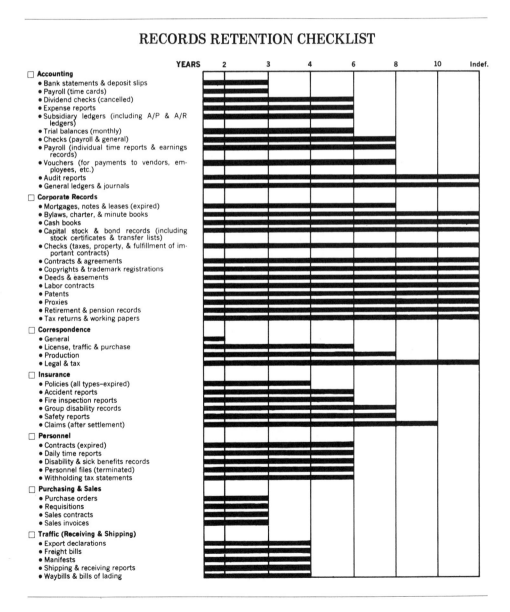

Statute of Limitations

Many businessmen feel that they must keep all original records for at least a certain time (six years is most quoted), after which no action can be brought against them. In fact, there is no single statute of limitations—there are dozens of them, and the time period for each statute varies depending on the particular law and state. Hence, record-keeping policies must be guided by the rule of reason and the probability and dollar amount of risk involved—not by statutes of limitations alone. For further information, obtain a copy of *Guide to Record Retention Requirements*, Government Printing Office, Washington, DC 20402 ($1.50).

CHAPTER 14

TAX TECHNIQUES

INTRODUCTION

Value of Tax Savings

Too many business managers get caught up in the day-to-day operation of their businesses and are content to let the accountant look after the taxes. Sometimes this works out just fine, but other times the manager is choosing to ignore or surrender responsibility for one of the most significant sources of income, tax savings.

A manager will stay up all night to save a few dollars in costs on his operation, but he is unwilling to spend even a few minutes looking at the more lucrative possibilities for saving taxes in his business. The absurdity of this attitude toward taxes is vividly illustrated in the Tax vs. Cost Savings chart that compares tax savings with dollars saved in costs.

TAX VS. COST SAVINGS

Before taxes profit margin on sales	Amount of sales needed to equal $1,000 savings in cost	Amount of sales needed to equal a $1,000 saving in taxes @ 48%
3%	$33,333	$69,444
5	20,000	41,666
10	10,000	20,833
15	6,667	13,888
30	3,333	6,944

Sources of Tax-Free Income

The following are a few of the more important sources of tax-free income.

Children's income. It is taxed to the child, not the parent.

Damages for personal injury.

Death benefits.

Discount on tax exempt bonds.

Dividends—up to the $100 exclusion.

Gifts.

Home—gain realized on sale of home if you buy or build another home.

Health insurance gains.

Inheritances.

Insurance proceeds from accidents.

Insurance proceeds for additional living expenses.

Interest from insurance that is included in payments to surviving spouse up to $1,000 per year.

Interest on tax exempt bonds (state or local).

Life insurance proceeds.

Loans.

Salary advances from your employer that you will repay.

Social Security benefits.

State unemployment compensation.

Stock dividends.

Workmen's Compensation Act payments.

In addition to the above sources of tax-free income, your business can also be a source of tax-free income. This is especially possible for stockholder-employees in a close corporation.

How to Get Money Out of Your Business and Pay Minimum Taxes

Like everyone else, stockholder-employees of close corporations want to reduce their tax expenses. As much as possible, they want to avoid having income taxed twice; first at the corporate level and then as a dividend at the personal level. The following is a checklist of ways to extract cash from a going corporation and pay minimum taxes. These items will be discussed in greater detail later.

Stockholder-employee benefits

- *Medical expense reimbursement.* Medical expenses for stock-holder-employees and their families may be paid directly by the corporation or through an insurance company with the premiums paid by the corporation. These payments are deductible by the corporation and tax free to the employee.
- *Meals and lodging.* The cost of meals and lodging for overnight travel away from home is deductible by the corporation and nontaxable to the stockholder-employee as long as a valid business purpose exists and the expenses are substantiated. Entertainment expenses are also deductible as long as they are reasonable.
- *Life insurance.* A corporation can provide up to $50,000 of group life insurance tax free to a stockholder employee.

Premiums on insurance in excess of $50,000 are treated as taxable compensation to the employee. In most cases, however, the tax imputation is considerably less than the actual cost of the insurance.

- *Pension plans.* The corporation can pay any reasonable amount into a pension trust. The payments are deductible by the corporation and nontaxable to the employee until he begins drawing the funds when he retires and is presumably in a lower tax bracket. Such plans can effectively favor the stockholder-employee by stipulating tough qualifications and eligibility requirements and by tieing the benefits to wage levels and social security benefits.

Payments to stockholder-employees

- *Salary.* The corporation may deduct the payment of a reasonable salary to a stockholder-employee. The salary that costs the least in combined corporate and personal taxes is the best. High salaries must have a justifiable business purpose, or the IRS may hold part of the salary as a "constructive dividend" and deny the corporate deduction while still taxing the individual.
- *Rent or lease payments.* The stockholder-employee can lease or rent real estate or equipment to the corporation at *reasonable* rates. This may be useful if the stockholder is already making a maximum reasonable salary. Excess payments are again subject to treatment as constructive dividends. Check the preference income rules of the 1976 Tax Act.

Other ways to get cash

- *Borrowing from the corporation.* A stockholder can borrow cash from the corporation, but there should be a note evidencing the debt and stipulating a fixed repayment schedule. There should be a reasonable interest rate on the loan to avoid the IRS position that an interest-free loan represents a constructive dividend equal to reasonable interest.
- *Payments that exceed earnings from deficit corporations.* If a corporation has an accumulated deficit and pays out dividends in excess of earnings for the current year, the excess is treated as a tax-free return of capital rather than a dividend. Pay out dividends equal to two years' earnings every other year, and only the portion equivalent to the current year's earnings will be taxed as a dividend. Be sure, however, to have your accountant or lawyer check state laws.

- *Subchapter S election.* A subchapter S election generally avoids federal taxation at the corporate level. For the first five years there must be ten or fewer shareholders and only one class of stock. Not more than 20% of gross income can be from "passive" sources (i.e., rents, interest, etc.). All corporate earnings may then be distributed to shareholders and will be taxed only once—at the personal level. Family taxes may be reduced if stock ownership is spread among family members who are in low tax brackets.

In light of the value of a tax dollar and the wealth of sources for such savings it is vital for an alert business manager to be aware of his tax possibilities, if not an expert on them. The key to being a good manager is understanding what is going on and knowing where to get more information if necessary. But now the question arises as to how far you dare go with tax savings.

When Does It Pay to Push Your Luck?

Tax avoidance is both lawful and ethical. It is making the best use of legal procedures to reduce the amount of tax you have to pay. On the other hand, *tax evasion* is not legal. Tax evasion is the willful misrepresentation of fact or the concealment of information to evade lawful tax. There may be some doubt in your mind as to the propriety of certain tax deductions if you seek to avoid tax, but if you are evading tax, there will be no question in your mind about what you are doing.

Tax issues are often complicated. It isn't surprising that tax courts hear hundreds of cases each year in hopes of straightening out some of the questions. Therefore it is understandable if you (even with the aid of your accountant) are unsure of the legality of certain deductions. If you have no clear guidelines on the correct procedure in regard to some of your deductions, go ahead and take the deduction. If your accountant also doesn't know how clear an issue is, have him say so in writing to protect yourself in case the IRS disagrees with your judgment.

In deciding how far you should push your luck, you must consider how much you stand to gain and how much you could lose. If you have a reasonable deduction, try for it. If the IRS says no, you've still had use of that money over the time it took them to get around to your case. Furthermore, be clear that such things as honest disagreements do occur in some areas of tax. Even if they go against you, you don't have to feel like a criminal. And of course, if you get no challenge from the IRS, you will have made yourself some money.

Usually, you don't risk much by taking chances on deductions. The IRS may make you pay back the sum with interest, but you probably decided beforehand that the possible loss in interest costs were worth gambling for the possible saving. This idea of pushing your luck does not mean you can make statements you *know* to be false because falsehoods can lead to questions of fraud and tax evasion. The penalties in these areas can be stiff indeed.

HOW TO GET MAXIMUM MILEAGE OUT OF TRAVEL AND ENTERTAINMENT EXPENSES

Travel deductions

For any business travel to be deductible, the IRS imposes two main requirements. First, the travel must be reasonable, have a necessary business purpose, and be "away from home." Second, the amount of the deduction cannot be lavish and must generally be substantiated. "Home" is defined as the taxpayer's place of employment, regardless of where his family residence is located. You do not receive a deduction for commuting to and from work, but you would for any other business travel, even if it is in the city where you live. The cost of meals on a business trip is also deductible but *only* if staying overnight. Of course, if the traveler manages to combine meals and business conversation with clients, then the cost would be deductible whether you stay overnight or not.

The amount of time spent on business during your travels will determine the extent of the deductions allowed. Here's how IRS looks at it:

- If your trip is *all business*, then all reasonable expenses for food, lodging, and transportation are deductible.
- If the trip is *mostly*—but not all—*business*, you may deduct the business related expenses and the transportation costs.
- A trip that is *mostly pleasure* with a little business thrown in is not deductible except for the expenses directly related to business. You may not deduct transportation costs.

You must be able to document your travel expenses if you wish to use the travel deductions. Documentation is a receipt, a bill marked paid, or some other verifiable document proving the expense. Here are the items for which you will need documentation.

- The number of days you spend away from home overnight and the exact dates you were away.
- Where you went—city, state, or town.
- Business reason for the trip. What you hoped to gain by the travel.
- Amount spent on lodging, transportation, and food. If you like, you may use a general category for such things as meals and gas and oil, as long as the total amount is reasonable.

Automobile expenses—itemized deductions vs. standard mileage deductions To the extent that auto travel is related to business, the following expenses may be itemized and are deductible:

- *Auto operation.* This includes gas, oil, maintenance, washing and polishing, garaging, and auto club membership.

- *State and local assessments.* This includes any use taxes, registration fees, sales taxes, and license fees.
- *Depreciation.* The full cost of the car may be depreciated over a period as short as two and a half years. If a three-year life is chosen, the double-declining balance method may be used.
- *Insurance.* All insurance premiums including liability, fire and theft, and collision are deductible.
- *Theft and casualty losses.* To the extent not reimbursed by insurance, you may deduct all such expenses without regard to the business use limitations described below.

If a car is used for both business and personal travel, the expenses may be allocated by either, determining the number of business and personal miles and then prorating them or basing the business deduction on the weekly percentage of business use. For example, if the car is used five days a week for business, 5/7 of expenses may be deducted. But whatever method is used, it must be a fair representation of actual business-related expenses and proper records to substantiate the deductions must be kept.

Rather than itemize expenses, owners may use a flat mileage allowance of 15¢ per mile for the first 15,000 miles and 10¢ a mile thereafter. The previous rate was 12¢ and 9¢ respectively. This allowance may be taken no matter what age or type of car. However, the flat rate may not be used when the owner previously itemized and used an accelerated-depreciation method. If you have a new car, it may be a good idea to itemize using straight-line depreciation while the car is new and then shift to the flat mileage allowance after the car is fully depreciated. Be sure to compute the deductions both ways each year and use the one that gives more tax savings. You may switch back and forth as often as you like.

For example, John Johnson has a new car that costs $6,000. He drives it 25,000 miles a year, of which 20,000 are for business. Estimated trade-in value of the car is $1,000 after three years.

As can be seen below, while the car is new, it is more advantageous to itemize. However, in the fourth year after the depreciation allowance runs

THE TAX FREE RAISE

Itemized method		*Standard rate method*	
Straight-line depreciation (3 years)	$1,667	15,000 miles × $.15	$2,250
Gas	1,200	5,000 miles × $.10	500
Oil and lube	100		
Tires	200	20,000 business miles	$2,750
Repairs	300		
Insurance	350		
	$3,817		
4/5 business use = $3,054 deductible		= $2,750 deductible	

out, the standard rate method will yield significantly higher deductions. Note that with both methods a deduction may be taken for investment credit, sales tax, and any interest paid to finance the vehicle.

An employee doesn't have to account for specific auto expenses if his company reimburses him for using his car on a straight mileage basis which is not more than 15¢ per mile, according to the IRS. So you can use the 15¢ per mile reimbursement rule to give an officer or employee a tax free raise. This can be done because an employee, officer, or officer-stockholder does not pay tax on excess compensation paid out on the 15¢ per mile reimbursement. Thus, if you want to increase a company officer's salary without arousing IRS suspicions about an unreasonable salary, have him use his own car on company business if he can operate it at a personal cost of less than 15¢ per mile.

Here's how it works: Simpson drives his own car on company business 10,000 miles and is reimbursed by his company at 15¢ per mile which equals $1,500. But the driving really only costs Simpson $500. Therefore he gets an excess of $1,000 and neither he, nor the company pays tax on the real increase in his compensation. This works whether it's a matter of reasonable salary for a company officer or a matter of saving on workman's compensation, Social Security tax, etc. for an employee's raise.

Per diem allowances In addition to car expenses, an employer may pay an employee a daily allowance in lieu of subsistence without requiring detailed substantiation of the expenses other than time, place, and purpose of travel. The allowance was formerly $36 per day and is now $44 per day. Any executive who owns more than 10% of his company's stock cannot use per diem reimbursement. If you fall into this category, you must continue to give a full account of all food, lodging, and similar expenses.

Travel Inside and Outside the United States Transportation, lodging, and meals are deductible when travel inside the United States is primarily for business reasons. Extra personal expenses during the trip are not deductible.

However, if the trip inside the United States is primarily for *pleasure* and only incidentally for business, you may not deduct transportation costs, only the costs that are directly related to the business you conducted during the trip.

If you are outside the United States for less than a week on business you deduct as if it had been a "primarily business" domestic trip. The same goes if you stay outside the United States for more than a week, but spend more than 75% of your time doing business. But if you are abroad more than a week and are working less than 75% of the time, you pay transportation expenses in proportion to the time spent on business (i.e., in France two weeks and only one week is business, you pay 50% of your transportation costs and one week's living expenses).

Entertainment

You "entertain" business associates anytime you take them out to dinner, to a night club, the theater, a country club, or on a sporting trip. Any social or recreational activity is entertainment and it can be a deductible expense if it meets any of the following tests:

- The entertainment is *directly related* to business i.e., although you combined business and pleasure, the primary activity was business. For example, a "clients only" cocktail party.
- Entertainment *associated with* business is deductible if you can show that it took place the same day as the business meeting and that the business was the real reason for getting together. To be associated with business the entertainment must directly precede or follow business.
- "Quiet Business Meal" is a term applied to those situations where you either have a quiet meal with a business associate or buy him or her a drink in an establishment that has a minimum of distractions. The idea here is that you get together in a place that is conducive to conversation. Taking a businessman to the fights does not qualify here.

Other Kinds of Entertainment. Generally, expenses incurred attending business seminars or conventions are deductible, unless the IRS feels there was more pleasure than business at the convention. If the IRS says the convention was primarily for pleasure, travel costs will not be deductible but costs directly related to business will be. Expenses for wives or husbands who are not directly affiliated with the business are not deductible unless the spouse actively aids in the business activity. However, if it is inappropriate to exclude a client's spouse, you may invite your own spouse and deduct for all four people. From now on, the deductibility of attending *foreign* conventions is severely curtailed. If you anticipate going overseas for such a convention, check with your accountant before leaving. You must produce stringent documentation of all expenses and the actual time you were in attendance.

Goodwill entertaining at a restaurant may be deducted as a "quiet business meal" and theater tickets may be deducted as "associated with" business if the business was conducted on the day the curtain went up.

Expenses for depreciation and upkeep of lodges, yachts, resorts, and recreational equipment are deductible in proportion to their use for business purposes—if they are used for business entertainment more than 50% of the time. The same is true of dues paid for use of recreational facilities (country club) when 51% of the use is business. However, if you use the facilities less than 50% of the time for business, you may not deduct any expenses whatever for upkeep, dues, or depreciation. Note however that out-of-pocket expenses, like expenses for bait or sandwiches on a fishing trip are deductible business expenses regardless of the boat's (the facility's) deductibility.

Keeping Entertainment Records. Like travel expenditures, entertainment costs are not deductible in virtually any category unless you can document them according to IRS specifications. Generally, you must be able to document the following:

- The date of your entertainment expenditure.
- The location and type of entertainment.
- The precise cost of the entertainment. (Taxi money and other incidental costs may be listed on a daily basis by their various classifications instead of by individual incident.)
- The purpose of the entertainment, the nature of the business discussion and the benefit you anticipate from the entertainment.
- The business relationship of your guest to you. You should show his firm, his name, and title.

Business Gifts

You may make gifts to business associates, but you may claim no more than $25.00 tax deduction per person per year. A gift to a member of a businessman's family is considered a gift to him. Promotional items under $4.00, like pens or paper weights, advertising displays, and awards to employees (under $100.00) for service, are not considered gifts.

Keeping Gift Records. If you want your $25.00 deduction for a business gift you must be able to document the following:

- The identification of the recipient: his name, title, and firm.
- The reason for giving the gift or else what you hoped to gain by it.
- The nature of the gift. A brief description of it would suffice.
- When the gift was given.
- How much it cost.

A Gift or Entertainment? Suppose a business client comes to town and you just happen to have tickets for a performance that night by his favorite singer. Can you give him the tickets and put it down to entertainment or do you have to use up your gift deduction by calling the tickets a gift? The rule is that if you do not accompany him to the performance, but you do spend time with him that afternoon talking business, you may call the tickets "entertainment associated with business" and save the gift deduction for Christmas.

What if the IRS Disallows Your Deductions?

The reason for being careful about keeping travel and entertainment records is that the IRS will hit you with a double tax if it disallows your deductions. Your company loses the business deduction and you, who received reimbursement for the expense, are taxed for receipt of additional income. For this reason it is worthwhile to plan ahead for your travel and entertainment expenditures by having standard procedures for recording the expenses.

WHAT YOU SHOULD KNOW ABOUT THE INVESTMENT CREDIT

The investment credit and accelerated depreciation rank as the two most important sources of tax savings for the average business. Originally introduced in 1962, the investment credit has had a varied history. Suspended in 1966, restored in 1967, and repealed by the Tax Reform Act of 1969, it was revived by the Revenue Act of 1971 and extended through 1980 by the 1976 Tax Act. The idea behind the investment credit was the stimulation of a sagging US economy. The tax saving made possible by the credit can be substantial.

The investment credit grants up to a 10% *dollar-for-dollar credit against federal income taxes for investment in certain qualified business assets.* This credit is worth more to you than an expense deductible from gross income because the credit is applied directly to your yearly tax bill. Suppose your taxes for a year were $10,000. But you purchased a qualified asset that year for $25,000 and were entitled to an investment credit of 10% or $2,500. The $2,500 comes directly off your $10,000 tax liability and you pay only $7,500 to the IRS.

The investment credit is generally available only to property purchased in the year the tax credit is claimed which meets all of the following tests:

- *Depreciable.* The investment must be in property that declines in economic value because of use.
- *Useful life.* The property must have a useful life of at least three years.
- *Tangible.* The property may be: (a) personal, (b) used as an integral part of manufacturing, production, transportation, etc., or (c) a research and development facility.

See the table showing various items that do and do not qualify for the investment credit. If you have doubts about whether or not your property qualifies, consult your tax adviser.

QUALIFICATION OF PROPERTY FOR INVESTMENT CREDIT

Qualify	*Do not qualify*
• *Tangible personal property.* Office equipment and furnishings; manufacturing and production equipment; automobiles, trucks, boats, and planes.	• *Land and any improvements.* Such as grading, sidewalks, etc.
• *Integral part of production process.* Printing presses, railroad tracks, and oil pipelines.	• *Buildings and most structural components.*
	• *Patents, copyrights, licenses, and other intangibles.*
• *Livestock (except horses).*	• *Inventory.*

There are restrictions on the amount of credit allowed.

- *New property.* The cost of all qualified new property is eligible for investment credit. There is no limit on new property. If you purchase a new asset for $180,000, you may compute your investment credit on that figure. However, there is a limit on the amount of credit that can be claimed in one year, as is explained below.
- *Used property.* There is a $100,000 yearly cost limit for investment credit on used property. If you purchase $110,000 worth of qualified used property in one year, you may compute your credit on only $100,000 of cost. Excess cost may not be carried over to another year. Naturally, if you acquire different used properties that collectively cost more than the $100,000 limit, you would choose to take the investment credit on the properties with the longest useful life in order to maximize your credit.
- *Useful life.* The portion of an otherwise qualified investment on which the credit may be computed depends on its expected life. (See chart)

Annual Credit Limitation

You may claim investment credit on as much qualified new property as you want, but there is a limit to the amount of credit you can claim for both new and used property in any one year. The amount of credit in one year cannot be greater than your total tax liability, or the first $25,000 of tax liability plus 50% of tax liability over $25,000. The lesser of the above figures will be your annual limitation. For example, suppose your total tax liability is $40,000 and you want to claim an investment credit on new and used property of $38,000. Can you do it? No, because the first $25,000 of your tax liability plus 50% of the liability over $25,000 ($25,000 + 1/2 × $15,000 = $32,500) is less than the credit you want, the $38,000. Your limit in this case then is $32,500.

Recapture. If you dispose of an asset before the end of its estimated useful life, any excess credit you took must be added to your current tax. For example, if you acquired a qualified asset for $100,000 with an estimated life of eight years, you could take 10% × $100,000 = $10,000 as a tax credit.

INVESTMENT CREDIT ALLOWANCE

Useful life of investment	Amount of investment which qualifies for 10% credit (new or used)
Less than 3 yrs.	0
3 yrs. or more, but less than 5 yrs.	33 1/3%
5 yrs. or more, but less than 7 yrs.	66 2/3%
7 years or more	100 %

If the asset only lasts six years, the credit to which you should have been entitled is only 66 2/3% × ($100,000 × 10%) = $6,667. Therefore, you must pay an additional $10,000 – $6,667 = $3,333 tax in the year you dispose of the asset. Before selling property on which you have claimed an investment credit, check with your accountant to find out if the sale will trigger recapture rules.

Depreciation base. Note that even though your effective cost for new equipment is only 90% of its actual cost (Uncle Sam paid the remainder by reducing your taxes), the depreciation base is unchanged—you can still use a full 100% of the purchase price as the depreciable cost. Check with your accountant on various ways to maximize the investment credit in your business. With the government paying 10% of the bill for much of your equipment, it is an opportunity you should not overlook.

Investment Credit Strategy

The following are ways in which you can make the investment credit work for you. Areas that are of interest to you should be investigated further with the help of a tax adviser.

Maximizing Estimated Life. Since the amount of credit offered increases with the estimated useful life of the asset, it is to your advantage to make the most optimistic estimate of that asset's life. If you overestimate, you may have to repay part of the credit, but you have had use of that money for some time. If you underestimate the useful life, tough luck. You can't go back and reestimate it.

Used Equipment. If you sell old property and within sixty days you buy used property to replace the old, your investment credit is computed on the cost of the replacement less the basis of the old property. But if you wait sixty-one days before buying the replacement, your credit is computed on the *full* price of the replacement property. Or, you could buy the replacement, use it alongside the old property for sixty-one days and then sell the old property. This way, too, you can compute credit on the basis of the full cost of the replacement. Also, since you can't take more than $100,000 in credit on the purchase of used equipment in one year, you might consider waiting until next year to buy the equipment which would drive costs beyond the allowable limit. Or, you might find that it is almost as inexpensive to buy new equipment with the credit as it is to buy old equipment without it.

Leasing. The lessor of new equipment gets the investment credit when he buys the equipment. Therefore, if you intend to lease new equipment, try to get the lessor to pass the credit on to you or at least reduce the cost of the lease. After all, without your company's business, he wouldn't have purchased the equipment at all.

Stimulate Sales. If you sell qualified equipment, use the investment credit as a sales device by reminding customers that they get an automatic tax credit. With the credit and the additional first year 20% depreciation coupled with double declining balance depreciation, the customer could recover a large part of his investment in the first year.

Incorporation. If you plan to incorporate and you also plan to acquire qualified property, buy the property *before* you incorporate so you can use the investment credit on your personal income tax where it should be more valuable. Later, after incorporation, you can transfer your property to the corporation without incurring recapture penalties.

THE TAX BENEFITS OF AN INSTALLMENT SALE

Too often business people sell property and merchandise without considering the tax consequences. Suppose you agree to sell a capital asset for $100,000. The down payment is $40,000, and $30,000 per year will be paid for the next two years. A nice simple transaction, but the tax treatment could be very unpleasant. If the property is carried on your books at $10,000, you'll have a $90,000 capital gain. *You will be taxed this year on the entire $90,000 gain even though you won't receive the full proceeds from the sale for two more years.* Let's see how you could structure the sale differently for a better result.

There are three general ways you can receive fixed payment for a sale of property: (1) You can receive full payment in cash or other property at the time of sale, in which case the full amount of any gain is taxable. (2) You can have payment deferred or made contingent on some specific occurrence. (3) You can receive partial payment at the time of sale and the remainder over time. In this situation *you can report taxable gain as installments are received* if you meet any of these three tests:

- You are a *dealer in merchandise* and regularly *sell on the installment basis.*
- The property being sold is *real estate.*
- The transaction is a "casual" sale (i.e., you are not a dealer) and the sales price of the property (other than real estate) is *more than $1,000.*

In the latter two cases of a real estate transaction and a casual sale over $1,000, there is one final test—*payments in the year of the sale can't be more than 30% of the purchase price.* Taking our above example, if the owner agreed to take a down payment of $30,000 or less and the balance over time, any income would be recognized *pro rata as proceeds were received,* instead of all in one lump sum. Real estate and casual installment sales will be covered in more detail in chapter 19.

If you are a *merchandise dealer* and regularly sell on an installment basis, you have a choice. You can report the full profit from an installment sale in the year of the sale or report the profit proportionately as you receive the money. Furthermore, you can choose *which accounts* you want to report on the installment basis—the IRS doesn't have to approve anything.

If one year you have booming sales, but you know they'll probably be down the next year, you can defer much of the income to the following year by converting accounts to an installment basis. Here are several points to watch for:

1. *Proper filings.* You may elect installment sale by filing a written statement with your return. While a dealer can switch to installment reporting at will, including which accounts are to be reported, the IRS insists that all installment sales be recorded on your tax return in the year of initial sale. This notifies the IRS that tax on certain sales has been deferred.

2. *Regularity of Payment.* The reasonable size and timing of the payments must be stated in the sales contract.

3. *Treatment of receivables.* Installment receivables can be handled in two ways. You can either *discount* them (i.e., sell them at less than face value to a bank or finance company), or you can *pledge* them (i.e., borrow against the receivables as collateral). To preserve the tax benefits, installment receivables can only be pledged. If they are discounted, the proceeds are taxable, negating any benefits of deferred taxation.

4. *Record keeping.* Your records should clearly show the year of initial sale of each installment receivable. A good method is to use a file card for each installment sale with different color cards corresponding to different years.

5. *Interest.* If the sales contract does not call for at least 5% interest, the IRS may declare the contract a tax avoidance tactic. If the IRS rules the avoidance excessive, they may recompute the contract at 7% interest.

6. *Gains and Losses.* The long-term capital gains tax rate is not affected by a sale by installment. However, a loss on an installment sale must be reported in its entirety in the year of the sale. Loss may not be prorated over the payment period.

7. *Advance payments.* If you receive advance payments for the property—deposits, options, etc.—these payments will be included by the IRS in the total payment received in the first year installment. Therefore, count them in yourself. Don't wait for the IRS to add them in because you don't want that initial payment to suddenly exceed 30%. If it does, you lose the whole installment tax benefit in one fell swoop.

Tax Strategy

If you are in a high tax bracket and are *selling* an asset on an installment plan, you want the price to be higher and the interest on the installments to be lower. The reason is straightforward. The higher the price, the greater the amount subject to capital gains tax and the less you must compute as ordinary income (the interest). The amount of money you receive remains the same, but its tax treatment is more favorable. Naturally, if you are a high tax bracket *buyer*, you usually want greater interest deductions because interest can be deducted immediately whereas depreciation on the asset is deducted over time and is subject to recapture. Whatever your position, however, be sure you don't negotiate the interest below the 5% mark lest you arouse the wrath of the IRS.

There is, however, an exception to the interest rate guideline. Payment of interest on an installment sale may be waived entirely if the sale meets one of the following conditions: all installment payments are made within one year; or total sales price is equal to or less than $3,000. If the sale meets one of these conditions, the seller may arrange the sale as a no interest sale by specifying accordingly in the agreement. In a no interest sale the price goes up to encompass most (but not all) of the money that would otherwise come to the seller as interest. The effect is that the seller takes the whole gain as capital gain instead of receiving the interest over time as ordinary income. Because this affords the seller a tax break, the seller is willing to reduce the price. The buyer then pays less overall for the asset and his increased depreciation "basis" is often high enough to offset the loss of his interest deduction. Needless to say, the IRS is sensitive to those who try to use the no interest sale to take tax breaks to which they are not entitled. If the IRS decides that your installment sale does not meet one of the two requirements for a no interest sale, they will do their tax computation on the basis of 7% interest instead of your zero interest. This could easily have an unpleasant effect on your tax strategy.

TAX ELECTION CHECKLIST

Taxpayers have a variety of elections that they can make under the Internal Revenue Code and IRS regulations. Some are binding for only one year, others until revoked. In certain cases IRS approval is needed to make the election; in others, it is at the taxpayer's discretion. Here is a rundown and brief explanation of the elections most important to the businessman:

Bad Debts

- *Specific charge-off vs. reserve method.* Bad debts may be deducted by one of two methods. The specific charge-off method allows the taxpayer to deduct bad debts in the year they become worthless. Under the reserve method bad debts are not deducted directly from income but are charged against a bad debt reserve.
- *Election.* An accrual-basis taxpayer filing his first return can select either method with IRS consent. The selected method must be used in subsequent years unless approval to change

is obtained. A cash-basis taxpayer does not need a bad debt election, since only actual cash collections are reported as income.

- *Changing method.* Application for changing methods must be made within 180 days after the beginning of the tax year for which the change is desired.

Depreciation

The taxpayer has two elections: (1) whether to use the "class life system" and (2) which depreciation method to use.

- *Class life.* Enacted by the Revenue Act of 1971, class life may be elected for assets placed in service after 1971. This system permits depreciation based on "guideline lives" established by the Treasury.
- *Depreciation method.* The taxpayer may choose among three general depreciation methods: (1) straight line, (2) declining-balance, and (3) sum-of-years digits.
- *Additional allowance.* Election to take an additional 20% first year allowance for "tangible personal property" is at the taxpayer's discretion and is made by attaching depreciation computations to the relevant tax return.

Installment sales

Dealers in personal property may report sales on the installment basis, that is, proportionately as collections are made. No permission is needed to go from the accrual basis to the installment basis.

Inventory valuation

The taxpayer can elect one of two methods for valuing inventory used in his business: (1) cost, or (2) cost or market, whichever is lower.

- *Measurement of "cost."* To measure cost, four general methods may be used: specific identification; first-in/first-out (FIFO); last-in/first-out (LIFO); or average cost. In addition, retailers can use the "retail" method, and manufacturers can (with IRS consent) use the "allocated cost" method when the inventory consists of several kinds, sizes, and grades. Application to change methods is made on Form 3115 and must be filed within 180 days after the start of the tax year. All elections can be changed only with IRS permission.
- *LIFO.* If the last-in/first-out method is chosen, IRS approval must be obtained. Application to use LIFO is made on Form 970 filed with the return for the first year the method is to be used. The election is irrevocable. (For a full discussion of LIFO and FIFO, see p. 108.)

Accounting methods

Cash, accrual, or any other method that clearly reflects income may be used. Where inventories are involved, the cash method may not be used. Application to change accounting methods is made by filing Form 3115.

Long-term contracts

The taxpayer has the option of reporting on the "percentage completion" or the "completed contract" basis. No consent is required to use either method.

Subchapter S

Election is made by filing Form 2553 along with consent statements from each shareholder. The election is made either the month before the beginning of the tax year for which the election is made or in the first month of the tax year. The election is effective for all later years unless revoked.

Tax attorneys and CPAs furnish competent tax advice. But they can never have complete knowledge of your business and must be asked *competent questions* in order to be efficient and effective. Know your tax options before you seek professional help. You probably won't have the answers—but at least you will be asking the right questions.

HOW TAX SHELTERS WORK

Too often investors do not understand how tax shelters work or the meaning of such terms as "soft dollars," "flow through," or "depreciation shield." The result is that they make unwise investments—or avoid shelters altogether when they could have been used effectively to legally reduce taxes.

How tax shelters work

Net personal taxable income above $44,000 for married couples filing joint returns is taxed at a minimum of 50% and at higher rates if the income is from unearned sources, such as rents and dividends. For single taxpayers, the 50% bracket begins at $32,000. If a taxpayer in that bracket can somehow reduce his taxable income by $1, he can save somewhere between 50¢ and 70¢. By investing in a particular venture, the investor takes deductions that reduce taxable income (and taxes). The most popular tax shelter is a limited partnership.

The limited partnership

The limited partnership structure is used for most tax shelters because the partnerships are not taxed directly—all profits and losses "flow through" to the partners, and any tax due is paid individually by them. The principal disadvantage is that the partners are usually jointly liable for any debts or other liabilities of the business. This drawback is overcome by the use of a *limited* partnership—the investor can participate in profits, but his liability is limited to the amount of his investment. The *general* partners run the day-to-day operations of the venture. They may be a corporation or a group of individuals, but they do not enjoy limited liability. (See chart below.)

Sources of tax deductions

The most common limited partnership tax shelter involves the ownership of real estate. The tax deductions for limited partners may be taken in the following ways:

Depreciation.   Often called a "depreciation shield" because it can be used to offset income, depreciation is a key ingredient of most tax shelters. Let's take a hypothetical example. Suppose you are a 10% investor in the construction of a $1,000,000 apartment complex. (For purposes here, we will assume that the land — which is not depreciable — has been leased. Therefore, the full $1,000,000 cost of the apartment building is depreciable.) By borrowing 90% of the purchase price ($900,000) in the form of a non-recourse mortgage (i.e., no one is personally liable for the loan), each 10% partner would only have to put up $10,000 of the $100,000 in equity money. Yet the basis for depreciation would still be the full price of $1,000,000. Using accelerated depreciation (200% of straight line) over 25 years, the first year's depreciation would come to a total of $80,000. This would mean a total tax deduction of $8,000 on your investment of $10,000, yielding a tax saving (if you are in the 50% bracket) of $4,000. Such tax savings are often called "soft dollars." You effectively get $4,000 of your investment back and have your "hard dollar" investment in the project reduced to only $6,000. Furthermore, you would continue to receive depreciation deductions in future years and still own 10% of the project. However, depreciation reduces your taxable basis in the property and when the property is finally sold, a tax must be paid on the gain. Part of this gain may be taxed at ordinary income tax rates because of depreciation recapture rules. There is still a significant advantage, however, in that taxes can effectively be *deferred* for many years, allowing you to use the tax money saved for other productive purposes.

Operating losses.   If there are operating losses (as opposed to those result-

STRUCTURE OF LIMITED PARTNERSHIP

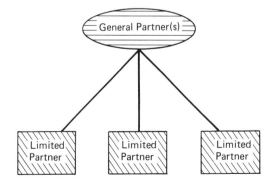

ing from interest on borrowings or depreciation deductions), they are also deductible by the partners. Limited partners can deduct losses in *excess* of their investment if the partnership and financing are appropriately structured.

Interest. Using the example above in which $900,000 was borrowed, almost $90,000 of interest deductions would result in the first year alone based on a 10%, 25-year mortgage. To the extent that these deductions were not offset by operating revenue, they should be deductible pro rata by the partners. However, watch this area carefully. The Tax Act of 1976 is unclear on this point and the IRS may attack such interest deductions.

Investment credit. The recent increase in the investment credit from 7% to 10% makes this an even more significant tax shelter component. The investment credit passes through as a direct dollar-for-dollar credit against individual taxes. The result for a 50%-bracket taxpayer is that this credit is twice as valuable as a deduction for interest or depreciation, since the latter items are deducted from income rather than directly from taxes due.

Tax shelters are not immoral—the laws facilitating them were purposefully designed to facilitate investment in higher risk and socially necessary ventures. But they are also not for the unsophisticated; always retain a competent tax advisor.

TRUSTS: NOT JUST FOR THE RICH

Trusts are just for the rich and super-rich, right? Well, not exactly. In fact, trusts are relatively easy to set up and are a convenient way for almost any person with modest resources to shelter a portion of his income from tax. But, no one is going to come to you with the inside knowledge. You must take the initiative.

How to Give a Tax Free College Scholarship to Your Children

Your daughter is three and your son is eight. Within ten years your oldest will be starting college. You've been setting aside a little money for their education and now your fund has $10,000 and earns 7% or $700 per year in interest. The problem is you are in a 40% bracket (including state taxes) so $280 per year goes to taxes, plus the remainder gets eaten up by inflation. A real treadmill. What would you say if:

- Most, if not all, the interest from the fund could accumulate completely *tax free* for your children's education, and,
- *You* would still retain effective control of the original investment.

Here's how it would work for your oldest child.

- Using what is known as a short-term or "Clifford" trust, you would turn the $10,000 over to a trustee, naming your son as beneficiary of all income from the trust.

- The trust will hold the $10,000 and credit any interest income to your son's account.
- Your son (not you, his father) will be liable for tax on $700/year of interest income, but
- Your son has a personal exemption of $750, so he pays no tax at all *plus*
- You, as father, *still* get a dependency exemption for all the years the trust is accumulating money so long as you contribute at least half to your son's support and he is under nineteen or a full-time student.

When your son goes to college in ten years, over $9,679 (thanks to compounding) of tax free money will be ready for him plus the original $10,000 reverts free and clear to you. It can then be used for your daughter's education or in any other way you desire.

Note that in this situation, you do not have to pay any gift tax and that your basic financial situation is unaffected (husband and wife may make tax free gifts of up to $6,000 per year to each child).

Obviously, the general idea here is to make a short-term gift to someone who is in a lower tax bracket in order to lower your own tax liability. The gift is income-producing property and the beneficiary pays the taxes instead of you. Later on, the principal reverts back to you and the beneficiary keeps the income he has paid tax on. This is a very useful tax tool for increasing the family income, but be sure to consider the following when you think about setting up a short-term trust.

- Retain competent legal counsel to set up the trust.
- Make sure the trust is irrevocable for over ten years.
- Protect yourself against emergencies by putting a clause in the trust agreement that you may borrow the cash/securities when secured by adequate collateral.
- Do not specify the purpose of the funds in the trust.
- Do not attempt to use the income for your own benefit in any way.
- Keep the accumulating interest and the original investment segregated.
- Check carefully with the attorney whether in your state it would be better for you or an outsider to be trustee.
- Never commingle trust and personal assets.

Note that in some states a father may be considered required to put his children through college as part of his duty of support. In these cases, using trust income for education may make it taxable to the father. If the age of majority in your state is eighteen, this should be no problem. If it is twenty-one, it may be better not to use the son's income for college expenses until age twenty-one.

A trust may be arranged so its income is retained or paid out annually to the beneficiary. If the beneficiary receives the income annually, he must pay income tax on it according to his personal income tax rate. On the other hand, a trust that accumulates the income pays the income tax according to the rate used for individual taxpayers. Later, when the beneficiary receives the accumulated income, he pays no tax on it. There is, however, an important stipulation in regard to trusts that accumulate income and pay tax. If the tax paid by the trust is less than the amount that would have been paid by the beneficiary had he received the income, the beneficiary must make up the difference to the IRS.

Other Possibilities

Thus far, we have been concerned with what are known as living (or in legal parlance, "inter vivos") trusts, which are created during lifetime (but many continue after death). They are highly effective whenever there is an appreciable difference between the tax bracket of the grantor (the father in the above example) and the beneficiary (the son). For example, you may wish to use a trust arrangement to accomplish any of the following:

- Accumulate savings for your spouse or some other member of the family. If you want to establish a short-term trust for your wife or husband, remember that if the trust pays out the income to the beneficiary annually, the beneficiary must pay tax on it. If you file a joint return and yours is not an accumulation trust, the tax benefit is lost. Also, in some states it is illegal for a trust to accumulate income for an adult.
- Provide support for a parent or some other dependent without the necessity of first passing income through your higher tax bracket.
- Accumulate funds within the trust for estate liquidity purposes.

Testamentary Trusts

There is another broad classification of trusts known as "testamentary" trusts that are created by will and become effective at death. They offer the same flexibility and variety of benefits as the living trust. Income can be paid to one or more beneficiaries, accumulated, or "sprinkled" among a group of beneficiaries at the discretion of a trustee. Principal can be paid in specified sums at various ages or times, upon occurrence of certain events, or at the discretion of the trustee or a third person.

More information concerning sprinkling trusts can be found in Chapter 22, "Estate Planning".

WHAT YOU NEED TO KNOW ABOUT CAPITAL TRANSACTIONS

Gains and losses in capital transactions receive different tax treatment depending upon the nature of the capital assets, how long they have been held, and who holds them. The difference in the tax treatment because of these three factors leads to some frustrating complexity, but most businessmen can obtain a useful understanding of capital transactions if they take the subject one step at a time.

Basic Definitions

What are Capital Assets?   A capital asset is anything you own, with the following exceptions:

- Depreciable property used in your business.
- Inventory (property intended for sale).
- Real estate used in your business.
- Accounts receivable.
- Some short-term government discount obligations.
- Some copyrights, literary work, etc.

Naturally, there are exceptions to the exceptions listed above. Although depreciable business real estate and property are considered noncapital assets, such properties when used for more than a certain time, may be taxed as if they were capital assets if there is a gain on their sale. This kind of business property is known as "Section 1231" property.

What is a Capital Transaction?   Generally, a capital transaction is a sale or exchange of capital assets. Usually, this results in capital gains or losses. In addition, the results of the following types of transactions will also sometimes be treated as capital gains or losses:

- Dividend liquidation.
- Distributions from pensions, stock bonuses, or profit sharing.
- Involuntary conversion of property used in trade or business.
- Worthless securities.
- Default by non-business debtors.

Section 1231 Property.   Normally, gain on the sale or exchange of property used in business (noncapital assets) would be treated as ordinary income. As noted, however, there is a special category known as Section 1231 property. Under this section property used in business for more than twelve months (nine months in 1977) may be treated as a capital asset if there is gain upon exchange or sale. As a result, the property is subject to the lower capital gain tax. Here are some further stipulations in regard to Section 1231 property.

- Gain on the sale of business property held *less* than twelve months (nine months in 1977) is treated as ordinary income.
- *Loss* on the sale of business property—no matter how long it is held—is regarded as ordinary loss.
- Gains on casualty or theft insurance settlements are taxed as long-term capital gains. Losses are deductible from ordinary income.
- Gain on the sale of Section 1231 property realized as a result of *depreciation* will be subject to depreciation recap-

ture rules. Generally, the recapture provisions call for the gain to be treated as ordinary income.

You can save tax money by making sure that you don't sell Section 1231 property at a loss in the same year you realize a gain from the sale of another Section 1231 property. Section 1231 property gains and losses in a given year must be netted so the gain offsets the loss. But gain is capital gain and loss, ordinary loss. Thus, you could be offsetting a capital gain with a 100% deductible loss. This would cost you an unnecessarily high amount of tax dollars. The strategy here is take the gain in one year and the loss in another.

How Net Capital Gains and Losses Are Computed and Taxed

Short-term capital gains and losses result from the sale of property held for twelve months or less (nine months in 1977). Long-term capital gains and losses result from the sale of property held more than twelve months (nine months in 1977). To find your *net* capital gains and losses, you separate the year's transactions into two categories. You offset all long-term gains against all long-term losses to compute your annual long-term gain (or loss). Similarly, short-term gains are offset by short-term losses to give you your net short-term result.

Once the net *amounts* of the capital gains or losses are known and *categorized* (short term or long term), the final factor is whether the capital gain or loss pertains to a corporation or an individual. The chart on page 238 summarizes the tax treatment of all possible capital gain or loss situations.

YEAR-END TAX PLANNING CHECKLIST

Too many businessmen don't think about tax strategies until their returns are prepared, two or three months after the books are closed. But a few simple moves to shift your income and expenses could minimize your tax liability and save you hundreds or even thousands in tax dollars.

Overall Corporate tax strategy

The basic corporate tax rate is 20% on income up to $25,000, 22% on the next $25,000, and 48% after that. Long-term capital gains are taxed at 22% if income (including the long-term gains) is below $25,000; above $25,000 the rate is 30%. There is also a 15% minimum tax on certain "preference income" items that include accelerated real estate depreciation.

To take maximum advantage of the lower tax rates, profits should be spread as evenly as possible from year to year. For example, a lower total tax will result from two years with $50,000 income each than from one with $15,000 and the other with $85,000. If you just signed a big contract that you know will net an unusual amount of income next year, start planning now to shift as much income as possible into the current tax year to avoid being taxed at a higher rate.

TAXATION OF CAPITAL GAINS AND LOSSES

Capital Gain and Loss Situation	Individual	Corporation
Net long-term gain.	50% of net long-term gain is taxed at regular individual tax rate OR first $50,000 of gain is taxed at 25% and excess at 35%	Pays normal 20–22% or 48% tax on ordinary income plus net long-term gain OR pays normal tax on ordinary income plus 30% tax on gain.
Net long-term loss.	May deduct 50% of loss from ordinary income, up to $2,000 in 1977 and $3,000 thereafter. All excess loss may be carried forward until it is used up.	May not deduct capital losses from current income, but may carry back loss three years to offset previous capital gains or five years forward to offset gains.
Net short-term gain.	Fully taxed as ordinary income.	Fully taxed as ordinary income.
Net short-term loss.	Deduct full amount from other income up to $2,000 in 1977 and $3,000 thereafter. Excess can be carried to succeeding years.	Carry back/forward to offset gains.
Net long-term gain & Net short-term gain.	Add 50% of long-term gain and 100% of short-term gain to your ordinary income and it will be taxed at the rate of your other income OR use the "first $50,000" alternative listed above under net long-term gain.	Add all short-term and long-term gain to ordinary income OR add short-term gain to ordinary income and compute long-term gain tax at the alternative 30% rate.
Net long-term gain & Net short-term loss.	Long term gain minus short-term loss and if: (a) remainder is a loss, deduct it from ordinary income up to $2,000 in 1977 and $3,000 thereafter. Carry over to later years if necessary. (b) remainder is a gain, add 50% to other income OR use "first $50,000" alternative listed above.	Deduct the short-term loss from the long-term gain and if: (a) loss exceeds gain it can be carried back/forward to offset capital gains in other years. It may not be deducted. (b) gain exceeds loss, excess gain can be added to ordinary income OR be taxed at alternative 30% rate.
Net short-term gain & net long-term loss	Short-term gain minus long-term loss and if: (a) gain is greater, add remainder to other income. (b) loss is greater, remaining net long-term loss is deductible under normal rules for net long-term loss.	Deduct the loss from the gain and if: (a) gain exceeds loss, gain is added to ordinary income. (b) if loss exceeds gain, loss can not be deducted, but it can be carried back/forward to offset gain in other years.
Net long-term loss & short-term loss.	Losses may be applied to offset up to $2,000 of ordinary income ($3,000 in 1978 and subsequent) in the following manner: (a) apply short-term loss and then the long-term loss. (b) Carryovers retain their identity as short-term or long-term losses in later years.	May not deduct capital losses, but may carry them back/forward to offset capital gains.

How to accelerate or defer business income

Open account vs. consignment sales. To speed up income, switch to open sales; title then passes and income is recognized when the goods are turned over to a common carrier. To defer income, sell on consignment; that way income is not recognized until the purchaser sells the merchandise.

Outright sale vs. approval. Outright sale with right of return results in immediate recognition of income. By switching to approval sales, income is not recognized until the goods are accepted and approved.

Collection policy. If on a cash basis, defer income by slowing up on billings and collections. Conversely, if collections are increased, income is greater. Speed up payments by giving discounts. If the business is on an accrual basis, speed up or slow down (as needed) on the completion of contracts and the closing of sales.

Installment sales. If you sell merchandise on the installment plan, you can spread the profit over the collection period while taking expense deductions in the current period. To speed up income, you can sell the installment obligations to a third party. Note that you can switch to installment reporting without IRS permission. You can also decide whether or not to use the installment plan with each sale.

Long-term contracts. If the contract is over twenty-four months, you can postpone recognition of income and expenses until the contract is completed ("completed contract" method). Alternatively, you can report on the "percentage of completion method" and pick up income and expenses as you go.

Equipment trade-in. If the trade-in value of a piece of used equipment is higher than its tax basis, sell it outright to a third party to capture the gain. Conversely, to avoid recognition of the gain, trade the equipment in.

How to shift business expenses

Acquire assets. If you plan to buy needed equipment, time the purchase to give you expenses when you need them. By acquiring assets before the end of the year (even if you buy on time), you get a triple benefit: depreciation deductions; 20% first-year additional depreciation allowance, and 10% investment credit, which means you effectively pay only 90% of the asset's cost.

Repairs and supplies. To accelerate expenses, make needed repairs, remodel if needed, and buy supplies now. Hold off if you want the expenses next year.

Prepayments. If on a cash basis, pay all bills by December 31 for a deduction this year. To defer the expenses, wait until January. Certain expenses can also be prepaid, such as office expenses, travel expenses, as well as *next year's* real estate taxes and state income tax. Note: Payment by check at the end of the year will give a current deduction, even if the check doesn't clear until next year.

Worthless property.

- *Bad debts.* If a debt is questionable, press hard to prove it is worthless for a deduction this year. Otherwise wait until next year.

- *Inventory.* To get a current deduction, aggressively write down any items damaged, obsolete, or unsalable at current prices. Otherwise hold off.
- *Equipment.* To get a current deduction, junk or abandon any worthless equipment before December 31.

Advertising. You can plan and prepay for advertising programs this year even though the programs will not go into effect until next year. The expense can then be applied to this year even though you will not benefit from the advertising until next year.

Contested Liability. If someone claims that your firm owes them a given sum of money, but you disagree, you have a contested liability. If you refuse to pay it, you cannot take a current deduction for it, but you may pay the amount into an escrow account and take the tax break in the current year. Later, if the settlement gives you a refund from the money you put into escrow, this refund is treated as ordinary income in the year received. Similar tactics may be applied to a contested tax bill, allowing you to make use of a tax problem to save tax dollars elsewhere.

Effect on Money Use. When you accelerate deductions and defer income you temporarily lose the use of the money involved. However, if you defer deductions and accelerate income and taxes, you improve your cash flow.

Inventory policy. To reduce income, switch to the last-in, first-out (LIFO) inventory accounting method. First-in, first-out (FIFO) generally results in higher income. Note: These changes cannot be made at will. Get further details from your tax consultant. Also, some businessmen have the impression that loading up on inventory at the end of the year will reduce income and taxes. This is not true. All that happens is cash is exchanged for another asset—inventory.

Personal Tax Planning

It will always be to your advantage to take the time to coordinate your business tax strategy with your personal tax strategy. Secondly, establishing an effective personal tax strategy may necessitate a change in your spending habits. The idea is to time your deductible expenditures so you have an option in regard to the year in which you claim tax deductions. This option will allow you to be flexible enough to accommodate changes in your own income from year to year as well as changes in tax rates.

Timing Cash Payments. According to the IRS, an expense is not deductible until it is paid and it is considered to be paid on the day you put your check in the mail. Therefore, if you can arrange to have some of the year's predictable expenses fall due in December, you can either pay them in December and take the tax deduction that year, or wait until January to pay them so you can take the deduction in the following year. Similarly, you can manipulate the year's income by arranging to have certain annual incoming monies come available toward the end of December, allowing you either to pick them up and have them counted in the current year's income, or delay picking them up until January.

Charitable Contributions. In general, you should plan your strategy in regard to charitable contributions later in the year when you will be able to judge if the year will produce high or low income. You get your personal deduction for contributions when the check is mailed, not when you promise to pay. If you donate long-term property, appreciation is included in determining the amount of contribution. Short-term property is deductible only on the basis of its cost. Appreciation isn't counted on short-term property.

Personal Property Taxes and Real Estate. Sometimes you can prepay taxes on personal property and real estate and in this way control the time of your deduction. This isn't always permissible so you should be sure it is an allowable procedure with your local government before you include it in your strategy. A deposit on future tax is not a deductible expense when it is paid.

Installment Payment of State and Local Income Tax. Estimated installment payments of state and local income taxes are deductible on your federal return in the year they are paid. Refunds for any overpayment of estimated tax are treated as income in the year you receive them. Therefore, you can shift this year's income into next year by purposely overpaying estimated state and local taxes this year. The deduction comes this year, but the income from the refund comes back next year.

Prepayment of State Income Tax. You may deduct current year state income tax from current year federal tax if you report the state tax and prepay it on a tentative state return before the end of the current year. This is a good tactic when you have an unusually high income in one year because the deduction goes in the same year as the federal return that reports the higher gross income. The taxable income is therefore reduced by the deduction for the state tax.

Medical Expenses. Try to shift medical expenses so that the bulk of the expenses fall into every other tax year. The point is this: you can only deduct the part of your total medical expense that exceeds 3% of your adjusted gross income. (Included in your medical expenses is the part of the total cost of drugs and medicines that exceeds 1% of your adjusted gross income). So if your adjusted gross income this year is $20,000, and your total medical expenses this year is $800, you may only deduct $200 for this year [$800 − (.03 × $20,000) = $200]. If you have the same income and medical expenses next year, your total deduction over the two years will be $400. However, if you could somehow shift $300 of this year's medical expense into next year, you would have no deduction for this year, but you would get a $500 deduction next year ($800 + $300 = $1100 − 3% of $20,000 = $500.) and thus save yourself an extra $100 over the two years.

To shift medical expenses into the next year, you should schedule non-emergency treatment like check-ups, minor surgery, and dental work for December and then delay paying the bills until January.

Half the cost of medical insurance premium that you personally pay is deductible up to $150. The 3% limit does not apply to this half but the other half of the premium cost is included in the 3% limit. Therefore, if you carry a policy that costs at least $300, half of that is deductible.

If you pay for a medical examination that is required for your job, you can deduct its cost as a business related expense. The 3% limit does not apply unless treatment is prescribed after the examination. The cost of the treatment is subject to the limitation.

If you pay for more than half the support of a parent who is 65 or over, you may deduct any medical expense you pay for that parent. For this reason it makes sense to have the parent assign his medical expenses to your half of his support costs and pay the other half with his own income.

Miscellaneous Deductions. The following are some deductible expenses that should be scheduled for payment in December to give you the maximum flexibility in determining the more advantageous tax year for them. They are expenses for: investment advice, safe deposit box rental, tax counsel, purchase of clothes needed in your work, business association dues, and other business related expenses that cannot be charged off through your work.

Offset Capital Gains and Losses. If you have capital gains or losses this year, think about selling other property that will offset this year's gain or loss.

Itemize One Year, Take Standard Deduction the Next. You have an option each year of taking the standard 16% deduction on adjusted gross income or itemizing your deductions. By alternating the itemizing system and the standard deduction (which allows deductions up to $2,800 on a joint return, you can save additional tax dollars. Here is how it can work: If you itemize $4,000 this year and $4,000 the next, you get a two-year total of $8,000 in deductions. But if you shift $3,000 out of one year and into the next, you may itemize $7,000 in one year and take the $2,800 standard deduction in the other year, a total of $9,800 deducted. You gain $1,800 in deductions that, when multiplied by your tax rate, gives you the money saved over the two years.

Gifts. If you want to make a gift to a family member, think about taking advantage of this year's $3,000 annual gift tax exclusion. This means you may give a gift of up to $3,000 each year without paying gift tax. If you plan to pass your estate on to your children, you can start this year and avoid a large estate tax later on. If your wife also makes a gift, the limit for the exclusion is doubled to $6,000, but remember, a gift by check to a family member must clear the bank in December to be counted in that tax year.

These are just a few suggestions for personal tax planning. Depending upon your individual tax situation, there may be many more ways in which you can reduce your yearly tax liability by careful planning.

HOW TO HANDLE OPERATING LOSS CARRYBACK/FORWARD

If a corporation has an operating loss, that loss may be carried back three years to offset previous highly taxed income. This may yield a tax refund. If the loss is not used up in offsetting income of the previous three years, it may be carried forward seven years to offset future income. If, after being carried forward seven years, the loss is still not used up, the excess loss is wasted and may no longer be used to offset income.

This carryback/forward rule may allow you to gain a substantial tax saving by shifting income into the coming year to create a loss in the current year. This loss may then be used to offset past income and to gain a tax refund.

For example, suppose your business paid 48% tax on an income of $40,000 in 1975, but now in the year 1978 you anticipate only breaking even. However, you can foresee that in 1979 your fortunes will rebound somewhat and your tax rate will be 22%. Here's how you save money. By deferring income into 1979 and by accelerating depreciation, you create a current 1978 loss of $6,000. You may now carryback that loss to 1975 and get a refund of 48% of $6,000 or $2,880. In 1979 you then pay 22% tax on the monies that were deferred into that year, but it still totals out to an incremental tax saving.

It's an unpleasant thought, but there's always a chance that a business will suffer losses that are too great to be absorbed by either the three-year carryback or the seven-year carry forward. What then? Well, here's one way you might be able to use up the excess loss in offsetting future income, despite restrictions.

Just to pick a figure, suppose you still have $5,000 of loss left over after the seventh future year of carryforward that will be wasted. You notice, however, that in the following year you anticipate $500 per month income from rental of some equipment. You may want to approach the renter and offer a $1,000 discount on the annual rent if he'll pay it for the whole year in advance. If he agrees, that $5,000 comes into the current year's income and allows you to utilize the $5,000 loss carryforward that otherwise would have been lost. The net tax savings, if your business is taxed at 48%, is $5,000 × 48% = $2,400. Of course you gave up $1,000 as a rental discount, but you are still well ahead.

TAX-FREE (SECTION 1031) EXCHANGES

Tax-free exchanges are treated under Section 1031 of the Internal Revenue Code. Basically the regulations state that *no gain or loss will be recognized on property held for business or investment purposes if it is exchanged for other property of like kind.* In practice, what this means is that if you swap real estate you presently own for other similar property, you can effectively defer any tax you would have owed on gains, had you sold the property outright. Hence, the term, "tax-free exchange."

For example, ten years ago you purchased a piece of land for your business for $10,000. Today it has a market value of $60,000 and you want to get rid of it so you can move your business to a new location. The new location you want happens to be owned by Mr. Smith and it, too, let us say, has a present market value of $60,000. If you sell your old property outright, you must pay capital gains tax on $50,000, which amounts to $12,500 tax. But if Smith will agree to a direct exchange of properties, you may indefinitely defer payment of the capital gains tax. Of course, should you decide to sell your new property outright years later, you would then have to pay the capital gains tax.

But what if Mr. Smith isn't interested in swapping for your property? Suppose he wants cash? Then you must bring in a third party. Here is how it is done by real estate professionals, step by step:

Step 1. You find a person who wishes to buy your property and have him sign an agreement to purchase the property from a *third party* at the agreed price.

Step 2. With this agreement in hand you locate a seller of suitable replacement property that you would like to own. The definition of like kind property is quite broad. For example, you could exchange improved city real estate for an unimproved farm, an apartment house for a building lot, or a leasehold of thirty or more years for raw land.

Step 3. You and the seller agree to *exchange* your properties. Any difference in price can be balanced with cash, notes, or other considerations. (Of course, the person receiving the additional consideration, be it cash, a mortgage assumption, or something else, must pay tax on this additional consideration.)

Step 4. At the closing you convey your property to the seller, and he conveys his property to you. Assuming all other considerations are properly handled, you have met the requirements of a direct exchange and have legally postponed any capital gains tax.

Step 5. One final step remains. The seller does not want your property. The problem is solved, however, because you arranged for him to convey it to your original buyer immediately after the exchange. Everyone is happy, and the circle is complete. The seller merely acted as a conduit in the transaction.

Section 1031 exchanges offer the sophisticated businessman and investor a valuable and straightforward technique to achieve nonrecognition of otherwise taxable gain. Unless you do not intend to reinvest the proceeds of the sale in real estate, always consider an exchange instead of a sale. In any transaction of this type, however, you should retain the services of competent professionals to assist you.

THE TAX SAVING POSSIBILITIES OF CHARITABLE CONTRIBUTIONS

You can save a substantial amount of tax dollars when you make a donation to a qualified charity by donating property instead of cash. Appreciated property, which would yield a long-term capital gain if sold, can be donated for a deduction equal to the fair market value at time of donation. This will be explained in depth shortly, but first we should review the basic rules that apply to charitable contributions.

An individual may donate up to 50% of his adjusted gross income to a church or public charity and get a full deduction on his donation. But if the donation is appreciated property that would otherwise qualify for long-term capital gains, the limit for the deduction is 30% of the gross adjusted income. Also, if the donation is made to a private charity, the deduction is limited to a donation of 20% of the gross adjusted income. A carryover of five years is permitted for any contribution to a public charity.

A corporation may deduct a donation up to a limit of 5% of its taxable income and it too may use a five year carryover period for excess donation.

The Type of Donation

The type of property contributed determines the tax treatment given to the donation.

- *Cash.* You may deduct the amount of cash contributed.
- *Depreciable Property.* You may deduct the fair market value of depreciable property minus any recapture of depreciation. A recapture of an investment credit is also a possibility.
- *Long-Term Capital Assets to Public Charity.* A donation to a public charity of a capital asset held more than twelve months (nine months in 1977) may be deducted according to its current fair market value. The fair market value would include any and all appreciation in value.
- *Long-Term Capital Assets to Private Charity.* If you choose to donate appreciated long-term assets to a private charity, you may deduct the cost basis plus 50% of any appreciation in value.
- *Short-Term Capital Assets.* A donation of capital assets held for investment for less than twelve months (nine months in 1977) may be deducted according to its cost basis or its fair market value—whichever is less.
- *Other Contributions.* If you hold a flea market sale for the benefit of a charity, donate personal, tangible property, preferred stock received as a nontaxable dividend or any other type of contribution, check with your tax advisor about the allowable deductions because these items can sometimes invoke some complicated restrictions.

An examination of the nature and treatment of charitable donations reveals that the best kind of donation from a tax standpoint is the contribution of long-term capital assets to a public charity. Here's how you can save tax dollars on such a donation:

Suppose you want to donate $2,000 cash to your church. You are in the 30% tax bracket. You get a deduction of $2,000 which reduces your tax by $2,000 × .30 = $600. But, if instead you give property worth $2,000, which you bought six years ago for $800, you get the tax deduction of $600 plus you avoid a capital gain tax of ($1,200 gain × 50% capital gain deduction × 30% tax rate) = $180.

In regard to charitable donations note that:

- You must keep records of contributions and if the contribution exceeds $200, you must attach a note to your tax return giving details of the contribution (to whom, where located, etc.)
- You may not deduct for personal services rendered the charity nor for the use of property.
- Gifts to charities reduce your income tax and also reduce your taxable estate.

Small Items That Add Up

Sometimes you can make a respectable tax saving at the end of the year by adding up all the little charitable contributions you made during the year. For example:

- The cost of materials used to make an item that is donated to charity is deductible whether the item is a Stroganoff casserole and the deductible ingredient is meat or a picnic table made of 35 board feet of redwood.
- Household goods donated for the church bazaar are deductible and if the charity won't appraise them upon receipt, figure them at 20% to 35% of new cost.
- If you go to a charity ball, you may deduct the price of the ticket, although you may not deduct the price of tickets for charity lotteries, or bingo.
- If you wear a special uniform while performing a charitable service and that uniform can't be worn elsewhere, you may deduct the cost of the uniform.
- If you drive your car for a charitable purpose you may deduct 6¢ per mile in expenses.

Get into the habit of keeping records on this kind of charitable contribution and add them up at the end of the year. Every little bit helps.

YOU MAY SAVE MONEY BY INCOME AVERAGING

If you have income this year that is substantially greater than your income in the previous four years, you may be able to use income averaging to reduce your income tax liability. Subject to conditions described below, an individual may use income averaging if a yearly income is more than $3,000 greater than 120% of his average income over the four previous years. This system, originally designed to aid artists and inventors who might spend years on a project before realizing any income from it, allows an individual to put the unusually high income into a lower bracket for computation. It does not allow you to spread out tax payments over a number of years.

Who Can Use It?

Only individuals may use income averaging. Corporations, estates, and trusts are not allowed to use it. If you were not a resident or citizen of the United States during any of the four years you will use to determine your income average, you may not use income averaging. If you did not pay at least 50% of your support during the years upon which you will base your income average (as in years spent in school), you may not use it. This provision is designed to prevent new college graduates who land high paying jobs from using their student days for income averaging.

Definitions

For ease of further discussion, definition of the following words is needed.

- "Computation year" is the year in which you receive the income you hope to average.
- "Base period years" means the four preceding years upon which you base your income average.
- "Taxable income" means gross adjusted income less exemptions and deductions.

What Kind of Income Merits Averaging?

Again, if your income is $3,000 higher than 120% of your average income over the previous four years, you may average almost all of your income. This includes 50% of net long-term capital gain. But you may not average: throwback trust accumulation distributions; excessive or premature distributions from self-employment retirement plans; or other income subject to a limitation on tax.

Suppose your average income over the last four years is $10,000 and this year you earn $16,000. You may use the income averaging in this case since 120% $\times$ $10,000 = $12,000 and $12,000 + $3,000 equals $15,000, which is less than your current income. Note that your marital status, the property laws of the state in which you live, and the place where you earned the income may affect your computation of tax.

How to Average Your Income and Compute Your Tax

IRS Schedule G of Form 1040 details the procedure for averaging income and computing tax, but the general idea is as follows:

1. Find your income average over the last four years.
2. Determine "base income" by multiplying average income by 120%.
3. Subtract base income from this year's income to find your "averageable income".

4. Take averageable income and divide it by five. Add this to your "base income".
5. Use Schedule G to compute the tax on your base income (from step 2) and then compute tax on base income + averageable income ÷ 5. Now subtract the one total from the other to get the tax difference.
6. Take this tax difference and multiply it by five. Add this number to the tax on your base income to get your final tax liability.

How Much Can You Save?

Without averaging, an individual with an average income over four years of $10,000 pays $3,820 tax when he ends a year in which he makes $18,000. With averaging this same individual pays only $3,760, a saving of $60.00.

A taxpayer with an average income of $17,000 over four years suddenly comes into a year in which he doubles his income. Without using income averaging he pays $9,500 tax. However, by using income averaging he pays only $9,138, a tax saving of $362.

The determining factor in income averaging isn't the amount of increase in income, but rather the proportion of increase over the previous four year income average.

When Should You Use Income Averaging?

You may use income averaging whenever you meet the requirements for it. You must elect to use it by filling out schedule G on the 1040 form. You may elect to use income averaging up to three years from the time the tax return was due or within two years from the time the tax was paid, whichever is later.

Disadvantages of Income Averaging

Usually, income averaging will yield a worthwhile tax saving, but bear in mind the following factors when you consider using income averaging. If you elect income averaging, you may not in the same year take advantage of:

- maximum 50% tax on earned income
- exclusion of income earned outside the United States
- alternative capital gain tax
- optional tax tables

CASUALTY LOSSES—SOFTENING THE BLOW OF DISASTER

Casualty losses are property losses sustained as a result of a "sudden, unexpected, and unusual . . . identifiable event," according to the tax code. Furthermore, the tax code stipulates that the loss must stem from an event that is "an accident or sudden invasion by a hostile agency or force," like a forest fire that burns your home, a high velocity wind, or a tidal wave. But sunlight damage to curtains, termite damage to outdoor furniture, and breakage of family crystal due to your own clumsiness, doesn't qualify. Common daily misfortunes of this sort are not deductible casualty losses.

Naturally, the issue isn't always black and white. Sometimes the individual suffering the loss will see the event as a natural disaster, but the IRS will disagree. If necessary, the court will settle the matter. If you're not sure if the deduction will be allowed, check with your accountant about deducting it anyway. At worst, IRS will make you pay it back later.

How to Determine the Deduction

For complete or partial loss of *non-business property* you may deduct the difference between the before and after fair market value. The difference, however, is limited to the adjusted basis of the property. For a *complete loss* of *business property* you deduct the adjusted basis of the property. For *partial loss* of business property, you apply the rules used in regard to loss of non-business property. Note, however, that the cost of the repairs necessary to restore property to its pre-casualty condition is an acceptable indicator of the property's loss in fair market value. If the value drops more than repair costs, the court has ruled that you may deduct the actual drop in value.

You may only deduct the amount of a non-business loss that exceeds $100. In other words, if a flood hits your basement and destroys your $120 carpet down there, you may deduct $20 and no more. But what if that same flood also destroys your $1,000 furnace, a $200 antique basinette, and does $150 damage to your pool table? In that case you subtract the $100 from the total loss suffered from the single casualty act and the remainder is deductible. In this case $120 + $1,000 + $200 + $150 = $1470 and then you subtract the $100 and your total deductible loss is $1370.

Other Casualty Loss Considerations

- An uninsured casualty loss in inventory will show up in your inventory account. You may take a separate loss deduction only if you make a corresponding adjustment in your inventory account.
- You may not take a casualty loss on money or property that "just disappeared." You must document a theft either by reporting it in writing to the police or by obtaining a copy of their report of the theft.
- You may not deduct for sentimental or aesthetic value of non-business property.
- You may not claim a casualty loss deduction on property that you do not own. If you damage your neighbor's boat, you may not deduct the amount it costs you to repair it because it's his property, not yours.
- You may deduct costs incurred in attempting to recover

stolen property and you may deduct costs for cleaning up after a deductible casualty loss.

Precautions

It helps in clearing up matters of casualty loss if you can prove condition and value of property before and after the accident. Save purchase checks, expert appraisals, newspaper clippings relating to the event, and anything else that will help document your casualty claim. Also, before and after photographs of property can help to quickly expedite claims. Therefore, you might consider taking periodic photos of your property. All these things can, in the event of a deductible loss, bring about greater tax savings and greater ease of obtaining the savings.

Fear of Insurance Premium Increases

Some people refuse to file for insurance reimbursement after a casualty loss because they fear an increase in insurance rates. However, the IRS usually tries to disallow the casualty loss deduction if you don't claim insurance reimbursement when you are clearly eligible for it.

HOBBY EXPENSES AND LOSSES MAY BE DEDUCTIBLE

The expenses and losses of your hobby are deductible if you can show that you engage in the hobby activity for a profit. When a hobby yields a profit it becomes a secondary business activity and as such is entitled to deductions usually permitted for a regular business. Also, a loss from the hobby may be deducted from other income if the hobby is deemed a business activity. Examples of profit-making hobbies might be: refinishing old automobiles for resale, painting saleable works of art, or stamp collecting for profit.

Many people would like to deduct the costs of their hobbies. Consequently, the IRS had to find some way to define those hobbies that are entitled to business deductions. Section 183 of the IRS Code was designed to provide this definition, and to some extent it succeeds. Generally, an activity is deemed to be engaged in for profit if it produces a profit in any two of five consecutive years—unless the IRS can prove otherwise. The hobby of raising horses is an exception. You must make a profit on your horses in any two of seven consecutive years to qualify for hobby deductions. Section 183 applies only to individuals and Subchapter S corporations. It does not apply to regular corporations.

Proving Profit Motive

If you claim profit on your hobby for the required two out of five years, it's up to the IRS to disprove your claim if they want to disallow your deductions. Conversely, if you don't claim the needed two years of profit, you've got a long uphill fight ahead of you to prove that your activity is nevertheless a profit-motivated hobby. The following are nine important considerations used to determine the validity of profit motivation in a hobby:

- How much time is spent at the hobby? Is anyone else employed to continue work when the claimant isn't there?
- Will the assets used in the activity appreciate in value?
- Are accurate business-like records kept of expenses and profits?
- How is the track record of the hobby enthusiast? Has he made a profit at this kind of thing before?
- Are losses and expenses in accord with reasonable expectations for the start up of a business?
- Are profits reasonable in relation to initial investment and claimed losses?
- To what extent is the hobby recreational or pleasureable? (The old idea of work cannot be fun.)
- Is there substantial income from other sources?
- Have experts been consulted to set up or run the activity?

It would hurt a taxpayer's claim if IRS decided that initial losses were too great, that there was too much income from other sources, and/or the hobby was too much fun. It would help the individual if he could answer affirmatively to the other questions. In judging a claim all the above factors must be taken into consideration. A disadvantageous answer to one or even a majority of the questions need not automatically mean the profit motivation will be disbelieved.

Tax Strategy for Hobbies. Keep your activity on a cash basis rather than an accrual basis so you can take advantage of opportunities to shift income and expenses into advantageous years to create a small profit for two of the five or seven years. You want those two years of profit, if you can get them, because then the burden of proof rests with the IRS.

What You May Deduct Even If It's Not Primarily a Profitable Hobby. You may not deduct loss on your hobby from your other income if yours is not a profitable hobby at all. However you may take normal deductions for casualty losses, interest, and state taxes (and local taxes too). It doesn't matter if you turn a profit for these deductions. You may also deduct depreciation and other expenses up to the point where total expenses equal any profit, however small.

UNIFORM GIFT TO MINORS ACT

The UGMA is designed to facilitate the transfer of property to minors. Its simplicity is its most outstanding attribute. If you wish to make a gift of property to your child under the UGMA you need only register the securities or the savings account in the following manner:

John L. Smith, as custodian for John L. Smith, Jr.,
under the Uniform Gifts to Minors Act.

Once this is done the property transferred belongs to the recipient (ownership cannot be revoked by the custodian) and interest or earnings are taxable to the minor.

Custodianship

Any adult may be the custodian under the UGMA. The custodian may buy and sell securities or deposit the proceeds in a savings account subject to his judgment but he must act with reasonable circumspection and honest intentions.

Under a short-term trust (see page 233) the donor can reclaim ownership after ten years and a day, but not so with the custodianship. When the child reaches the age of majority, he owns the property.

Additional Considerations

- You may continue to claim your child as a dependent as long as you pay more than 50% of his support costs.
- A parent may not use the custodial account to pay for the child's support. If the parent is legally obligated to pay for such support and he uses the custodial funds, the payment will be taxed to the parent.

How to Use the UGMA to Save Money

If you wanted to set up a savings account for your child's education, you could do it in your own account and never bother with custodianship. However, the tax you pay on the interest from a savings account in your own name would be determined on the basis of your personal tax rate. Usually, the tax you would pay on the interest or earnings from your own account would offset any real interest gains. On the other hand, if the account is set up in your child's name with you as custodian, the interest earned on the principal would be taxable to the child which is to say in most cases, it would be tax free. If you intend to save a few hundred dollars a year for your child's education, a custodianship under the UGMA could save you more than $1,000 in taxes over a ten to fifteen year period.

The Best Stock for a Gift

If you wish to make a gift of stock to your children, be sure the stock's market value is as close as possible to your cost basis. If there is unrealized gain or loss when you give the stock, the recipient will either have to pay capital gains or give up some standard shelters for capital loss.

If there is *unrealized gain* on the gift stock, the child will pay capital gains tax when he sells it. The basis of the stock to your child will be your basis plus the amount of any gift tax paid.

If there is *unrealized loss* on the gift stock and the recipient sells it at a loss, his basis is your basis plus gift tax or the market value at the date of gift, whichever is less. Furthermore, you don't get to offset the loss against other gains and neither does your child.

Therefore give your child stock with a market value that is closest to your cost basis. And when you make the gift, include with it a memo stating relevant tax information like purchase date of the stock, commissions paid, gift tax paid, and the market value at the time of the gift.

IMPORTANT ASPECTS OF INVOLUNTARY CONVERSION

When an owner is compelled by circumstances beyond his control to give up ownership of his property, an "involuntary conversion" occurs. If, for example, a thief relieves you of the burden of ownership of your car, this is an involuntary conversion. Similarly, if the government compels an owner to give up land so a freeway can go through, the property has undergone an involuntary conversion. Sometimes you are reimbursed by insurance for the conversion and other times you may receive money or other property from a party which is obligated to compensate you for your loss.

Involuntary conversion may result in a gain or a loss to the original owner. These gains and losses are treated as capital gains/losses and the duration of the ownership of the converted property determines whether the gains are long-term or short-term.

If you realize gain on an involuntary conversion (you have depreciated the value of the car to $1,000 but when it was stolen and destroyed, insurance paid you $2,000) you may elect not to recognize the gain now and thus you will pay no tax on it now. However, you must reduce the basis of replacement property by the amount of the gain. This way, when you sell it later, the sales price and the basis will reflect the conversion gain and the gain will in effect be subject to tax at that time.

In general, you may elect not to recognize gain from involuntary conversion if the replacement property serves the same purpose as the converted property. If you buy a new tugboat with the insurance compensation to replace the old sunken tugboat, nonrecognition is not a problem, but if you replace the old tugboat with a yacht, you might run into problems. The more latitude you take in defining a like replacement for the old property, the more trouble you are likely to have convincing the IRS of your right to nonrecognition of gain.

Usually, it will be better for you to elect not to recognize gain from involuntary conversion and to thereby avoid the immediate tax on the gain. But always do your homework. Sometimes you can make a significant tax saving by recognizing the gain, paying capital gains tax, and depreciating the new property at its full value. Making the extra effort to put the numbers into columns and doing a little arithmetic can save you money.

HOW TO HANDLE BAD DEBTS

There are two kinds of bad debts, business and personal, and each receives a different tax treatment. A bona fide business bad debt is fully deductible from ordinary income. A business bad debt may be deducted when it is completely worthless or partially worthless. But a personal bad debt may only be deducted when it is completely worthless and even then it may only be deducted as a short-term capital loss which may be used to offset capital gains up to $1,000 each year. A personal bad debt may be carried over from year to year until it is used up.

Business Debt vs. Personal Debt

Since the tax treatment of the two kinds of debt differs, there is often some confusion over what is in fact a business debt and what is a personal debt. Strictly speaking, a business debt is one that is acquired in the course of an individual's trade or business. A personal debt is one that is created outside of business. But to be more specific, here are some guidelines for distinguishing business debts from personal debts.

The following situations lead to bad *business* debts:

- Making loans to customers, suppliers, or lessees when such loans aid your business.
- Your primary business is loaning money.
- Merchandise was sold on credit and the recipient of the merchandise will not or cannot pay for it.
- Loans that are necessary to protect your business reputation.
- Accounts receivable, retained after the liquidation of your business, become uncollectable.
- You make a loan to your employer in order to keep your job.
- A loan to a corporation when that loan is instrumental in protecting your credit for a similar business activity you are engaged in.
- A loan to your partnership.

The following situations lead to bad *personal* debts:

- Debt from investment situations is not considered business debt.
- Money lent to someone else when he needs it for his business is, with some exceptions, considered a personal loan. It isn't your business, so to you, it's a personal debt.
- You make a loan to a corporation that you own to keep it on its feet. This is not a business loan because the corporation is a separate entity and as such its business is not your business.

Naturally, if you have any question about the nature of a bad debt, consult a tax expert. The above situations are only designed to give you some idea about the differences between the two kinds of debt.

HOW TO CUT YOUR UNEMPLOYMENT TAXES

Many business managers are being hit with shopping increases in their unemployment insurance tax rates. Remember that if any of your former employees collect unemployment benefits, the state charges your unemployment tax account. Obviously, the more charges, the higher your future rate will be. Here's how to keep your rate as low as possible.

In a typical state, an employer may pay $35 per employee per year for unemployment taxes. If just a few ex-workers draw on his account, that amount can easily jump to $250—an increase of over $200 per employee. Many employers are shocked to learn that an employee who they thought had quit of his own accord or was fired for a good reason can collect benefits for one reason or another. Here's why:

- *Change in job conditions.* If an employee is transferred from the day shift to the night shift (or vice versa) and then quits, unemployment benefits can be collected because job conditions were changed. To avoid this, first learn whether or not the employee will work nights. If so, the departure would have been voluntary, and no benefits could be collected.
- *Employer's convenience.* An employee who was constantly tipsy or late to work was finally told he had to go as soon as a replacement could be found. In this situation the employee can collect because the departure was timed to suit the employer's convenience. The employee would not be able to collect if after giving the employee an ultimatum, you immediately dismissed him when he disregarded your warning.
- *Language difficulties.* If a foreign employee was fired because he smoked in an area clearly marked "no smoking" where explosive solvents were kept, he can collect on the argument that his dismissal was based on instructions he couldn't understand. Therefore, be sure directions and procedures can be clearly understood by all employees.

Here are several easy steps that can cut your unemployment taxes:

Get a free ride. If two applicants are equally qualified, always hire the one presently receiving unemployment benefits. This worker's last employer (at the time he filed for benefits) is considered his most recent employer for a full year, no matter how many jobs he holds in the interim. You can hire him and let him go within the year without having your account charged for any benefits.

Be specific. If you let someone go, state the exact reason. A worker can only be disqualified for benefits for the following reasons: misconduct (cheating, stealing, absence, insubordination, etc.); quitting; refusal to work; or inability to work.

Amend your employment application blank. Ask such questions as: Will you agree to work on any shift, as assigned? Will you work on weekends or holidays, if required?

Know who is collecting from your account. Past employees whom you can prove are clearly unqualified may be collecting. Check with your local employment office frequently.

Watch the calendar. If a new employee doesn't make the grade, let him go before *three months elapse.* If he cannot obtain another job, suggest that he file for unemployment because most states will not count you as the most recent employer, since the employee didn't work a full quarter on your payroll. As a result, any benefits he collects for the following twelve months cannot be charged against you. It's the indirect taxes—unemployment taxes, workmen's compensation, FICA—that can add up. Start to cut your payroll tax costs now. A few hundred dollars savings per employee may make a substantial difference to your business.

THE TAX SAVING POSSIBILITIES OF A MEDICAL REIMBURSEMENT PLAN

Without a medical reimbursement plan an individual taxpayer who itemizes his deductions may deduct medical expenses for himself and dependents only to the extent that they exceed 3% of adjusted gross income. In addition, the taxpayer can deduct medical insurance costs of up to $150 per year as well as expenses for drugs that exceed 1% of adjusted gross income. But a good medical reimbursement plan through your company can permit far greater savings on the high cost of today's medical care.

You can avoid paying medical expenses and premiums personally by having your corporation set up a medical reimbursement plan and pay all these expenses for you. With such an arrangement, the payments are *deductible as an expense to the corporation* and *tax free to the individual.* There is no personal tax wastage due to the 3% and 1% limitations mentioned above. Also, the plan can be very flexible and can be tailored to cover a few employees or individual executives. Furthermore, benefits can range from minimum amounts to virtually unlimited coverage. Funding for the plan may entail direct reimbursement to the employee, direct payment to the doctor or medical facility, or purchase of insurance by the company.

Small companies must exercise caution

The IRS and courts make it clear that the plan must be for *employees.* In small corporations where most or all the officers and employees are also shareholders, the IRS sometimes construes the payments as dividends, claiming that payments are made because a person is a shareholder rather than because he is an employee. Here is how to avoid any problems:

Put the plan in writing. Although not required by the IRS, a written plan will support the company's position that the plan is strictly for the benefit of employees (although they may also be stockholders).

Be specific about who is covered. The written plan should spell out exactly who or what class of employee is covered. For example, if you specify management only, be sure that all management personnel are included whether they are shareholders or not. The courts have ruled that if all employees are shareholders, medical expenses for one are paid for by the others and the plan is therefore tax free since those covered benefit more as employees rather than as shareholders. But if the plan covers only one shareholder-employee, the plan will not be tax free because he benefits more as a shareholder.

Formal announcement. While it is not required, announcing the plan to covered employees will substantiate your claim that the plan is employee oriented.

Establish a maximum limitation on benefits and keep benefits in line with salary and services performed. The amounts under most benefit programs tend to be in relation to compensation and services rendered by the employee, and few employee benefits are open-ended. Therefore, placing reasonable restrictions on the amounts of medical reimbursement coverage will help support its employee orientation.

Treat dependents equally. Dependents of stockholder-employees should not be favored over other dependents in the same employee class.

A medical reimbursement plan is one of the finest tax-free benefits available to an individual and his dependents. It can cover all expenses for medical and dental care, drugs, health insurance premiums, as well as eyeglasses. Unfortunately, sole proprietors and partnerships are not considered to have employees and cannot use a medical reimbursement plan. However, Subchapter S corporations and closely held or family corporations do qualify.

IRS AUDIT SURVIVAL CHECKLIST

Almost inevitably either your business or personal tax returns will be audited by the IRS; yet few taxpayers are really prepared to handle an audit. Keep this checklist handy for eventual reference.

The agent

The first step you should take when you meet with any IRS agent is to examine his or her credentials. If the agent is a *revenue agent*, the audit is probably routine. If, however, you discover that you are dealing with a *special agent*, immediately terminate the interview, answer no questions, and phone your attorney. Revenue agents are concerned with ordinary *civil* tax questions whereas special agents investigate *criminal* tax fraud matters. While a special agent is supposed to read you a summary of your rights, they sometimes try to keep a low profile by quickly flashing their identification papers or working as a team with a revenue agent. Know which type of agent you are dealing with. Be firm but courteous in all your dealings with these agents.

Scope of audit

The second step is to ask the agent to outline the scope of the audit and what records he would like. Generally, the agent is only looking for supporting evidence for certain claims you have made. By knowing exactly what the agent is looking for, you and your accountant can prepare the necessary documentation to support your case and quickly complete the audit. Answer all questions but *do not* volunteer information or give overdetailed answers. There is obviously a fine line between being evasive, which will only engender suspicion and prolong the audit, and being too helpful. *Never allow an agent to casually browse through your papers or records.* It will only lead to more questions and may expand the scope of your audit.

Settlement and the Revenue Agent's Report (RAR)

Once the audit is complete, the agent will prepare a RAR stating his recommendations concerning the investigation. You will then be asked to sign a waiver Form 870 indicating that you agree with the agent's assessment of taxes due. If the amounts are small or the agent has discovered obvious mistakes, it is generally best to sign the form and conclude the audit. But if the agent touches on gray areas where you feel your position is defensible, you should tread carefully. If you agree to settle too quickly, the agent may feel that you have other things to hide that merit further investigation. Many agents shoot high, expecting to compromise eventually. In these situations and where the sums involved are substantial, it is preferable to let your accountant or tax attorney argue the technical points for you.

Postaudit and appellate procedures

Tax experts generally agree that a case should be settled as early as possible— preferably at the audit stage. However, if you do not agree with the agent's findings and cannot come to a settlement, you will have to appeal the case, either through the IRS *administrative* process or through the courts, which is a *judicial* process. In the administrative appeal, it is advisable to have a professional tax advisor or legal counsel accompany you. You should definitely have legal counsel for any judicial proceedings.

Administrative Process

The "30-day" and "90-day" letters. If you do not agree with the agent's assessment and refuse to sign Form 870, you will receive a copy of the RAR with a preliminary note advising you that you have thirty days to appeal your case. If you ignore the letter, you will then receive a ninety-day letter advising you to pay or petition the tax court for a redetermination.

The district conference. After receiving the thirty-day letter but before receiving the ninety-day letter, you may request a district conference with the IRS. Here you will meet with an official who is independent of the revenue agent who conducted your audit. The official has broad discretionary power to resolve disputes if the tax deficiency is less than $2,500 for the year in question and more limited power in cases involving greater amounts. About two-thirds of all cases that go to a district conference are resolved with taxpayers agreeing to settlements that average 41¢ for each dollar originally claimed by the revenue agent.

The appellate division. If you lose at the district conference or if the amounts involved are larger than $2,500, you may resort to the appellate division of the IRS. The appellate division settles about two-thirds of the cases before it with an average of 37¢ on each dollar of originally assessed deficiency.

The written protest. To make an administrative appeal you may need to file a written protest with the District Director. You do not need to file a written protest if you are appealing to the district conference staff and, (a) the disputed amount is less than $2,500 or, (b) the audit was conducted by correspondence or by interview in an IRS office. Similarly, you need not file a written protest for an appeal to the Appellate Division if, (a) the disputed amount is less then $2,500 or, (b) you already filed the protest at the district conference level. If required, the protest letter should be submitted in duplicate within the thirty-day period allowed by the preliminary letter. Contact your tax advisor or the IRS for further specifics.

Judicial Process

At any time after a tax deficiency has been determined, you may elect to bypass the IRS administrative process and proceed directly to the tax court, court of claims, or your US district court. These courts are independent judicial bodies and have no connection with the IRS. Your chances of success may be greater in court than with the IRS—about three-fourths of the cases brought to court are resolved out of court, and settlements average 30¢ for each dollar of original deficiency. These settlements, however, vary between IRS districts.

Tax Court. If your case involves a disagreement over whether you owe additional income tax, or estate or gift tax, you may go to the US tax court. To do this, ask the IRS to issue a formal letter, called a "statutory notice of deficiency." You have ninety days from the date this notice is mailed to you (150 days if addressed to you outside the US) to file a petition with the tax court.

Note that if your case involves a dispute of $1,500 or less for any one taxable year, a simplified alternative procedure is provided by the tax court. Upon your request and with the approval of the tax court your case may be handled under the Small Tax Case procedures. At little cost to you in time

APPEALS PROCEDURE CHART

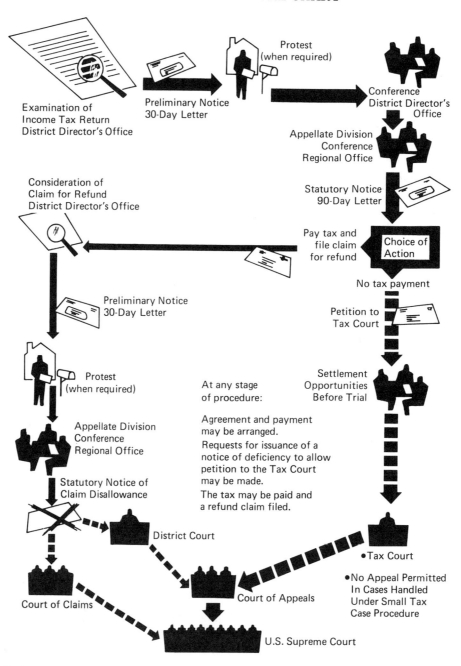

or money, you can present your own case to the tax court for a binding decision. If your case is handled under this procedure, the decision of the tax court is final and cannot be appealed. You can obtain more information regarding the Small Tax Case procedures and other tax court matters from the Clerk of the US Tax Court, 400 Second Street, NW, Washington, DC 20217.

District Court and Court of Claims. You may file a claim for refund if after you pay your tax you believe the tax is erroneous or excessive. If the IRS hasn't acted on your claim within six months from the date you filed it, you can then file suit for refund. A suit for refund must be filed no later than two years after the IRS has disallowed your claim. You may file your refund suit in your US district court or in the US court of claims. Generally, your district court and the court of claims hear tax cases only after you have paid the tax and have filed a claim for refund. You can obtain information about procedure for filing suit in either court by contacting the clerk of the district court in your area or the Clerk of the Court of Claims, 717 Madison Place NW, Washington, DC 20005.

An IRS audit is no reason for panic and it does not indicate that the IRS intends to delve into all of your personal or business affairs. As you can see, appeal to higher authorities generally results in a lower settlement, but, of course, costs more in legal fees.

MAKING THE MOST OF BUSINESS INTERRUPTION INSURANCE

What Is It? Business interruption insurance is insurance that pays an owner for overhead expenses and loss of profits if the business is closed down for a while due to fire or some other casualty. Most businesses carry some form of business interruption insurance. There are two kinds of interruption insurance, "valued" and "nonvalued."

A nonvalued form of business interruption insurance pays for the estimated loss of profits due to casualty and the reimbursement money is taxed as ordinary income. The amount of payment depends on the amount of estimated profit lost.

A less common form of interruption insurance is the valued form which pays a fixed amount to the business during the loss of operations due to casualty. The payments are not based on the estimated loss of profit. However, the income from valued form is taxed at the lower capital gains rate. If the money is used to replace damaged property, it may be treated as a nontaxable exchange and the capital gain tax can be deferred.

It could mean a substantial tax saving if you can take the time to look into the valued form of business interruption insurance. In some states this form is not allowed, but it can't hurt to find out.

TAX EXCLUSION ON AN EMPLOYEE DEATH BENEFIT

The motivation behind a presentation of money to the family of a deceased employee will determine the tax treatment given that sum.

Compensation

In general, payment made by a company to the widow or other beneficiary of a deceased employee is tax-free income to the beneficiary up to $5,000 if the payment was made in compensation for the death. (This, of course, assumes that the deceased did not have a nonforfeitable right to such payment before his death.) Not only can the beneficiary take the money tax free, but the amount is also fully deductible to the company as a reasonable business expense. It doesn't matter if the payment was made because of a written contract or because of a sense of duty on the part of the company.

Gift

If a larger payment of, say, $10,000 is made out of charity, respect, or for some other reason besides legal and moral obligation, it is considered a gift and as such is completely tax free to the recipient and is deductible up to $5,025 for the company as a reasonable business expense. In this case the company gets the normal gift deduction of $25 plus the $5,000 maximum deduction for the death benefit payment.

Additional Compensation

If, however, the $10,000 payment is considered additional compensation— and the amount of additional compensation is reasonable—the company may deduct the full $10,000 as an ordinary business expense. The beneficiary would pay tax on only $5,000—the remainder is tax free. Usually, the IRS regards death benefit payment as additional compensation. It's often a struggle to prove it is a gift.

PERSONAL DIVIDEND DEDUCTION

The IRS allows you to take a $100 exclusion on income you receive from stock dividends. Therefore, if you have $300 in income from your stocks, you pay tax on only $200.

However, if you have a wife and a child and they have no income from dividends, you may transfer some stock to each of them and in this way get two extra $100 exclusions on the dividend income. Even if you and your wife file a joint return, she retains her exclusion.

Therefore, in the above case, the family would use its three $100 exclusions to escape tax on the entire $300 dividend income. If the original stock owner is in a 40% tax bracket, this means a tax saving of $120 per year.

DEDUCTING FOR BAD DEBTS
WITHIN THE FAMILY

You may not claim a bad debt deduction for an uncollectable loan to a
member of your family unless you can prove to the IRS that it was a loan
and not a gift. The way to prove it is a loan is to write it down in a business-
like form stating maturity date and interest paid. It sounds rather cold for
family business, but it could save you tax money if, for some reason, the
family member decides not to pay you back.

DEDUCTING SUPPORT OF A
DEPENDENT PARENT

If you pay more than 50% of the cost of supporting a parent, you may take
the $750 deduction for a dependent. Here's how this can work to save you
tax money.

Suppose you support a parent who gets $1400 a year from social security
and other sources. The parent's medical expenses come to $200 a year and
you give the parent $100 per month to help with living costs. That adds up
to only $1,400 in support per year, but if you gave the parent $100.50 per
month, your yearly support total would be $1,406 which would put you
safely over the half-way mark. Then you claim the parent as a dependent,
take the $750 exemption and add the parent's medical costs to your own
for later tax deductions.

CHILD'S INCOME

A child is entitled to a $750 personal deduction and a low income allowance
of $1,700 which combined allows him $2,450 of tax-free "earned" income.
However, if the child has "unearned" income, he may not use the $1,700
low income allowance to offset it. A child's unearned income may be offset
by his personal $750 deduction and by the $100 dividend exclusion if part
of the unearned income is from dividends. Here's how it works. If a child
has a total annual income of $2,700 with $1,700 of earned income and
$1,000 of unearned income, he may offset the $1,700 with the low
income allowance ($1,700) and use his personal $750 deduction plus the
$100 dividend exclusion to reduce his taxable unearned income to $150.
The child's total taxable income in this example is, therefore, only $150.

You can shift income from your own higher tax bracket to your child's
lower bracket by (a) employing your child in your business or (b) transferring
income-producing property to your child. However, keep in mind the following bits of information in regard to a child's tax situation.

- The parent may still claim the $750 dependency exemption if he provides more than half of the child's support and the child is under nineteen years of age or attends school five months or more per year.
- If the child is under twenty-one and is employed by a father-and-mother partnership or by a parent who is a sole proprietor, his wages are exempt from Social Security and federal unemployment taxes.
- If your child is employed by your corporation or by your sole proprietorship, his wages can be deducted as ordinary business expenses. Of course his wages must be reasonable in relation to his work and he must really work for you and make a contribution to the profit making capabilities of the company.
- Children may claim exemption from income tax withholding by filing form W-4E with their employers—providing they did not pay tax in the previous year and do not expect to pay tax in the current year. This rule applies unless the child earns more than $2,450 or has a gross income over $750 that is comprised in part by unearned income.

DISC

The term DISC actually stands for Domestic International Sales Corporation. To stimulate exports and improve the balance of payments, Congress authorized in 1971 the creation of this new type of corporation. Specifically, a DISC is granted special status and tax benefits in return for acting as an export agent for its parent (if the DISC is a subsidiary) or for other unrelated manufacturers of export products. Here are some of the benefits a DISC can provide.

Taxation

The DISC itself is *not* subject to income tax. Instead, 50% of its profits are taxable to its *shareholders* in the year earned. So long as export sales grow, the IRS considers the balance taxable to the shareholders only when actually distributed to them. Hence, the tax on one-half of profits can potentially be deferred indefinitely.

Producer's loan

Under the proper conditions, the 50% of the DISC's income on which income tax is deferred may be loaned ("producer's loan") to the parent or shareholders without being considered as distributed and, hence, taxable.

Freedom from transfer-pricing problems

The DISC provides "safe havens" from the strict and complex intercompany pricing rules found elsewhere in the Internal Revenue Code. Rules governing

DISCs effectively allow a liberal portion of the profit from an export transaction to be allocated to the DISC (when it receives the tax benefit) rather than to the manufacturer.

Requirements to set up a DISC

Because the DISC legislation had a definite purpose in mind—to increase exports—the law provides strict qualifying criteria:

- The DISC must be domestically incorporated, although it can operate in foreign countries.
- Not more than one class of stock may be oustanding, and capital must be maintained at $2,500 or more.
- At least 95% of the DISC's assets and receipts must be related to its export function.
- The export corporation must make an election to be treated as a DISC.

To qualify for the 50% tax deferral granted to DISC's, the law (1971 Revenue Act) says that the shareholders must make an election to have the corporation treated as a DISC *ninety days prior to the beginning of the taxable year* for which they want the deferment. Your accountant or attorney should have the proper form for making the election.

For further information contact your local IRS office, Commerce Department, or obtain a very informative booklet by the Treasury Department entitled, *DISC—A Handbook for Exporters.* Write to Government Printing Office, Washington, DC 20402 and ask for Stock #4800-0194 (40¢).

RULE OF 78s—ACCELERATED INTEREST

The Rule of 78s allows the acceleration of interest payments on installment loans made at a discount and on discount loans. If the borrower needs greater interest deductions in the first year and/or the lender needs greater income from interest in the first year, each would be well advised to consider using the alternative Rule of 78s to compute interest payments.

How It Works

Normally, interest is prorated evenly over the payment periods. You pay the same amount of interest on the first payment as you do on the last one.

But under the Rule of 78s, you determine interest payments by multiplying the total interest on a loan by a declining series of fractions.

The numerator (top part of the fraction) is determined by the number of months the loan has yet to run. The denominator (bottom of fraction) is computed by adding up the months of the loan (the denominator of a twelve-month loan would be $1+2+3+4+5+6+7+8+9+10+11+12 = 78$—hence, the name, Rule of 78s. The denominator of an eighteen-month loan would be $1+2+3+ \ldots +18 = 171$).

So, if the total interest on a twelve-month loan was $2,000, the interest due on the first payment under the Rule of 78s would be:

$$2,000 \times \frac{(\text{Number of months yet to go} = 12)}{(\text{sum of months} = 78)} = \$307.60$$

The second month it would be $2,000 $\times \dfrac{11}{78}$ = $282.00.

The third month it would be $2,000 $\times \dfrac{10}{78}$ = $256.40.

The fourth month it would be $2,000 $\times \dfrac{9}{78}$ = $230.60, etc.

If you are contemplating the use of the Rule of 78s, keep the following in mind.

- This accelerated computation of interest yields no tax benefit if the loan is for less than twelve months.
- If you want to switch from the standard pro rata method to the Rule of 78s, you must let the IRS know by filing form 3115.
- The lender and the borrower may use different methods of accounting in regard to the interest. Each does as he pleases.
- A cash basis taxpayer may not deduct the interest expense until he has actually made the payment.

DEDUCTING STATE SALES TAX

Since few, if any, taxpayers are likely to save all receipts as proof of state sales tax payments, the IRS does not require such proof for income tax deductions on the sales tax. Instead, the IRS provides a table in your Form 1040 by which you may estimate the amount of state sales tax paid and deduct accordingly. The following are a few suggestions for increasing the amount of your deduction for state sales tax.

Estimate According to Your Entire Income. The IRS estimates of sales tax in the 1040 form are based on average sales tax paid by people in certain income levels. But the income you report on page one of the 1040 form isn't necessarily the income by which you may estimate your state sales tax. In determining your state sales tax deduction, you should include in your total income all nontaxable income for the year. This may be dividends deducted under the $100 exclusion, the other half of your long-term gain that was not subject to tax, tax exempt interest, and so on. By estimating by the higher income level, you get a greater sales tax deduction.

Out-of-State Purchases.   Not all state sales taxes are the same. If you have made significant purchases in a state with a higher sales tax rate, you may estimate the additional amount of sales tax paid and add that to your official estimate.

Rare Purchases.   The sales tax paid on an automobile should always be added to your official average amount of sales tax. This is an unusual purchase and its contribution to your sales tax total is important. Of course, any other major and unusual purchases like a boat or a new set of golf clubs should be added.

SELLING YOUR HOME

Most people know that if you sell your house, you may use the proceeds to purchase a new house without paying tax on the proceeds of the sale of the old house. What most people don't know, however, is that the regulations governing this change of residence can be pretty strict. So if you want to take advantage of the tax benefit allowed you on the sale or purchase of a home, pay close attention to the following:

The Principal Residence

If you want the house you sell to qualify for a "tax-free exchange", the house must be your principal residence. Sale of your skiing condominium at Vail, Colorado, doesn't qualify unless you can prove that it is your principal residence. The profits from the sale of your principal residence will be liable for tax unless they are spent on a new principal residence. If you rent a garrett and buy a sailboat with the money acquired from the sale of your home, the sale will not be tax free.

Gain on the Sale

If you make a gain on the sale of your home and that gain is not invested in your new home, it is taxable to the extent that it exceeds the cost of the new home. However, if you paid for cosmetic improvements on the old house in order to sell it, those expenses may be deducted from the amount of gain. Building a new garage onto the old house or putting in a swimming pool don't qualify as expenses that affect the adjusted sales price of the home. But painting the living room or exterior, laying in new sod on the lawn, or wallpapering do qualify and you may adjust the sales price to reflect these expenses.

Price of old home	$50,000
Price of new home	45,000
Taxable gain	5,000
Cost of presale cosmetic changes	3,000
Total taxable gain	2,000

Note, however, that cosmetic costs to fix up the house before sale must be done within ninety days prior to the sale or within thirty days after the sale date in order to be used to adjust the sales price.

To maintain the tax free exchange treatment of your home, you must occupy your new residence within eighteen months of the sale of the old house. It may be eighteen months before or after the sale, but you must eat and sleep in the new home to qualify as occupying it. Stuffing it with furniture is not occupying it.

If you build a new home you must occupy it within twenty-four months of the sale of the old home. If your contractor suddenly decides he can't finish the new home in that time, you're out of luck. Therefore, it is wise to put a clause in the construction contract that grants you damages (to cover any tax loss due to delay in moving in) if he doesn't finish your home on time.

Suppose you don't like your new home and decide to move out before you have lived in it eighteen months. Can you then sell the new house and enjoy the benefits of the tax-free exchange? No. You must live in the new house for at least eighteen months before selling it if you want the tax benefit from the sales.

If you are over 65 years of age, the first $35,000 (up from $20,000) of the sales price of your home is tax free, whether you buy a new home or not. If your house sells for $35,000, the entire price is tax free and you don't have to build a new home at all to keep the money. Tax on gain for individuals 65 and over is computed on the basis of the ratio of the sales price to the $35,000. See the example of how it's done:

Cost basis of home	$30,000
Adjusted sales price	50,000
Gain	20,000
$35,000/$50,000	= 70%

You then exclude 70% of the gain from tax. Here the seller pays tax on only 30% of $20,000 = $6,000 of taxable gain.

Loss on the Sale

Selling Your Home at a Loss.   Not everyone makes a profit on the sale of his home. And unfortunately, a loss on the sale of your personal residence is not deductible. However, if you can convert your personal residence into a property held for trade or business, you can deduct the loss completely. You do this by renting your home for a year before you sell. Rented property becomes business property, according to the tax court. But in order to qualify as a rental property, the house must be rented for a full year. A short-term rental does not make it in the eyes of the IRS.

Selling a Relative's Home at a Loss.   If you inherit a house, and the house is not your personal residence, a loss on the sale of that house is deductible as a capital loss up to $1,000 per year until the loss is used up.

If, however, the house was up *for rent* before it was sold, you can take the entire loss in the year of sale.

Losses From a House That Won't Sell. If you are unable to sell your house, but the upkeep is getting expensive as it sits idle on the market, look for legal deductions that can cut some of these expenses. You can take quite a few deductions if you handle it correctly. First, the interest expense on a mortgage is deductible regardless. But what about all the upkeep expenses while the house is empty? The IRS says that if you are holding property for possible income production or profit, you can deduct any expenses for up-keep. You should either offer the house for rent with an option to buy (income production) or be able to demonstrate that by holding the house it may appreciate further in value (profit motive). This will allow you to deduct all reasonable expenses while the house is still on the market.

TRANSFER OF A LEASE

Rental income is taxable as ordinary income, but if you can sell your lease instead of subletting, your gain is taxed as capital gain. Here's how it can work:

Your firm has a fifteen-year lease on a building, but you want out after ten years. Happily, Mr. Smith's firm is willing to move into your old building. You were paying $5,000 per year and (what with inflation and all) Smith is willing to pay $6,000 per year. If you sublet the property to Smith, you have $1,000 per year ordinary income for five years; $5,000 taxed at your ordinary income rate.

However, if you sell the lease outright to Smith for $5,000, the money comes to you as capital gain and is subject to the lower tax rate. If you give Smith a break on the price to entice him to go along, he is happy because he saves money (he can still amortize the cost) and you are happy because you save tax dollars.

Naturally, you don't want the IRS to suspect that the sale of the lease is actually only another form of sublet. Therefore, after you've arranged things with your landlord, write up a bill of sale for the lease and use terms like "buyer" and "seller," avoid any right on your part to repossess, and have the lease assigned to Smith. These little details help you to avoid trouble later.

SELLING INVESTMENT OR BUSINESS
REAL ESTATE

If you intend to sell investment property or business real estate that you have held for more than twelve months, you might consider the tactic of spending more money for repair of the property, jacking up the price to cover those repair costs, and then taking a tax profit on top of your sales profit. The key here is that profit on the sale of property is capital gain, but repair costs are deductible against ordinary income.

How it Works to Save Tax Dollars

Suppose you have a business property to sell, but the property could use some repairs. Your tax bracket is 25% and you have to pay $1,000 for the repairs. How can spending more money save you money?

1. Since repairs are deductible against ordinary income, these repairs have just created a $250 deduction in your ordinary income tax.
2. You raise the price of the property by $1,000 to recover the money spent on repairs. The profit on the property is taxed at your capital gain rate ($\frac{1}{2} \times$ normal ordinary income tax rate). Therefore the capital gains tax on the repairs will be $\frac{1}{2} \times 25\% \times \$1,000 = \$125.00$.
3. So you have increased your capital gain tax on the property by $125.00, but you have lowered your ordinary income tax by $250.00. Therefore you have a net saving of $125.00 which was brought about by spending more money! Of course, you must always be wary of recapture on depreciation in this kind of arrangement. Check with your accountant if you have doubts.

INCORPORATING BEFORE YOU HAVE A BUSINESS

Most people say that they would want to investigate very carefully before forming a new business, but sometimes you can actually save money when considering a new business by going into business first and worrying about the nature of the business later. Sounds odd? Here's how it can work.

The Cost of Obtaining Information on a Business

*   *When It Relates to Your Present Business.* When you are investigating new possibilities for your present business, you may deduct the expenses of your investigation as necessary to your business. As long as the expenses are related to your present business, the IRS won't bother you.
*   *When It Involves an Unrelated Business.* If you are in the business of making cotton candy and you suddenly decide you want to look into making life rafts for submarines, you may not deduct as ordinary business expenses the costs incurred while investigating the submarine life raft industry. Expenses for investigating a business not related to your present business are capital expenditures that may be deducted later through amortization, depreciation, sale, or abandonment—if you proceed with the new business. Of

course, if the investigation leads to a dead end and you don't form the new business, you're just out of luck in regard to the money expended for the investigation.

Form the New Corporation First

Because of the restrictions on business deductions, you may find that you will save money by simply forming the new company before you investigate the new business. Of course, this discussion is primarily aimed at investigations that require significant amounts of money. The idea here is to form a minimum capitalized corporation and then write off the investigation expenses to the corporation to which they are directly related. Later, if the new business doesn't seem feasible, you can deduct the expense of the investigation as an abandonment in a discontinued corporation.

DEDUCTING EXPENSES FOR EDUCATION

You may deduct expenses for your education as long as the education is to maintain or improve the skills needed for the business *in which you are already established.* You may not deduct expenses for education if that education will train you for a different business or even for a new job in the same field.

Related Skills

If you make a living as a cowboy and want to go to school to learn electrical engineering, you may not deduct the expenses of your education. However, if you are an electrical engineer and you want to take an updated course on a new kind of circuitry now being introduced into your field, the deduction will probably be allowed.

Sometimes there is a very fine line between related and unrelated education. The tax court has held that an accountant who wanted to deduct the cost of his study for his CPA exam was not entitled to the deduction because the CPA qualification would have made him eligible for a new job. However, as suggested in the introduction to this chapter, when in doubt, try it. If you are not sure if your education is related to your present business, assume that it is and let the IRS worry about it.

Travel Expenses

If the education is job related, how much can be deducted for any travel expenses?

Primarily for Education. If you can show that the primary purpose for the travel expenditures was education, you may deduct transportation costs, meals, lodging, and other costs related to pursuing education away from home.

Partly for Education. If you travel to a seminar or some other educational meeting, but the primary reason for the travel is pleasure, you may deduct for meals, lodging, and expenses while the educational function is underway, but you may not deduct transportation costs. You will notice that the restrictions here are similar to those governing business expenses as outlined starting on page 219.

SAVING TAX MONEY ON GROUP TERM INSURANCE

You might be able to save tax dollars by taking another look at your group term life insurance arrangements. Of course, many businessmen know that up to $50,000 of group term life insurance can be provided tax free to an employee—with costs deductible to the corporation. But often unknown is the fact that the corporation can provide more than $50,000 coverage to *favored* officers or employees and still receive a full tax deduction. The recipient, however, must include the cost of the coverage above $50,000 as taxable compensation to himself. But, the "cost" is not the true cost of the extra coverage (as paid by the corporation). Rather it is computed according to a schedule provided by the IRS.

COST OF EXTRA COVERAGE COMPUTED BY IRS

Age	Cost Per Month Per $1,000	Age	Cost Per Month Per $1,000
20–29	8 cents	45–49	40 cents
30–34	10 cents	50–54	68 cents
35–39	14 cents	55–59	$1.10
40–44	23 cents	60–64	$1.63

As you can see, because these rates don't include any loading charges, they can be substantially below the actual cost of the insurance.

THE AVERAGE FOR ITEMIZED DEDUCTIONS

Sometimes, when you are figuring your itemized deductions for a tax year, it is helpful to know the national average for these deductions.

You are, of course, entitled to all deductions that are legal, and there can be no firm standards. However, the IRS does publish the average itemized deductions taken by taxpayers. If your return has a deduction well above average, it will probably be flagged for an audit. Of course, just because your return is average doesn't mean it won't be audited, but its chances will be considerably less.

AVERAGE ITEMIZED DEDUCTIONS

Adjusted Gross Income	Contribution	Interest	Taxes	Medical
$ 9,000- 10,000	$ 326	$ 950	$ 791	$533
10,000- 15,000	364	1,153	1,013	506
15,000- 20,000	416	1,360	1,361	404
20,000- 25,000	517	1,516	1,722	409
25,000- 30,000	643	1,786	2,123	402
30,000- 50,000	921	2,262	2,897	497
50,000-100,000	2,005	3,871	4,952	651
100,000 or more	9,630	12,074	12,361	989

If you seem to be above average in one or more categories, you might want to attach extra documentation to support the extra deductions. This may forestall an audit. Also, if you are significantly below the average for your income group, take another look at your allowable deductions to be sure you haven't overlooked anything.

Part III
HOW TO SELL
(OR BUY)
A BUSINESS

CHAPTER 15

HOW MUCH IS
YOUR BUSINESS WORTH?

Would you know how to set a fair price if someone wanted to acquire your company? How will the government value your business for estate tax purposes? These are vital questions for the business manager. However, unlike Wall Street for public corporations with actively traded securities, there is no common denominator for valuing a smaller, closely-held company. Other methods must be used. Basically, these fall into two categories: those that consider the value of *physical assets* and those that are based on the value as a *going concern.*

Value of physical assets

The three most common asset approaches to valuation are:

Liquidation value.   This is the value of the assets if the business were liquidated. Generally, this value is computed because it represents a *minimum price* and tends to put a floor under the valuations reached by other approaches.

Reproduction value.   Many business managers value their companies based on the cost to *reproduce the assets of the business at current prices.* The major difficulty here is that an investor buys a business on the basis of what similar businesses sell for, not on the basis of the assets' current market price. This method tends to yield a *ceiling price* on valuations reached by other methods.

Book value.   The excess value of assets over liabilities represents the net worth or book value of the business. While there are refinements to this approach, any business manager will recognize its problems. For example, most closely held businesses use two sets of books, one for taxes and the other for business purposes. Also, the true value of the assets may be difficult to determine because of accelerated depreciation and LIFO/FIFO conventions. Finally, the net worth of a company may be high because it has accumulated earnings over a considerable time period. Yet its recent earnings may be down, and its future prospects depressed.

Because of these shortcomings, the book value is most useful for appraising companies with mostly liquid assets subject to accurate accounting valuation, for example, banks, insurance companies, and investment trusts. Even in these cases, book value is seldom used alone as a criterion of value. Nevertheless, it provides a useful benchmark when used in conjunction with other methods.

Going Concern Value

While businesses are often bought and sold solely on the basis of asset value, most investors are more concerned with the *profits* these assets can generate. The most common technique used to measure going concern value is the "capitalized earnings" method. In this method the company's true annual earning capacity is first estimated based on past performance and future prospects. These earnings are then multiplied by a "capitalization factor" to arrive at a final value as explained below:

Estimate of true earnings. Past earnings are usually a good indication of what can be expected in the future. To arrive at an annual earnings figure, most analysts take the average earnings for the past five years. However, several adjustments must be made: (1) any extraordinary profit or loss must be eliminated, such as gain from the sale of part of the business or a loss from inventory write-offs, (2) salaries and special perquisites to shareholder-employees must be deducted from earnings, and (3) any nonstandard accounting practices must be adjusted, e.g., certain expenses may have been capitalized when they should have been written off.

Determining the capitalization factor. Suppose that an investor wants a guaranteed 10% return on his money. If you have an investment that yields a guaranteed $8,000 per year, he should be willing to pay you $80,000 for it. This is the amount he can afford to invest and still receive a 10% return. The investor capitalized the investment at ten times that return by taking the reciprocal of the yield he wanted and determining how much he could afford to pay (1/.10 $\times$ $8,000 = $80,000). The chart is a rough guide to capitalization factors. Keep in mind, however, that because of special economic circumstances, solid companies sometimes sell below book value.

Guidelines for Determining the Capitalization Factor

Depending on the *growth potential* of the business and the *risk* that projected earnings may not be realized, capitalization factors vary. The higher the growth potential and less the risk, the smaller the return that the investor will accept and the more the business is worth. Several other considerations that affect the value of a business are:

- *State of the economy.* How vulnerable is the company to economic change and what is the projected state of the economy?
- *Position in the industry.* Is the company a leader in its field or is it highly dependent on the actions of others? Is the company's business seasonal or affected by scarcity of certain key resources?
- *Financial.* How dependent is the company on debt? Will

TYPICAL CAPITALIZATION RATES

This chart, showing typical capitalization rates, was compiled many years ago. While the factors may be high in today's economic climate, it is a useful guide to relative values of various types of businesses.

Business	Capitalization Factor (number of times earnings paid for the business)
Established business with considerable growth potential.	10+
Established business with solid position in market and good management. Limited growth potential.	10
Established business requiring managerial attention but otherwise sound.	8
Business relatively vulnerable to general industry or economic fluctuations.	6-7
Small, highly competitive industrial, retail, or service business where capital investment is relatively small.	4-5
Industrial, retail, or service business dependent on the special skills of one or a few managers. Capital investment is small and business is highly competitive.	2-3
Personal service business requiring little capital. Highly dependent on present owner.	1

heavy interest expenses or possible acceleration of debt re-
payments cause problems?

- *Management.* Will present key management stay with the
company or must new (and unproven) executives be re-
cruited. (Note: This is an especially critical point for a small
business heavily dependent on one or two individuals.)

An Actual Example

Now that you understand some of the factors that need to be evaluated in
placing a price on a business, lets use some real numbers to see how these
systems can work to give a clearer picture of a company's net worth.

VALUE OF COMPANY XYZ

Physical Assets:

Liquidation Value	$50,000
Reproduction Value	$150,000
Book Value	$75,000

Going Concern Value

5 Year Annual Average Earnings (after tax)	$10,000
Amount of Extraordinary Earnings	0
Capitalization Factor	10
Going Concern Value ($10,000 × 10)	$100,000

Influence of Fluctuation in Economy	none
Position in Industry	good
Management	good/stable
Financial	no substantial debt
Estimate of Price	$100,000

When you attempt a reasonable evaluation of a business, keep in mind that
generally, a business owner's estimate of the value of the stock held for his
close corporation has been shown through cases in tax court to be about 1/3
the estimate given by the IRS. Usually, the court settled the value about half
way between the two estimates.

CHAPTER 16

BUYING OR SELLING A PROPRIETORSHIP

When a sole proprietorship is bought or sold, it is no longer a single entity, but rather a group of separate assets, according to tax laws. The assets are divided into three categories: capital assets, noncapital assets, and Section 1231 assets. Each receives different tax treatment. (Explanation and tax treatment of each of these type assets is discussed on pp. 235–238.) These assets may all be sold or purchased at the same time, but they must remain separate when it comes time to determine tax. The key to a successful sale or purchase, once the overall price is agreed upon, is the most advantageous allocation of price to the three kinds of assets. Generally, what is good for the buyer is bad for the seller and vice versa. But if these things aren't clearly settled in the sale, the IRS will allocate value for you and it will probably not be to your liking.

Advantage to the Seller

If the seller could have it all his way, he would have most of the sales price allocated to his capital assets and Section 1231 assets (depreciable business property held longer than the long-term capital gains period) because gain on these is taxed as capital gain rather than as ordinary income. Sale of noncapital assets produces ordinary income that is taxed at a higher rate so the seller does not want much price allocated to things like inventory and accounts receivable.

Goodwill, which is the premium over the book value of the business that is paid for brand name, and prestige, should have high value in the sale from the seller's point of view because it is considered capital gain and is taxed at the lower capital gain rate. Unfortunately, it is not deductible to the buyer so he won't be anxious to agree to a high value on goodwill.

Advantage to the Buyer

For the most part, the opposite of what the seller wants is the arrangement the buyer wants. He wants low price allocation to capital assets, high allocation to prepaid expenses, and medium or low allocation to Section 1231 property.

The chart below provides a general summary of the price allocation desired by seller and buyer. In this case the assets are assumed to have been held for more than twelve months (nine months in 1977) and to have been sold at a gain. Selling an asset at a loss reverses the party's position on that asset (i.e., if the buyer wanted it high, he now wants it low, and if the seller wanted it low, he now wants it high).

Other Considerations

When you weigh the possibilities of the sale or purchase of a sole proprietorship, here are a few other items to keep in mind.

Investment Credit. The seller should note that the sale may trigger recapture of investment credit which can have adverse tax consequences.

Installment Sale. Under the restrictions of an installment sale, inventory is not included in the installment method of reporting income. This means that you can sell the inventory in a sale of a proprietorship separately to increase the total first-year payment without affecting the maximum 30% first-year payment for installment sale.

Accounts Receivable. The seller's allocation to accounts receivable should equal the value of the accounts after reducing them by the bad debt reserve. If not, the reserve will be deemed taxable income.

Depreciated 1231 Assets. When you sell a depreciated 1231 asset, capital

PRICE ALLOCATION DESIRED BY SELLER VS. BUYER

Seller	*Class of Asset*	*Buyer*
I. Non-capital		
Low. It is treated as ordinary income.	Inventory or stock in trade.	High since cost of goods sold allows recovery.
Low. It is treated as ordinary income.	Accounts receivable.	High. The cost will be recovered as they are collected.
Low. Ordinary income.	Covenant Not to Compete.	Medium price since it may be recovered through amortization.
II. Capital		
High enough to cover unexpired cost.	Prepaid Expenses.	High. They are deductible against future income.
High. It is treated as capital gain.	Goodwill.	Low. It is not depreciable.
III. Section 1231		
High — capital gain.	Lease.	Medium. It is recoverable through amortization.
High — capital gain.	Land.	Low. It is not depreciable.
High — capital gain.	Buildings, machinery, equipment.	Medium. Can be recovered by depreciation.

gain is produced only if the gain exceeds depreciation recapture. Usually, a buyer wants a medium allocation to this type of asset, but he may gain by a higher allocation if he stands to get a large investment credit upon buying it. If there is going to be a large depreciation recapture on that asset, the seller wants a low allocation because the recapture will be taxed as ordinary income.

If you agree to an allocation that is favorable to the other party, you should receive in return some kind of concession on the price. And remember, if the allocation chosen is not thought reasonable by the IRS, they may reallocate in a more unpleasant manner.

CHAPTER 17

STRUCTURING THE SALE OR ACQUISITION OF A CORPORATION

At one time or another, almost every business manager will become involved in the purchase or sale of a business. There are many ways such transactions can be structured, and the tax consequences to the buyer and seller can be very important. Some transactions, for example, result in immediate taxable gain to the seller. In others, the transactions can be qualified as "tax free," meaning that taxes are deferred. Your knowledge of the basic methods of structuring an acquisition can save on legal expenses and negotiating time and can result in an arrangement that is highly favorable to your interests.

Taxable transactions

The most straightforward and frequently used method of purchasing a business is to offer *cash and/or notes* for the stock or assets. While any gain from such a transaction is immediately taxable to the seller, he presumably has enough liquidity from the sale to meet the tax bill. There are two ways such a purchase can work.

Purchase of stock If the business is a corporation and if it is desirable to transfer the business as a going concern, the buyer will normally purchase the stock of the corporation from the seller. Three potential problems must be watched: (1) The buyer must take steps to be sure he doesn't assume any hidden liabilities of the corporation and that accounts receivable are collectable; (2) the excess of the purchase price over the book value of the corporation is classified as goodwill and cannot be deducted for tax purposes, and (3) there may be a problem if minority shareholders of the acquired corporation do not wish to sell out.

Purchase of assets To overcome some of the problems of stock transactions, often only the *assets* of a business are sold. Such a sale avoids unforeseen liabilities, but it may be difficult to transfer certain leases or contracts if they are not specifically assignable. A great advantage to the buyer in this type of transaction is that the depreciable assets take on a stepped-up basis that yields increased depreciation deductions.

Tax-free transactions

The IRS recognizes three common types of acquisition transactions as tax free: Type A, Type B, and Type C "reorganizations."

Type A: Merger This transaction is sometimes called a "statutory merger" because it must be done in strict compliance with the merger provisions of the corporate statutes of a given state. It consists of combining two corporations into one as follows: (1) The shareholders of both corporations must approve the merger and (2) the shareholders of the disappearing corporation must retain a significant interest in the survivor. Generally, the IRS will accept a figure equal to 50% of the value of the shareholders' interest in the disappearing corporation as significant.

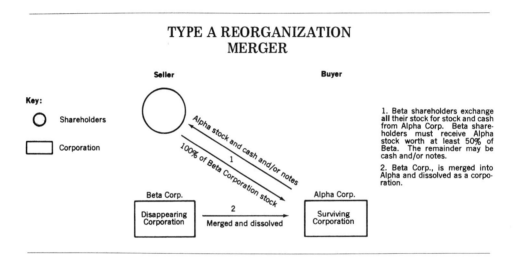

TYPE A REORGANIZATION
MERGER

Seller

Buyer

Key:

◯ Shareholders

▭ Corporation

Alpha stock and cash and/or notes

1

100% of Beta Corporation stock

Beta Corp.

Disappearing Corporation

2

Merged and dissolved

Alpha Corp.

Surviving Corporation

1. Beta shareholders exchange all their stock for stock and cash from Alpha Corp. Beta shareholders must receive Alpha stock worth at least 50% of Beta. The remainder may be cash and/or notes.

2. Beta Corp., is merged into Alpha and dissolved as a corporation.

Note that a Type A reorganization is the only one where the stock issued by the acquiring corporation does not have to be *voting* stock to obtain tax-free treatment. In fact, cash or debt may also be used as long as the seller pays taxes on it.

Type B: Stock-for stock acquisition This is the most common tax-free acquisition method. It occurs when the buyer exchanges *only* voting common or preferred stock for at least 80% of each class of the voting and nonvoting stock of the seller.

This type of acquisition is popular with small companies that sell out to larger public concerns. Since the stock received is not taxed until it is sold, the seller enjoys considerable flexibility as well as liquidity. Note that in this type of reorganization, the acquired corporation stays alive. As a result, there is generally less paperwork and expense than with other types of acquisitions.

Type C: Stock-for-assets acquisition In this type of transaction, voting stock of the buyer is exchanged for substantially all the assets of the seller. In practice, the IRS usually interprets this to mean that at least 90% of the seller's assets must be acquired and more than 80% of the consideration

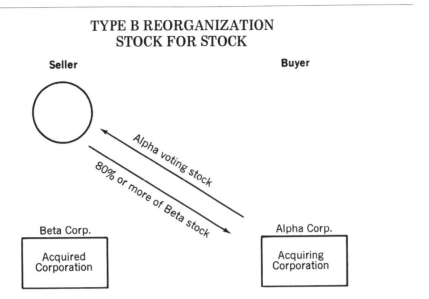

TYPE B REORGANIZATION
STOCK FOR STOCK

given by the buyer must consist of voting stock. The remaining 20% can be cash or debt. This type of acquisition is generally used when the buyer does not wish to acquire certain assets or assume certain known or any unknown liabilities of the seller.

Note that in this type of transaction, the sellers (Beta) retain the old corporate shell including any assets that were not sold. To obtain the Alpha shares, the Beta shareholders will normally exchange their Beta stock for the

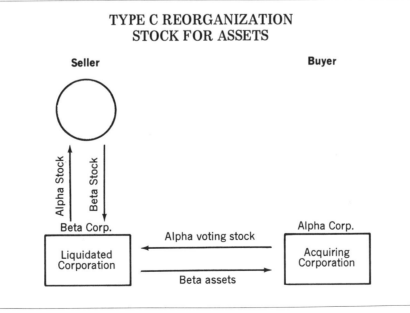

TYPE C REORGANIZATION
STOCK FOR ASSETS

Alpha stock and then liquidate Beta corporation. This exchange is noted in the chart above. If the exchange is accomplished properly, the sellers will not be taxed on their Alpha stock until they actually sell it.

While a basic knowledge of acquisition methods is valuable, it is a specialized area requiring expert assistance. Always retain competent legal and tax counsel to advise you.

CHAPTER 18

HOW TO SELL TO YOURSELF— THE SPECIAL CASE OF A DISPROPORTIONATE STOCK REDEMPTION

You've worked hard to build your business (which probably represents most of your personal assets). Naturally, you would like to cash in on some of the rewards. You could raise your salary, but the IRS would probably disallow any undue increase and treat it as a dividend. This would result in a double tax—once at the corporate level and once as ordinary income at the personal level.

Or you could sell a portion of your stock, but the other stockholders probably wouldn't have the money to buy your shares and you wouldn't want to sell to outsiders. However, there is a solution—one that few businessmen are aware of—a disproportionate stock redemption.

What is a 302 redemption?

According to the law whenever a corporation buys back shares from a stockholder during his lifetime, the proceeds are normally treated as a dividend for tax purposes. But if the redemption qualifies as disproportionate according to Section 302 of the Internal Revenue Code, the transaction is considered a "capital exchange" and is afforded capital gains treatment. Basically, a disproportionate redemption occurs when: (1) the selling shareholder owns 20% less stock after the redemption than before, *and* (2) the selling shareholder owns less than 50% of the outstanding voting stock after the redemption.

Here's a simple example: Suppose a corporation has 1,000 voting shares outstanding and you own 600. To qualify for capital gains treatment via a disproportionate redemption, you would have to sell at least 201 shares back to the company. According to the 20% rule, you would only have to sell 20% × 600 shares = 120 shares. However, to meet the second requirement of owning less than 50% of total voting stock outstanding after the redemption, you would have to sell a total of 201 shares. (1,000 shares - 201 shares leaves 799 outstanding after the redemption. You are left with 600 – 201

= 399 shares. These 399 shares will then represent less than 50% of the total stock of 799 shares outstanding after the redemption.)

The trap of "stock attribution"

When determining a stockholder's interest for purposes of the 20% and 50% tests mentioned above, the rule of stock attribution must be applied. This means that a stockholder is deemed to have a "constructive interest" in any shares owned by certain related parties. Here are five situations where stock attribution applies:

- *Family.* Spouse, children, grandchildren, and parents (but not brothers or sisters).
- *Partnerships and estates.* Any stock owned by a partnership or estate is considered owned *proportionately* according to the interest of the partner or beneficiaries. (If you are equal partners with three others and the partnership owns 100 shares of XYZ stock, you will have 25 shares of XYZ attributed to you if you redeem any personal XYZ shares you own.)
- *Trusts.* Proportional attribution applies (similar to partnerships and estates).
- *Corporations.* If an individual owns 50% or more of a corporation, any stock held by the corporation is attributed to the individual in proportion to the individual's ownership interest in the corporation.
- *Options.* Stock will be considered constructively owned and fully attributable if the individual has an option to buy it.

Complete redemption and termination of interest

You can also qualify for capital gains treatment by selling *all* your shares to the corporation, terminating your interest in the company. You will not have to worry about attribution rules as long as: (1) the retired shareholder retains no interest in the corporation other than as a creditor (an interest includes being an officer, director, or having a consulting retainer), (2) the retired shareholder does not acquire an interest (except by inheritance or bequest) for ten years.

How your spouse can help you convert dividends into capital gains. The great advantage of a complete redemption is that you can sell a substantial part of a family-owned company at capital gains rates—and still retain undiluted control of the corporation. However, it does involve a step-by-step ten-year game plan:

1. Give your spouse a substantial amount of stock when you set up the corporation or as soon thereafter as possible.
2. Make sure the stock is held for at least ten years.
3. Have the corporation redeem all your spouse's stock.
4. Make sure your spouse does not acquire any more stock or any other interest in the corporation for the next ten years.

As a result, all the gain is capital gain, and you retain complete control of the corporation. For example, suppose you form a corporation and issue 100,000 shares at $1.00 per share. You give 50,000 to your spouse and retain the other 50,000. After ten years the shares are worth $5.00 per share. You would like to get some money out of the company, but almost anything you do will be treated as a dividend—nondeductible to the corporation and fully taxable as ordinary income to the individual. The solution? Redeem all of your spouse's stock for $250,000. The first $50,000 is tax free—it's a return of capital. The remaining $200,000 will be taxed as a capital gain rather than as ordinary income. Finally, you will still have control of the company because you own the remaining shares. Here are several points to consider:

Gift tax. The shares you give to your spouse will potentially be subject to a gift tax. However, you are entitled to a gift tax marital deduction on the first $100,000 of gifts to a spouse and an annual exclusion of $3,000. Unless you have previously made substantial gifts to your spouse, no gift tax should be due.

Filings with the IRS. After receiving the stock your spouse must file an agreement with the IRS to notify them if any additional stock is acquired within ten years of the distribution. Furthermore, a timely return must be filed in the year of the redemption or the capital gains treatment may be lost.

Appreciated property. Your spouse's stock can be redeemed with appreciated property the corporation holds, such as land or securities. The corporation would escape tax on the asset's appreciation and preserve its working capital. The spouse still gets capital gains. Note: This type of redemption escapes the normally very restrictive new tax rules that apply to using appreciated property to redeem stock.

CHAPTER 19

SPECIAL CONSIDERATIONS

INSTALLMENT SALE OF REAL ESTATE

You may recall from Chapter 14, "Tax Techniques," that a businessman can realize substantial tax saving on the sale of property by making it an installment sale. To recapitulate, the drawback of an outright sale is that you must pay full capital gains tax in the year of the sale, regardless of whether or not you have really received the full payment on the sale.

So if you sell a property for $100,000 and the property is on your books at $10,000 you would pay tax on the full $90,000 profit if you don't elect to make an installment sale. Even if you only receive $40,000 down and the rest over two years, you still pay the tax on the full profit. However, you may report taxable gain as installments are received if you meet any one of these tests:

- You are a *dealer* in merchandise and regularly sell on the installment basis.
- The property sold is *real estate;* or
- The transaction is a "casual" sale. (This means you are not a dealer and the sales price of the property, other than real estate, is more than $3,000.)

We discussed the dealer's situation on page 227, but now let's take a look at the other two situations.

Real estate sale or casual sale over $1,000

In order for a real estate sale or a casual sale to qualify for installment sale tax treatment, the seller may receive *no more than 30%* of the total price in the first year. Therefore, in the above example the sale would qualify for an installment sale if the seller received only $30,000 in the first year. Then he would pay tax as the payments were received.

In addition to the 30% test, the sale must also adhere to the following guidelines:

Year of sale. Payments *in the year of sale* must not be more than 30% of the total selling price. Generally, this means the year (tax year rather than calendar year) when the sale is closed and title passes, not when the option to purchase was signed. Payment in the first year includes all payment received up to the year of sale. Any advance payments will count as first year payments whether they were actually received in the year the contract was signed or not.

What are "payments"? Payments in the year of sale include any cash, property, or tradable securities given the seller by the buyer. They do not normally include notes given by a buyer that are merely promises to pay, not actual payment.

The Interest Trap. The interest incurred on the installment payments must be 5% or more. If less, the IRS feels that the seller is trying to dodge his taxes and the IRS will compute the interest at 7%. Higher interest computation will reduce the overall price of the sale. If the price of the sale is reduced, the 30% test may fail. With reduced price the amount you had calculated to be 30% is now more than 30%. If the test fails, you may lose your entire installment tax benefit.

Be sure to work closely with your accountant or tax advisor when setting up an installment sale. The rules are relatively simple, but there are several pitfalls to watch for.

GOODWILL AND THE NONCOMPETITION COVENANT

Goodwill is a term applied to the amount paid for a business over and above the value of the tangible assets. It covers such things as the good reputation of the purchased firm, high morale of employees, and good management. Goodwill is treated as a capital asset and the seller treats the payment for it as capital gain. However, the buyer of the company may not deduct the cost of the goodwill. He gets his money back for the goodwill only when and if he sells the business.

Noncompetition Covenant. The buyer of a business would usually like some assurance that the seller won't turn right around after the sale and start a new, competitive company. Therefore the buyer would like to have a "covenant not to compete" and he is willing to pay extra for such an agreement. Usually, this noncompetition agreement states that the seller will not compete with the buyer for a set period of time or within a given geographical or market area. However, whereas goodwill is taxed as capital gain to the seller and is nondeductible to the buyer, a noncompetition covenant is taxed as ordinary income to the seller and is deductible to the buyer over the agreed upon time period.

How Much Are They Worth at Time of Sale? It stands to reason in light of the above that the seller is going to want a large price allocation to goodwill and the buyer will want a large allocation to the noncompetition covenant. Some strenuous negotiations will probably precede the final agreement on these matters.

Separate the Covenant Not to Compete. It is usually best for the buyer to establish the noncompetition covenant as being distinct and separate from the agreement for the sale of the business. This separation is important because if the covenant not to compete is deemed by the IRS to be a necessary condition for the enjoyment of the purchased goodwill, the covenant will be considered part of the goodwill and as such will no longer be deductible to the buyer.

DEDUCTING THE COST OF A CUSTOMER LIST

In the buying and selling of firms like publishing houses, insurance agencies, and many service industries, the purchase of the customer list is an important part of the deal, especially if you are buying out a competitor. But too often the price of the competitor's customer list is included under goodwill and the buyer misses an opportunity to deduct the cost of this list.

Usually, the IRS will say that a customer list is a single asset and may not be broken down into individual accounts for the purpose of deducting losses. However, if the buyer can determine the dollar value of each account on the customer list by means of reasonable calculation, he may later deduct the cost of these accounts if he loses them. Or, he may take annual amortization deductions over the determined useful life of the list. Again, the calculation of the list's useful life must be made by means of reasonable calculation.

For example, if you were buying a dry cleaning business and you wanted to find the dollar value of the accounts on the customer list, you might find the average billing for an established account and then multiply it by the frequency of that customer's patronage. You might then discount the amount by the dry cleaner's turnover rate for this kind of customer, say 15%. Once a dollar value is established for that account, it becomes a separate asset and may be deducted later if lost.

Part IV
RETIREMENT,
LIFE INSURANCE, AND
ESTATE PLANNING

CHAPTER 20

RETIREMENT PLANNING

High on any hierarchy of human needs is security. In addition, during the last few years security at retirement has become a prime political, economical, and social problem. Employees know that social security alone will not provide a comfortable retirement, and the corrosive effects of inflation make it all but impossible to accumulate sufficient personal savings to provide for dramatically increased life expectancy. Hence, unless you are willing to effectively fire long-service employees, the question of a properly designed retirement program must eventually be addressed in almost any business. Here are the basic facts you need to know to develop and protect your business's most important asset—its people.

CORPORATE EMPLOYEES—QUALIFIED VS. NONQUALIFIED PLANS

Retirement plans fall into two broad categories—"qualified" and "nonqualified." A qualified plan is simply one that meets the stringent requirements of Section 401 of the Internal Revenue Code and qualifies for highly favorable tax benefits. Nonqualified plans, of course, do not receive such benefits. A typical nonqualified plan would be a deferred compensation arrangement in which a company agrees to pay an employee at some future date (usually after retirement) for services he is currently performing.

A Typical Nonqualified Plan—Deferred Compensation

Although a deferred compensation arrangement does not receive the tax breaks given to qualified plans, it does have other advantages. To begin, the employee does obtain a genuine tax benefit by deferring his extra income until retirement. And the corporation may also benefit if it anticipates jumping from the 22% corporate tax rate to the 48% rate by the time the employee retires. At the higher corporate tax rate the compensation will have a lower after-tax cost to the employer.

How It Can Work

Suppose you are a corporate officer, sixty years old, and in a 38% personal tax bracket. Your firm wants to give you a raise of $4,000 per year until you retire at age 65. The firm now pays the 22% corporate tax rate.

If you accept the raise now, you pay personal tax on it at your present rate (38% $\times$ $4,000) and take home just $2,480 per year [$4,000 - (38% $\times$ $4,000) = $2,480]. This raise has an after-tax cost to the company of $3,120, [$4,000 - (22% $\times$ $4,000) = $3,120]. Over the five years until you retire, you take home only $12,400. The after-tax cost of your raise to the company is $15,600 over those five years (5 $\times$ $3,120).

But, if you take the raise as deferred compensation, payable after retirement when you will probably be in a lower tax bracket—say 20%—you receive the $4,000 per year at the lower tax rate (20% $\times$ $4,000 = $800 tax) which is $3,200 take home. The corporation, which we will assume has expanded over the five years so that it now pays the 48% tax rate, has an after-tax cost of [$4,000 - (48% $\times$ $4,000) =] only $2,080 per year for your raise. Over five retirement years you take home $720 more per year, a five year tax saving of $3,600. Similarly, the company pays (5 $\times$ $2,080) = $10,400 after tax over the five years—a tax saving for the company of $5,200.

A nonqualified deferred compensation plan is not subject to the requirements of Section 401 of the IRS Code, but it is by no means unrestricted. It is still subject to the following guidelines established by the IRS. The tax court reasons that if these rules are followed, the tax on the income may be deferred because the employee doesn't actually get his hands on the extra money until he is in fact retired.

Rules for Deferred Compensation Plans

- The deferred compensation arrangement must be established before the employee actually earns the income.
- The employee must be on a cash basis.
- The agreement may not be unconditionally funded by placing the deferred payment in an escrow or similar type of account. The employee can have the company's promise of payment, but the compensation may not be secured in any way.
- The employee may not demand the compensation before the date agreed upon.
- The amount of compensation must be reasonable. If either current or deferred compensation is deemed unreasonable, it will not be deductible to the employer.

Usually, the employee agrees to the following in a deferred compensation agreement:

- The employee may not receive any part of the deferred pay

until he reaches the established retirement age or becomes disabled. His heirs may receive the compensation if he dies.

- The employee may not join the competition or engage in competitive activity.
- The employee must remain in the employer's service for an established period of time in order to receive the deferred pay.
- The employee will, as an outside contractor, be available for consultation if needed after retirement. Note: It is important that it is clear that the employee is acting as an independent contractor when he does consulting work for the company. There should not be confusion about the retiree's relationship to the company.

  Also, if the employee should die before all the deferred payment is made, his beneficiary will receive all or part of the remainder.

Advantages of Deferred Compensation

- No legal restrictions on who or how many employees can take advantage of deferred compensation. The plan may cover any number of employees.
- The employee makes a substantial tax saving by deferring part of his salary into lower tax years.
- The employer may make a substantial tax saving if he anticipates a higher tax rate in later years.
- The employer may have access to the deferred funds during the time of deferment.
- The arrangement is easy to set up.

Disadvantages of Deferred Compensation—And How to Beat Them

- There is no guarantee that the company will be able to pay the deferred compensation by the time the employee is ready to retire. After all, the company may go under two years after the employee retires.
- Since IRS regulations forbid unconditional funding via an escrow account, it may be a good idea to have the company purchase a high cash value type of life insurance policy on the employee with the employer as beneficiary. When it comes time for the employee to retire, the policy is cashed in and the monies are available for the deferred payment. Or, the company might set up a special fund with the deferred monies, taking care not to link this fund legally with the deferred compensation agreement or with the employee.
- The employee doesn't get the use of the deferred monies.
- Deferred compensation may not benefit a retiree with high

income. There is a 50% maximum tax on earned income, but deferred compensation is considered *unearned* income and is subject to tax up to the full maximum 70%.

Qualified Plans

As we have seen, in a nonqualified compensation deferment plan the employee, and often the corporation as well, winds up paying a reduced tax on the compensation. Furthermore, the nonqualified plan is free from the more stringent IRS requirements for qualified plans.

Qualified plans, on the other hand, have these advantages:

- *Current Tax Deduction.* Pretax corporate money goes into the plan as a deductible contribution.
- *Tax-Free Accumulations.* Income from investments in the plan may accumulate and be reinvested tax free.
- *Deferred Tax on Benefits.* Benefits are not taxed until actually received. Even if the entire amount due an individual is paid out in a lump sum, the distribution receives preferential tax treatment under a special seven-year averaging method.
- *Distribution of Securities.* Securities credited to an individual's account may be distributed, but tax is not due on any appreciation until they are actually sold.
- *Stockholders.* In no way are stockholders prohibited from participating in a qualified plan as long as they are also employees of the company.

Pension vs. Profit Sharing Many businessmen are confused by the difference between the two major types of qualified plans—pension and profit sharing. Under a pension plan the company has a *fixed* obligation to continue to contribute a certain amount of money each year toward the plan, rain or shine. With profit sharing there is no such fixed commitment—contributions are contingent on profits and can be skipped or reduced in a bad year. Usually, a formula is established that defines the way in which the employer's profit sharing contributions will be made. For example, it might be 15% of pretax profit over the first $10,000 in profit. But the retirement benefit under profit sharing will vary according to the amount of contributions and the fund's accumulated earnings.

Generally, profit-sharing plans tend to be more attractive to smaller or recently formed businesses with unstable, year-to-year profits. On the other hand, pension plans are generally more attractive to older management and employees who want the security of a fixed contribution by the company to the plan each year. A little known fact with profit-sharing plans is that retirement benefits do not necessarily have to be provided, and the plan can still qualify for the tax break. Other benefits, such as house mortgage financing, tuition assistance, and emergency loans, can be substituted. Hence profit sharing tends to be more attractive to younger individuals. The checklist summarizes the major differences between the two types of qualified plans.

COMPARISON OF QUALIFIED PROFIT
SHARING VS. PENSION PLANS

	Profit Sharing	*Pension*
Orientation	Favors younger employees.	Favors older employees.
Benefits	Retirement benefits need not be provided.	Retirement benefits must be provided.
	Other benefits, such as accident and health, may be provided.	Other benefits limited to disability coverage.
Contribution	At discretion of management and based only on profits. Cannot exceed 15% of total payroll.	Fixed obligation which must be made in both profit and loss years.
Forfeiture	May be allocated to remaining participants of plan.	Used to decrease employer's cost.
Distribution	After as few as two years.	Only on retirement, death, disability, or termination of employment.

Requirements to Qualify   To obtain IRS approval and the tax benefits, the main requirement is that a qualified plan be permanent and not discriminate in favor of a particular employee group, such as top management. It is generally possible, however, to design the plan so that long-term employees (including management) indirectly receive preferential treatment. For example, some plans stipulate rigorous "vesting" provisions. Any employee who leaves in the first five years of employment forfeits all contributions to the plan. (These funds then accrue to the remaining members in the plan.) After five years there is 50% vesting with additional 10 percent increments each year, resulting in full vesting only after ten years of continuous employment. Furthermore, there is no requirement with qualified plans that all employees receive the same amount of benefits. Allocation of contributions among participants can vary according to: (1) years of service, (2) age, and/or (3) compensation. A payout formula based on a combination of compensation and years service generally works out best for long-term employees and management.

Other Requirements for Qualified Plans

- *Who must be included.* Qualified profit sharing plans and pension plans must cover 70% of all employees who work more than 1,000 hours in twelve months. Also, an owner of two separate businesses may not establish a plan for one business that discriminates against his employees in the other.
- *Voluntary contributions.* In a profit-sharing plan a participant may pay extra money voluntarily into his retirement account. This is in addition to the amount payed in by the employer. There is, however, a limit to the amount of voluntary contributions and such contributions are not deductible

to the participant. However, once in the account, they do escape tax on their compounded earnings.

- *Benefit limitation.* The limit on the amount a retired employee may receive under a pension plan is the average compensation he received over his three highest paid years or $75,000—whichever is less. The benefit limitation on the profit-sharing plan is limited by the restrictions on the amount that may be payed into or credited to his account.
- *Benefit taxation.* Retirement benefits are taxed as ordinary income if they are disbursed as annuity payments. Of course, the ordinary income tax rate is significantly less as a retiree. A lump sum payment of the benefit—be it at retirement time or when the plan is terminated—is taxable as long-term capital gain if attributable to contributions and earnings made before 1974. Payments attributable to earnings after 1973 are treated as ordinary income subject to a special ten-year forward averaging stipulation.
- *What if a participant dies before retirement age?* Then the beneficiary of the employee may exclude $5,000 from income tax as an employee death benefit.
- *Allowable Investments.* In most cases funds contributed to a retirement plan may be invested in bonds, savings accounts, real estate, life insurance contracts, stock, or mutual funds. However, (1) a profit sharing plan may invest in the employer's real estate or stock only if the plan specifically permits such investment and the transaction is conducted at arms length; (2) loans may not be made from the plan to the employer or to any involved party; (3) a 10% investment limit is placed on defined pension plan investments in the employer's stock. Also, there is a diversification requirement in regard to such investment.
- *Rollover.* Rollover or "portability", is the term applied to the tax-free transfer of accumulated retirement benefits from one company to another or to an Individual Retirement Plan. Usually, an employee who terminates his employment is taxed on the vested interest he withdraws when he leaves. But if he transfers the amount taken out into his new employer's retirement program within sixty days, he is not taxed on his accumulated retirement benefits.

Two More Qualified Plans

Before moving out of this area of retirement planning it should be noted that there are two other common forms of retirement plans; a stock bonus plan and a "defined contribution" plan.

Stock Bonus Plan. Under a stock bonus plan a company contributes its own stock to the retirement plan instead of cash. In virtually all other respects it is the same as a profit sharing plan.

Defined Contribution Plan. This plan resembles a pension plan in that the employer must contribute a fixed amount annually to the retirement fund. However, the employee is not promised a specific amount of retirement compensation. Rather, when he retires, a pension annuity will be purchased with the money that has been allocated to his retirement account.

Conclusion

Employers are finding employees increasingly restive for catch-up wage increases. Rather than paying out higher salaries with attendant higher social security taxes, workmen's compensation, and other taxes, it might make sense to investigate a retirement plan instead. With the double benefits of a current corporate tax deduction for contributions to the plan plus tax-free accumulation of all proceeds, employees can be provided the security of a retirement program—at a net cost to the company of perhaps no more than current wage demands.

And, do not overlook the morale and loyalty factor involved here. Security can mean a great deal to an employee and it is likely to make him stay on.

Of course, pensions and profit sharing are no jobs for a novice to tackle. See if your trade association has any qualified plans already approved by the IRS for your industry. Then get the advice of your attorney and a good insurance agent.

SELF-EMPLOYED—THE KEOGH OR HR-10 PLAN

What is a Keogh Plan?

Prior to 1963 only those who conducted their business in the corporate form and employees of corporations received a tax break in their retirement planning. The estimated nine million self-employed business people were left out in the cold. However, in 1962 Congress passed the Keogh Act. Based on this law, any self-employed individual or partner could set aside a maximum of $2,500 per year as a tax-deductible contribution to a retirement plan. However, because of the relatively low amount that could be contributed, only an estimated 10 percent of those eligible had formed Keogh plans after twelve years. Under the 1974 Pension Reform Act the maximum deductible amount was tripled, and any self-employed person can now contribute 15 percent of his earned income, up to $7,500 yearly. Here are the specifics.

Contributions

General rule. If you own 10% or more of your business, you may set aside 15% of your earnings, up to a maximum of $7,500 per year. And no matter how little you earn, you may contribute and deduct $750. However, if you have employees, you must make equal percentage contributions for those who have been with you three years or more (i.e., if you contribute 15% of your wages, you must contribute 15% of their wages).

Voluntary contributions. If you have employees and made contributions on their behalf, you may voluntarily contribute an additional 10% of earnings (limit $2,500), making a maximum annual contribution of $10,000. This voluntary contribution is not tax deductible, but it does accumulate tax free.

Defined benefits. The system described above is called a "defined contribution" plan. It is also possible to set up a "defined benefits" plan. According to this scheme, you may contribute an amount each year sufficient to give you a certain income upon retirement—not less than $10,000 or more than the average of your three highest year's salaries ($75,000 maximum). For some self-employed people with few years until retirement, this can result in tax-deductible contributions well in excess of $7,500 per year.

Accumulations

Earnings on any money salted away accumulate tax free and *taxes are not paid until the funds are withdrawn.* For most people, this will be in their retirement years when their tax bracket is lower because of reduced total income and old-age dependency exemptions. The effect of pretax contributions and tax-free accumulation is shown below.

Roll Over

An account in a Keogh Plan may be rolled over tax free into a qualified retirement account at a corporation or into an Individual Retirement Account.

Vesting

Vesting begins immediately with Keogh Plans. Unlike the normal corporate procedures that call for forfeiture of any accumulated retirement funds if

THE EFFECT OF
KEOGH CONTRIBUTIONS

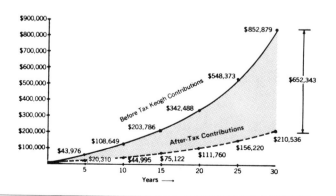

Note: This graph shows the difference between an investment of $7500 (before tax) in a Keogh Plan with the $3750 you would have available to invest each year after paying income taxes at a 50% rate. A constant 8% return is assumed and all income is reinvested.

the employee leaves before five years, a Keogh Plan demands that every dime you put in on behalf of your employee belongs to him starting with the first day.

Withdrawals

The whole idea of a tax-sheltered retirement program is to encourage savings for later years, and the law discourages with stiff tax penalties any "premature distributions". However, funds may be withdrawn without difficulty under these circumstances.

- *Normal retirement.* Fund withdrawal cannot begin before age 59½ and must start by age 70½. But employees may start drawing when they reach the age agreed upon in their retirement plan.
- *Disability.* Benefits may begin any time an individual becomes disabled, i.e., unable to engage in "substantial gainful activity because of physical or mental impairment which is expected to be of indefinite duration."
- *Death.* In the event of death, proceeds due an individual may be distributed to beneficiaries within five years. Alternatively, the funds may be used to buy an annuity payable over the beneficiaries' lives.

How to Begin

Setting up a Keogh Plan is not a do-it-yourself affair and it should be an integral part of your overall retirement plan. Contact your attorney or bank trust department, as they should have full information.

INDIVIDUALS—THE INDIVIDUAL RETIREMENT ACCOUNT

The Individual Retirement Account (IRA) is a plan that allows an individual who is not covered by any other retirement plan to set up his own tax-exempt retirement account. The IRA, part of the Employee Retirement Income Security Act of 1974, permits a qualified person to set aside up to 15% of earned income or $1,500 per year—whichever is less—for retirement investment. In the case where one spouse isn't working outside the home, up to $1750 can be set aside.

Like the Keogh Plan, the two most outstanding advantages of the IRA are: (1) contributions to the retirement fund are deductible from current taxable income; and (2) investment earnings are tax free until they are withdrawn at retirement age.

However, unlike the Keogh Plan: (1) the IRA allows a maximum contribution of only $1,500 ($1,750 if nonworking spouse included); (2) it need not cover employees; and (3) it is open to anyone who is self-employed or a corporate officer who is not otherwise covered for retirement.

Contribution Restrictions

- *General Rule.* The annual contribution must be made in money (i.e., no notes) and it is deductible from gross income.
- *Excess Contribution.* Contributions in excess of the deductible are subject to a penalty tax of 6%.
- *Spouse's IRA.* A working spouse may set up his/her own IRA and may contribute to it out of his/her income up to the limit. A joint return may include each spouse's deduction. The maximum total IRA deduction on a joint return is $2,250.

Investing IRA Funds

Investment of IRA funds may follow any one of three basic structures. In all cases the earnings compound tax free.

- The funds may go into an individual retirement annuity or endowment purchased from a life insurance company. However, the cost of the life insurance premium may not be deducted.
- Investments may go into an individual retirement account where contributions may be invested in savings accounts, mutual funds, trust accounts, or stock and bonds under the trusteeship of a bank or some other fiduciary. This must be done in accord with a written agreement with the IRS.
- You may also invest in special government retirement bonds.

Withdrawals

Like the other retirement plans, the idea behind the IRA is to put money aside for later. Therefore, if you try to withdraw the money before retirement, you will have to pay tax penalties. Here are the withdrawal regulations:

- Premature distribution (withdrawal of funds) is subject to a 10% penalty tax, except in the case of rollover, disability, or death.
- Funds may not be withdrawn until age 59½ but if you don't begin to withdraw by age 70½ the funds are subject to a 50% penalty tax.
- Withdrawals are taxed as ordinary income and may be eligible for regular income averaging.
- They may qualify for the retirement income credit.
- They are not excluded from estate tax and they may be subject to state income tax.

How An Employer is Affected By IRA

In addition to setting up his own IRA, an employer may also set up IRAs for his employees. Of course, there is no restriction on the number of employees who may be covered. Here are the guidelines for an employer-sponsored IRA.

The employer may deduct the cost of the contribution made on behalf of his employee and the cost of administration of the account. He must withhold social security and unemployment tax, but he does not withhold income tax. The employer may contribute all or part of the maximum contribution. Funds in an employer-sponsored account may go into a common investment account, but a separate accounting is required to establish the interest of each participating employee.

The employee must declare the employer's contribution as income, but he may take a corresponding deduction. He may contribute additional funds voluntarily to supplement the fund up to the limit allowed if the employer doesn't contribute the maximum.

Rollover

Retirement funds from an IRA may be transferred tax free to a qualified retirement plan in a new company if the monies are put into the new retirement plan within sixty days of withdrawal. Usually, such a withdrawal would be subject to the premature distribution penalty tax, but the penalty is avoided as long as the funds are rolled over into the new plan.

SOCIAL SECURITY: WHAT YOU SHOULD KNOW

In the foreseeable future, probably no single piece of legislation will affect you, your employees, or your company more than the Social Security Act. Yet, many businessmen are unaware of the basic provisions of this law and how it can influence their personal and business planning. Here are the basic facts you should know.

The social security law actually covers twelve major programs, but the benefits of most concern to the executive are these four: retirement benefits; survivor benefits; disability benefits; and lump-sum payment at death.

Retirement and Survivor Benefits

See the table that summarizes the retirement and survivor benefits available to the executive and his family. You can see that survivors' benefits are an especially valuable life insurance benefit for young families. If the head of the family dies or becomes disabled before age 65, the spouse and children under eighteen will each receive a monthly benefit. The amount of current life insurance you now have under social security depends on your age. If you and your wife are both 35, for example, with two young children, it can be worth about half-a-million dollars.

For an executive who retires at age 65 in 1990, the basic benefits will be $447 per month. In other words, you and your wife could expect to receive $447 per month plus her 50% if she is age 65, totalling $670 per month. And don't worry about that amount of money not buying a shoeshine—the 1972 revision to the basic act stipulates that all benefits are to be corrected for inflation using the Consumer Price Index.

RETIREMENT AND SURVIVOR BENEFITS

Individual	Status	Percent of Basic Benefits
Executive	Age 65 or over	100 %
	Age 62	80 %
Spouse	Age 65 or over or age 62 with child under 18, student under 22, or disabled child	50 %
	Age 62, no children at home	37½%
Widow(er)	Age 65 or over	100 %
	Age 60	71½%
	Age 50 and disabled	50 %
Child	Under age 18 (22 if full-time student, unmarried and dependent) or disabled child at any age if disability began before age 22	50 %

Disability Benefits and Lump-sum Payment at Death

There are two other social security benefits that should interest an executive. First, if you become blind or expect to be disabled for twelve months or more, you will receive 100% of your basic benefits at any age. Second, your survivors will receive in a lump-sum up to $255 toward your burial expenses at death.

Eligibility

The rules that must be met to be considered fully insured under social security are complex, but almost every executive, whether self-employed or working for an employer, should be fully qualified.

Watch These Gaps

While social security provides a base for you and your family's personal security, there are important gaps that you should consider. One concerns widows' benefits. If you should die, your spouse will get benefits only if she is over sixty or caring for a child under eighteen. Hence, you should consider an insurance program to meet this shortcoming. Also, if you become a widower with dependent children, it could cause a substantial financial burden. More and more executives are considering life insurance on their spouse to meet this unfortunate need. Another problem area is disability benefits; the government's definition of disability is exceedingly strict and it is often difficult to collect. Consider a private program to at least supplement social security benefits.

CHAPTER 21

INSURANCE PLANNING

SPLIT DOLLAR INSURANCE

With the stock market in veritable disarray and stock options in disfavor, many employees and employers alike are seeking refuge in new tax-attractive incentives and perquisites. However, the Tax Act of 1969 put an end to many attractive fringe benefits. But here's a little known one that came through unscathed—the "split-dollar".

Adequate life insurance is a concern of every executive. But during heavy spending years when an executive most needs insurance, he has the least money available to buy it. Furthermore, insurance premiums are not deductible to the individual and, hence, have to be paid with aftertax dollars. This is where split-dollar comes to the rescue. It provides a way for a corporation to assist executives with their personal insurance programs by *splitting* the premiums with them. Additionally, it is one of the few compensation benefits that can be awarded on a *discriminating basis* to selected individuals.

Split-Dollar in Practice

Every permanent life insurance policy (as opposed to the term variety) has two aspects: the cash value and the death benefit. With split dollar, the corporation pays that portion of each annual premium that represents *the increase in cash value* of the policy. The favored executive pays the remainder of the premium. With respect to the death benefit, two beneficiaries are designated—the corporation for the amount equal to the cash value of the policy at the time of death and the executive's beneficiary for the remainder.

Let's look at the numbers for a typical plan (see chart on following page). Consider the case of a $100,000 split-dollar policy on a 36-year-old executive. The first year, the policy has a cash value of $225, which the employer pays, and the executive pays the remaining premium of $1,940. (To make it easier, many companies advance executives the amount of their portion of the first year's premium which is then repaid out of future salary.) The second year, the executive's payment drops to $275, and the company pays $1,825. By the fifth year, the cash value increases as much as the premium, so that company pays the entire premium thereafter for the life of the policy.

At all times, the death benefit stands at $100,000 and eventually goes to the two beneficiaries—the company for an amount equal to the cash value (ranging from $225 in the first year to $37,000 by the twentieth) and the executive's widow or family for the remainder. In other words, with split-dollar, the executive receives far more insurance than he could normally afford if he bought it himself, and the employer is absolutely sure of getting back whatever was spent on the policy, whether the executive lives, dies, quits, or retires.

Tax Consequences

As stated, the tax consequences for both the company and executive were left untouched by the 1969 Tax Act that hit many other areas of executive compensation. If the executive dies, for example, his beneficiary receives the insurance proceeds free of income tax. There are ways to make the proceeds free of estate tax as well. The company, for its part, incurs no tax liability when its money is repaid.

During the executive's life, he must report as income and pay taxes on an amount equal to the cost of one year's term insurance at the employee's then age for the *net* amount of insurance coverage the executive has under the split-dollar plan. Insurance men have tables to compute the exact amount, but it comes to no more than a few hundred dollars a year premium the executive pays himself (IRS Ruling 64-328).

Advantages to the Employer

- The corporation can bind key employees more closely to the firm by giving them substantial life insurance at low cost.

SPLIT-DOLLAR PLAN

$100,000 Ordinary Life Policy — Annual Premium $2,350

Year	Dividend	Net Premium (Annual Premium Less Dividend)	Cash Value	Increase in Cash Value (Employer Pays)	Net Premium Less Employer's Contribution (Employee Pays)	Employee's Death Benefit
1	$ 185	$ 2,165	$ 225	$ 225	$1,940	$99,775
2	250	2,100	2,050	1,825	275	97,950
3	315	2,035	3,900	1,850	185	96,100
4	385	1,965	5,775	1,875	90	94,225
5	445	1,905	7,680	1,905	0	92,320
1-20	$12,600	$36,200	$37,000	$33,300	$2,490	$63,000 (end of 20th year)

- Tax-free death benefits in excess of the $5,000 exempt under Section 101 of the Internal Revenue Code can be provided by the corporation to an employee's family.
- There is no requirement that the plan be extended beyond selected employees and no approval is needed by stockholders, the IRS, or the SEC.
- The corporation's financial position is unchanged since all contributions remain as assets of the corporation. Furthermore, this cash value may be borrowed against or used to fund a retirement plan.
- The only cost to the corporation is the "opportunity cost" of having its money tied up. All money used to fund the split-dollar program will eventually revert to the company.

Advantages to the Employee

- Substantial insurance can be obtained at a time when it is most needed, but, because of family expenses, normally most difficult to afford.
- The net cost to the executive is low, and proceeds are free of income tax to the beneficiary.
- The plan can be continued after retirement or be arranged so that the policy is paid up at time of retirement.
- Death benefits to the employee's beneficiary can be kept constant by electing the so-called "fifth dividend option." In effect, part of the dividends from the policy are used to purchase term insurance equal to the cash value.

Split-dollar provides a remarkably versatile compensation device for executives of widely ranging age and circumstances. In addition, it can be used in creative estate planning to keep proceeds to beneficiaries out of probate and to solve a variety of business problems, such as getting money tax-free out of a close corporation.

MINIMUM DEPOSIT INSURANCE

Adequate life insurance can be expensive, and the premiums are not tax deductible. Many business people, especially those in their early years, feel that they can afford only term insurance, although they know its protection is temporary. It's surprising how few business people realize that they can purchase whole life insurance at less cost than term insurance.

Financing life insurance

Interest on house or car payments is tax deductible. If policyholders borrow to pay life insurance premiums, that interest is also deductible, leading to the innovative practice of borrowing against the cash value of whole life insurance to pay the premiums. Since the cash value normally grows by more than the premium each year, the policy can effectively become self-financing. When certain rules are followed, the result is a triple benefit:

- The expense of carrying the policy becomes tax deductible.
- All proceeds still pass to beneficiaries free of income tax.
- Whole life protection can be obtained at a cost considerably below that of an equivalent amount of term insurance.

Minimum deposit in practice

The Minimum Deposit Plan chart illustrates how a $100,000 minimum deposit policy could work out for a person 35 years old. The tax laws (Section 265 of the Internal Revenue Code) state that a deduction for interest payments to finance life insurance is allowable as long as at least *four full premiums are paid in the first seven years of the policy's life* ("minimum deposit"). All other premiums may be borrowed from the insurance company. Therefore, for the first four years, the full premium is paid (Column 5). In the fifth and subsequent years, the amount of the net annual premium is borrowed from the cash value of the policy (Column 6), and a tax deduction is taken for interest payments (Columns 8–9). Over a 20-year period the net cash outlay would total $16,960 (Column 10). However, to obtain the true net cost so that it may be compared with an equivalent amount of term insurance, the residual cash value must be deducted because term insurance normally has no cash value. As shown, the net cost is $273 per year, which works out to $3.07 per $1,000 of in-force coverage (Column 11). The result is permanent protection at a price considerably less than an equivalent amount of term insurance.

MINIMUM DEPOSIT PLAN

$100,000 Ordinary Life Policy — Annual Premium $2,300

(1)	(2)	(3)	(4)	(5)	(6)	(7)	(8)	(9)	(10)	(11)
	Premiums			How Paid		Cash Value	Interest		Outlay	In-Force Insurance
Year	Annual Premium	Annual Dividend	Net Annual Premium	Premium Paid by Insured	Premium Borrowed from Insurance Company	Cash Value (after loans)	Annual Interest (6%)	Value of Interest Deduction (40% tax rate)	Net Cash Outlay (Cols. 5 + 8 − 9)	Death Benefit ($100,000 − Col. 6)
1	$2300	$ —	$2300	-$2300	$ —	$ 500			$ 2300	$100,000
2	2300	115	2185	2185	—	2900			2185	100,000
3	2300	165	2135	2135	—	4900			2125	100,000
4	2300	240	2060	2060	—	6900			2060	100,000
5	2300	315	1985	—	1985	5900			0	98,015
6	2300	385	1915	—	1915	5625	119	48	71	96,100
7	2300	450	1850	—	1850	5730	234	94	140	94,250
8	2300	520	1780	—	1780	5740	345	138	207	92,470
°										
°										
°										
20	2300	1050	1250	—	1250	11,500	1440	576	864	74,900
Total			$33,780	$8,680	$25,100	$11,500	$13,800	$5,520	$16,960	$74,900

Calculation of Net Cost of Insurance	$16,960	(Total net cash outlay from Column 10)
	- 11,500	(Residual cash value from Column 7)
	$ 5,460	
	= $ 273/year = $3.07/$1000 of in-force insurance	

Note that as funds are borrowed against the cash value of the policy to pay the annual premium, the death benefit (Column 11) is reduced by an equal amount. To retain full coverage, many minimum deposit plans allow for application of part of the annual dividends to pay for one-year term insurance equal to the amount borrowed. This is referred to as the fifth dividend option. Each year as the policy loan increases and death benefits decline, the term will equal the full face value of the policy.

How to raid the cash value

As noted above, IRS regulations state that at any time during the first seven years of a policy, no more than the amount of three net annual premiums may be borrowed. Since the cash value grows faster than the annual premium after the first year, a residual cash value builds up (Column 7), that cannot be borrowed without jeopardizing the tax status of the previous loans. However, beginning in the eighth year, the full cash value not yet taken out ($5,740 for the above example) may be borrowed without upsetting the interest deduction. Since most people feel that they can obtain a greater return on funds than the 5% to 6% it costs to "raid" the policy, they normally withdraw all available cash value and make up the reduction in death benefits with additional one-year renewable term insurance.

Integration of minimum deposit with an existing estate plan

The minimum deposit concept can be applied to any existing whole life policy. Check with a competent insurance advisor for assistance. Also note that on a new policy the sequence of premium payments does not have to be the same as above. In summary, minimum deposit offers the following advantages:

- Whole life protection can be obtained at a net cost (after taxes) below that of term insurance.
- Even if more than three of the first seven premiums are borrowed, the interest deduction will be allowed as long as the need for the funds was in connection with *an unforeseen event* or the taxpayer's *trade* or *business*.
- The loan plan may be discontinued at any time, and the original premium rate will still be guaranteed for life, even though the individual may no longer be insurable.

SELLING YOUR LIFE INSURANCE POLICY TO YOUR CORPORATION

If you currently own your own life insurance policy, you may be able to realize substantial gain by selling that policy to your corporation, a transaction that is perfectly acceptable to the IRS as long as you are an important member of the corporation. Here are four ways in which you can gain by giving up ownership of your life insurance policy:

1. By getting tax-free money out of a corporation you own.
2. Increasing your annual spendable income.
3. Eliminating estate liquidity problems.
4. By removing surplus funds from the corporation at the lower capital gains rate.

Getting Accumulated Funds Out of Your Own Corporation Tax Free

One of the principal problems with incorporation is that the income is taxed twice, once at the corporation level and once again when it is distributed to the stockholders. However, if you could sell your life insurance policy to your own corporation, the cash value of the policy comes to you as a tax-free exchange and in this way you duck the second level of taxation on income. The results of this transaction are:

- Corporate earnings come directly to you without the second tax.
- The corporation's surplus funds are virtually unaffected since it can cash in the policy anytime.
- The corporation becomes the beneficiary of the policy.
- Upon your death your heirs receive your stock which has increased in value as a result of payment of the policy benefit to the corporation.

Of course, if the corporation pays you more than the actual value of the policy, the excess over the face value of the policy will be taxable to you as ordinary income.

One other advantage to this type of transaction is that selling to your corporation increases your income. This logic is very straightforward. If you are paying $1,000 per year for the life insurance policy that you own personally, and you sell that policy to your corporation at its fair market value, you no longer have to pay for the annual premium and you now have an extra $1,000 in spendable income.

Eliminating Estate Liquidity Problems

Suppose your main reason for carrying life insurance is to cover possible estate liquidity problems. But, by the time you're 55, you realize that the insurance you are carrying won't be adequate to cover estate liquidity needs. At this age you can't afford the higher premiums necessary for the additional coverage so you sell the policy to your corporation for its fair market value and the corporation buys the needed additional insurance coverage. Upon your death the corporation receives the benefit of the policy and your heirs may redeem an amount of stock sufficient to cover estate liquidity needs. Redemption proceeds will be taxed at capital gain rates, but there will be no income tax because the funds will be withdrawn as a Section 303 Stock Redemption. (See page 321)

Who Owns the Life Insurance Policy?

If you are planning to carry a life insurance policy through your business, be sure to establish who is in fact the owner of the policy. Confusion over true legal ownership can lead to substantial tax cost.

If you wish your corporation to own your life insurance policy you must be certain that you do not retain any "incidents of ownership," according to the tax court. These would include:

- The right to change the beneficiary.
- The right to use the policy as security in obtaining a loan.
- Your right or the right of the estate to any of the economic benefits of the insurance policy.
- Any power to benefit from the disposal of the policy during your lifetime.
- Your right to cash in the policy.

If you retain just one of these rights or incidents of ownership, you are considered the owner of the policy and the proceeds of the policy will be taxed accordingly.

CHAPTER 22

ESTATE PLANNING

WILL POWER

People write scornful wills, vindictive wills, and generous wills. They can be as short as Rabelais' one sentence will, "I have nothing, I owe a great deal; the rest I leave to the poor," or as long as a small publication. But even though most people would like a voice in the disposition of their affairs after they die, nearly three out of four people die "intestate"—without a will.

Outside of tax law, there is no federal law regarding wills. Each state has its own intestacy statutes, and your estate will be distributed according to the laws of the state of your legal residence. These laws fractionally divide an estate according to rigid formulas. And, of course, they cannot provide for the desired disposition of family treasurers, which are often sold to pay taxes and provide for the survivors.

It may surprise you to learn that if you die intestate, the bulk of your estate may not go to your spouse. The laws of many states award from one-third to two-thirds of the estate to the children. If there are no children or grandchildren, the state intestacy laws will probably give your parents, siblings, or other blood relatives a portion of your funds—even if they are less needy than your spouse. If you think your view of your affairs would differ from that of your state, you will probably decide to make a formal will and soon.

Even if you have a written will, it may not be accepted as valid by the court if it is:

- *Handwritten.* The statutes of many states hold that hand-written (sometimes called "holographic") wills are invalid.
- *Do-it-yourself.* Many standard will forms obtainable from stationery stores or books do not conform to the letter of the law and are easily contested and often declared invalid on a technicality.
- *Out-of-state.* Your will is administered according to the laws of your domicile, not where you had the will drafted. If you have moved, be sure your will conforms to the laws of your new state of domicile.

- *Witnesses.* Strict requirements are stipulated for witnesses in many states.
- *Marriage and children.* In most states, marriage and the birth of children cause automatic revocation or alteration of part or all of a will.

Modification of a Will

After it has been properly prepared and executed, it is not necessary to re-draft the basic will to make changes or updates. Instead, the changes are incorporated in a separate document known as a "codicil" that is appended to the will. However, the codicil must be executed with the same formality as the basic will. Under no circumstances should you simply cross out certain clauses in the will and insert changes.

Probate and Priority of Claim

No will is legal until the proper court or official declares that it meets all statutory requirements. This act is known as the decree of probate.

Once the will has been admitted to probate, several claims have priority before any distribution can be made under the terms of the will. While the exact order varies by state, they follow this general pattern:

1. *Funeral expenses.*
2. *Administration.* Fees due the court, attorneys, and others for administering the estate.
3. *Family allowance.* An amount, often set by the court, to provide for the immediate needs of the decedent's family while the will is being administered.
4. *US Government.* Any taxes and other claims due.
5. *Last illness.* Expenses pertaining to the decedent's final illness.
6. *State, county, and local governments.*
7. *Wages due others.*
8. *Claims secured by liens.*
9. *All other debts.*

Statements Outside the Will

Not all of your property and personal matters can be settled within the will. Here are some other arrangements you should consider:

1. *Contract benefits.* Ample life insurance is a good way to tide the family over until your estate is settled. The payments are made to the beneficiary named in the contract, apart from any will. However, the total value of the benefits may be treated as part of the taxable estate. Remember that the security of a paid-up life insurance policy does not obviate the need for a well-drawn will.

2. *Joint tenancy.* Securities, real estate, and bank accounts that are jointly owned can by-pass probate and go directly to the survivor. But you cannot avoid federal and state estate taxes by the use of joint tenancy—and at the death of the survivor, this property can be taxed again. Moreover, while you can easily change a will, some joint tenancy holdings create a legal title that cannot be changed without the consent of the other party.

3. *Last instructions.* If you have specific wishes regarding your funeral and interment, it is wise to leave a memo (a letter of last instructions) with a trusted friend or relative describing the funeral arrangements you desire. It should also give the location of the will, other important papers, ready cash, and valuables.

Watch These Items

If you presently have a will, here is a checklist of sometimes omitted items you should review with your attorney.

- Does the will take full advantage of the marital deduction that allows a tax exemption of up to one-half of the estate?
- Are inheritance taxes to be borne by the estate or the beneficiaries?
- Have all insurance arrangements been considered in the will?
- Have safeguards been provided to ensure minimum double taxation of the estate—once at the death of each spouse?
- Have proper provisions been made to establish who legally died first in the event of apparent simultaneous death of both spouses?
- Should the executor of the estate have the power to run or dispose of your business?

SECTION 303 REDEMPTION

In the event of the death of an owner of a closely-held corporation, stock owned by the decedent may be redeemed tax free or as capital gain up to an amount that equals funeral, administrative expenses, and death taxes. This provision is found in Revenue Code Section 303 and it is designed to avoid tax squabbles over the tax treatment of stock redeemed to cover estate liquidity of the owner of a closely-held corporation.

The problem was that the IRS sometimes viewed such redemption gains as ordinary dividend income and, by the time enough money was taken out of the company to pay estate taxes, the estate was valued in a higher bracket and thus was subject to ever greater tax.

Requirements for Section 303 Stock Redemption

All the following requirements must be met before a Section 303 redemption can be made.

- The decedent's gross estate (as determined for estate tax purposes) must include the stock that is redeemed under Section 303.
- The stock owned by the decedent at time of death must have a greater value than 50% of the adjusted gross estate. This applies to the stock held in his own corporation.
- If the decedent held stock in more than one corporation and 75 percent of the value of all such stock is included in his estate, all the stock is treated as if it were stock in a single corporation.
- The Section 303 redemption must usually be made within thirty-nine months of the filing of the federal estate tax return, unless you elect to pay in installments.

Of course, if stock is redeemed in excess of the established costs of estate liquidity, the excess is simply taxed as ordinary income.

HOW TO SET UP A SPRINKLING TRUST

A sprinkling trust is a trust established for the grantor's children or grand-children that is flexible enough to "sprinkle" funds out to the children in proportion to the varying needs. *Flexibility of distribution* of funds is the primary motivation behind a sprinkling trust, whereas primary motivation for other types of trusts may be avoidance of litigation; tax minimization; efficient management of funds; or reduction of administrative costs and court costs.

There are two common methods for structuring a sprinkling trust, fixed share and single fund. Although each has advantages and disadvantages, keep in mind the system you might use to provide for your children's needs if you were paying for them right out of your wallet.

Fixed Share

Under this method each child covered by the sprinkling trust is allotted a fixed share of the principal. The child's needs are then paid for by sprink-lings from his share of the income and principal of the trust. When the trust is terminated, the child receives whatever is left of his allotment.

Single Fund

The single fund approach provides that all the principal and income from the trust be kept in a single fund and that sprinklings be taken from the fund as needed to meet the different needs of the children. Therefore, if one child falls ill and another decided to go to graduate school, the extra expenses for each child are met by the whole of the trust fund instead of just by the children's individual shares. When the single trust fund is terminated, the remaining assets are distributed (usually) evenly among the children. Generally, the single fund method for a sprinkling trust is considered to be most flexible in meeting the needs of the children. Therefore, the bulk of this discussion will center on single fund sprinkling trusts.

When to Terminate a Single Fund. At some point you may want to terminate the single fund and distribute the principal to the children. When is the right time to do it? No matter when you choose to terminate the trust, the needs of one child will differ from the needs of the other at the time of distribution of the funds. You must gauge your optimal termination time upon your estimate of the needs of your family. Here are four common situations upon which terminations hinge:

1. *After a specified period of time.* You may choose to terminate the trust after fifteen years have elapsed. The advantage here is simplicity and apparent equality. But this is not always the case. What if the oldest child needs the principal to buy a house before the termination date or the youngest child—at age seventeen—will use his share to buy the motorcycle you never wanted him to have?

2. *When the oldest child reaches a specified age.* You might design the trust to terminate when the oldest child reaches a specified age, say age thirty. Again, a simple system, but what if the youngest child is only halfway through college and would be better served by a trust to cover his remaining costs of education?

3. *When the youngest child reaches a specified age.* Obviously, this one too has its problems. By the time the youngest no longer needs the trust, the oldest may be up to his ears in debt or may already have gone through bankruptcy as a result of not having access to the principal in his trust.

4. *A set age for each child.* If you establish the trust so each child's share is distributed to him upon reaching age twenty-five, you systematically reduce the principal of the youngest child. If there are four children, the first reaches twenty-five and withdraws his 25% of the principal. The second soon turns twenty-five and does the same thing. Finally, the third child withdraws his 25% and now the youngest is left with sprinklings from one quarter the original principal. The youngest enjoys only 25% of the financial security given the oldest child.

Switching to separate shares. Another alternative is to switch from single fund to separate shares when the first child comes due for his distribution.

Of course, this brings on the disadvantages of separate share method for the other children and the youngest gets the worst of it since he has only the separate share to rely on for the longest period of time.

Getting Around the Disadvantages

Although the disadvantages of these variations seem discouraging, they are by no means prohibiting because a sprinkling trust can often be designed with sufficient flexibility to get around most disadvantages. Here are a few ways some of the drawbacks can be dealt with:

1. *Special funds within the trust.* One of the drawbacks of terminating the trust when the youngest child comes of age is that the older children have to wait too long. This can be dealt with by having a separate fund within the overall trust to meet the specific needs in one area, like education or medical costs. Once this separate fund is set aside to meet special needs, the rest of the funds can be distributed.

2. *Special Distributions.* The trustee may be given the power to make special distributions as needed before the termination of the trust. So, if an older child needs to buy a house, the trustee can give him a special distribution of part of his share of the principal without bringing about a complete dissolution of the trust. Of course, these premature distributions would be deducted from the recipient's share of the trust upon final termination.

3. *The younger they are, the larger their share.* If it is clear that the needs of the younger children will for some reason be greater than those of the older children, it is sometimes best to give the younger children a larger share of the trust when you are using the separate share method. This is not more equal, but it may be more equitable.

Usually, a sprinkling trust can be as flexible as you need it to be to cover the needs of your children, but you should certainly be aware of the above variables when you approach your attorney to have him set it up.

GRANDFATHER TRUST

A grandfather trust is a trust set up to benefit your grandchildren, but it is set up in such a way as to allow your children access to the principal if they need it.

Suppose that your children are well established in their professional or business careers and have accumulated substantial estates of their own. It would be pointless for you to pass your property on to them, only to have it eventually taxed again in their estates. So, you would really like to leave your assets to your grandchildren. The problem, however, is that you want to provide for the contingency that your children may have financial setbacks and need money. The solution is to set up a trust benefiting your grandchildren but give your children the right to "invade" the trust if they need money to maintain their accustomed standard of living. If the so-called grandfather trust is set up this way, your property will pass to your grandchildren, escape needless tax in your children's estate, yet still provide your children if they should unexpectedly need money because of an unforeseen setback.

"FLOWER" BONDS—HOW TO GET THE GOVERNMENT TO HELP PAY YOUR ESTATE TAX

A flower bond is a certain issue of US Treasury Bond that can be at par value used to pay estate tax. If you've come to that time when you must consider ways to pay your estate tax, consult your bond broker about these.

What is the Advantage?

US Treasury Bonds pay taxable interest, but if you can buy flower bonds at a discount there may be a tidy tax-free profit to be made when your estate tax is paid. If, for example, you know that your estate tax will be about $20,000, you could buy twenty flower bonds at a discount cost of $900 each. These bonds pay 4% interest on a par value of $1,000 so that you have income from the interest to start. But later, the bonds may be used to pay your estate tax. The cost of the bonds was $18,000 but the par value makes them worth $20,000 when used to pay the estate tax. This gives your estate a nontaxable profit of $2,000 in addition to the taxable interest earned on the bonds.

INDEX